INTERNATIONAL SECURITY DIMENSIONS OF SPACE

INTERNATIONAL SECURITY DIMENSIONS OF SPACE

Edited by
Uri Ra'anan
Robert L. Pfaltzgraff, Jr.

International Security Studies Program
The Fletcher School of Law and Diplomacy
Tufts University
Medford, Massachusetts 02155

ARCHON BOOKS
1984

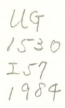

First published 1984 as an Archon Book,
an imprint of The Shoe String Press, Inc.
Hamden, Connecticut 06514

Composition by The Publishing Nexus Incorporated
1200 Boston Post Road, Guilford, CT 06437

Printed in the United States of America

The paper in this book meets the guidelines for
permanence and durability of the Committee on
Production Guidelines for Book Longevity of the
Council on Library Resources.

Library of Congress Cataloging in Publication Data
Main entry under title:

International security dimensions of space.

   Based on the Program's Eleventh Annual Conference,
April 27–29, 1982, held at the Fletcher School's Cabot
Center.
   Includes bibliographical references and index.
   1. Space warfare—Congresses. 2. Space weapons—
Congresses. 3. Space law—Congresses. I. Ra'anan, Uri,
1926–   . II. Pfaltzgraff, Robert L. III. Fletcher
School of Law and Diplomacy. International Security
Studies Program.
UG1530.I57   1983   358'.8   83-21450
ISBN 0-208-02023-3

Contents

About the Authors and Editors

Hans Mark is Deputy Administrator of the National Aeronautics and Space Administration. He has also served as Secretary of the Air Force, Under Secretary of the Air Force, and Director of NASA's Ames Research Center.

Barry J. Smernoff is Senior Fellow, Strategic Concepts Development Center, National Defense University.

Marc E. Vaucher is a Ph.D. candidate at The Fletcher School of Law and Diplomacy and is employed by the Bank of New England, Boston, as a Country Risk and Credit Analyst.

Uri Ra'anan is Professor of International Politics at The Fletcher School of Law and Diplomacy and Chairman of the International Security Studies Program.

Wallace E. Kirkpatrick is President of DESE Research and Engineering, Inc., Huntsville, Alabama. He is former Deputy Director of Management and Administration, Ballistic Missile Defense.

Clarence A. Robinson, Jr. is Senior Military Editor of *Aviation Week and Space Technology*.

Robert B. Giffen, Colonel, USAF, a graduate of the Air Force Academy received his Ph.D. from the University of Heidelberg and has flown in the Air Force as both a combat pilot and a test pilot. After working in space operations in Cheyenne Mountain, he attended the National War College, and is now Professor and Head, Department of Astronautics, USAF Academy.

Joseph E. Justin, Major, USAF, was an Assistant Professor of Astronautics at the U.S. Air Force Academy, Colorado, and a Rand Research Fellow at The Rand Corporation in California, prior to his current assignment to Headquarters, United States Air Force (Studies and Analyses), Washington, D.C.

Patrick J. Friel is President of the consulting firm Friel and Company, Inc., Lincoln, Massachusetts. He has been involved in U.S. strategic technology programs for twenty-five years and is a former Deputy Assistant Secretary for Ballistic Missile Defense.

Frederick W. Giessler, Colonel, USAF, is Assistant Director for Net Assessment in the U.S. Department of Defense.

David Leinweber received undergraduate degrees in physics and electrical engineering from M.I.T. in 1974 and a Ph.D. in computer science from Harvard University in 1977. He has been employed as an analyst of space and information technologies at M.I.T., Lincoln Laboratories and The Rand Corporation.

John M. Logsdon is Director of the Graduate Program in Science, Technology, and Public Policy of George Washington University, where he is also Professor of Political Science and Public Affairs. He is at present spending a year away from the university as the first occupant of the National Air and Space Museum Chair of Space History.

John H. Hoagland is Chairman of Hoagland, MacLachlan & Co., Inc., a consulting firm in Wellesley, Massachusetts.

John B. Gantt is the Vice President and General Counsel of COMSAT General Corporation, which is the major subsidiary of Communications Satellite Corporation.

S. Neil Hosenball is General Counsel for the National Aeronautics and Space Administration, Washington, D.C.

Harry H. Almond, Jr. is former Senior Attorney Advisor in International Law, the Department of Defense, Washington, D.C. He is presently Professor of International Law at the National War College in Washington, D.C.

Robert L. Pfaltzgraff, Jr. is Professor of International Politics at The Fletcher School of Law and Diplomacy, Tufts University, and is President of the Institute for Foreign Policy Analysis in Cambridge, Massachusetts, and Washington, D.C.

Bruno W. Augenstein, currently Senior Scientist at The Rand Corporation, has been involved in space activities since 1946. He has held positions as Chief Scientist for Satellite Systems at Lockheed, and with the Department of Defense as Special Assistant for Intelligence and Reconnaissance.

Marcia S. Smith is Specialist in Aerospace and Energy Systems, Science Policy Research Division, Congressional Research Service, Library of Congress, Washington, D.C., providing research and policy analysis to the members and committees of Congress on matters concerning U.S. and foreign space activities.

Preface

The International Security Studies Program of the Fletcher School of Law and Diplomacy continued its effort, this year, to focus public attention upon topics that are likely to emerge soon as themes of central significance for American security. In this quest, the Program once again decided to provide a forum for in-depth analysis and exchange of information among representatives of the institutions most directly concerned, in the anticipation that material of particular value to policy makers might result, as it had on previous occasions. With these considerations in mind, the organizers of the Program's Eleventh Annual Conference chose the subject "International Security Dimensions of Space." Nearly one hundred decision makers and experts from the executive and legislative branches of the United States and other governments, the armed services, the corporate and technological communities, "think tanks," and various academic institutions attended the conference on April 27–29, 1982, at the Fletcher School's Cabot Center.

The present book constitutes an outgrowth of the work initiated before and during that conference; it includes the bulk of the papers presented there, suitably amended and updated, and additional material commissioned by the editors. The subject already is becoming increasingly topical, and concepts that emerged from the conference are likely to have significant policy implications. It is hoped that this book may prove helpful to decision makers, and that it may stimulate further interest in the topic.

The editors note that, within weeks of the conclusion of the conference, a number of developments advocated by various participants began to be implemented. The conference had stressed the need for a coherent national space policy, encompassing both military and civilian objectives, and initial steps toward this goal were announced by President Reagan some five weeks after the conference. About two weeks later, the U.S. Air Force announced the formation of a new Space Command, a step that was viewed as essential at the conference, so that space activities of the military services might be consolidated. Some two weeks after that, the appearance of a Defense Guidance Document was reported, which indicated another move viewed as highly desirable by the participants, namely, acceleration of the development of a U.S. counter to the Soviet ASAT device that is now operational. More recently, on March 22, 1983, President Reagan made his now famous "Star Wars" speech, proposing that the United States develop space-based weapons systems for defense against nuclear missiles, fundamentally reshaping nuclear deterrence policy.

The editors do not claim, of course, that the conference was responsible for these developments, but they note with satisfaction that the International Security Studies Program of the Fletcher School of Law and Diplomacy had been able, in this as in other instances, to remain in the very forefront, not only of state-of-the-art technology, but also, more important, of the political and security ramifications that require urgent policy decisions.

Uri Ra'anan
Robert L. Pfaltzgraff, Jr.

Medford, Massachusetts

Introduction

HANS MARK

National-security-related space operations have been proceeding for two decades. The growth of these programs shows striking parallels with the development of military aviation. Military operations in the ocean of air above the earth have been conducted to provide observation and communication since the beginning of the nineteenth century. Observation balloons, for example, were used in the American Civil War and in the Franco-Prussian War in 1870 with good effect. In the field of communications, carrier pigeons were used for many centuries despite their low reliability.

Today, observations and communications are being conducted from space. Large communication satellites in geosynchronous orbit are profitably operated by private firms that responded to the high return on investment provided by space-based communications. The military services also operate a large space-based communications network because of the efficiency of space communications. This network is vital to military operations in peacetime and in periods of crisis. During an all-out war, however, today's satellite communication network would be less useful, because satellites in geosynchronous orbit probably can be destroyed by nuclear weapons. For this reason, a distinction must be drawn between national-security-related operations and military operations in space. Today's satellites are primarily useful for national-security-related operations in peacetime and in the resolution of crises before war begins.

Satellites also make observations from space, their second important contribution to national security. In 1978, President Carter announced publicly that the "national technical means of verification" referred to in the 1972 SALT agreement were satellites that provided photographs to verify arms-control agreements. It is important to recognize that the primary function of observation satellites is to provide timely information on the activities of other governments. The information provided by these satellites has helped stabilize the international situation.

Deployment in earth orbits of weapons of mass destruction is prohibited by a U.S.-USSR treaty; in fact, this agreement is largely symbolic, because it is not clear that nuclear weapons deployed in earth orbit have any real military value. The treaty says nothing about other weapons, however, and the Soviet Union has deployed non-nuclear weapons in space. Development and testing by the Soviet Union of an antisatellite weapon has continued over the past ten years, and a number of tests have been successful. The USSR anti-satellite system works by placing a small satellite with an explosive warhead in orbit next to the target satellite and then detonating a conventional explosive shrapnel system aboard the antisatellite, which then destroys the target.

Why have the Soviet leaders developed an antisatellite system? One explanation is that Western observation satellites are vital to gain information about security-related events in the Soviet Union, though Soviet leaders can use other means to gain similar information about events in the West. Perhaps this is the reason that the Soviet Union has placed a higher priority on antisatellite systems than has the West. We are now working on an antisatellite system, and we should have one; but, for the reasons mentioned, it may not be as important for us to have one as it is for them. We should not, however, let the Russians trap us into one-sided discussions about the deployment of weapons in space.

Weapons in space do not yet pose a major danger to populations on earth, and therefore they need not be high on the arms-control priority list. The more important questions with respect to weapons in space concern the roles of these weapons and the circumstances in which they would be used. Since Western development of tactical military doctrine for space weapons is years away, negotiations with the Soviet Union on space weapons have little to offer the United States.

Rather than pursuing a policy of arms control of weapons in space, the United States should recognize that internationalizing the current observation systems may be an appropriate option to consider in planning the future of space operations related to national security. A process of internationalization should start with collaboration among the United States and its allies. For instance, joint surveillance systems can reduce the uncertainties of national leaders throughout the West. Joint surveillance has been effective in the past, and the effort has strengthened relations among allies. In the next two decades, the United States will build manned bases in earth orbit from which all kinds of space operations will be conducted. Internationalizing the construction and operation of these manned platforms would reap dividends for the United States.

The United States has taken several important initiatives in the conduct of international operations in space. The Space Shuttle was developed by this country, but the primary payload for manned space flights using the shuttle is a European project. The Spacelab program, carried out under the management of the European Space Agency, is a billion-dollar effort to provide a manned capsule that fits into the Space Shuttle payload bay, from which experiments in space can be conducted. There is reason to hope that the Spacelab module will also be a building block for a manned space station.

It is difficult to overstate the importance of the effect that the Space Shuttle will have on space operations. The Space Shuttle is the first new launch vehicle that has been developed in over thirty years. Space operations for the last three decades have been conducted using unmanned launch vehicles that were essentially derivatives of the Intercontinental Ballistic Missiles first created in the late 1940s and early 1950s. The Space Shuttle is an important initiative because it incorporates the factors of human imagination and judgment as a matter of routine space flight. The presence of human judgment is important in space operations related to national security. An international space station that would conduct observations to assist national leaders during periods of crisis could be an important step toward a more stable world. International efforts based on Space Shuttle technology offer great potential for expanded cooperation among the Western nations, and can ultimately improve the prospects for world peace.

The world is a dangerous place. Our job is to see that operations in space serve to stabilize the world rather than to create more turbulence. I believe that space operations have done this in the past, and there is a good chance that they will continue to do so in the future. We must also work to enhance the importance of space operations for the purposes I have outlined. The Space Shuttle will undoubtedly make an enormous contribution to this effort because of its unique features, and it will permit the United States once again to assume a role of leadership, not only in technology, but in maintaining world stability.

1

Space As a Military Environment

1

A Bold Two-Track Strategy for Space: Entering the Second Quarter-Century

BARRY J. SMERNOFF

The second twenty-five years of the space age began on 4 October 1982. When Sputnik I was launched by the Soviet Union, few observers dared to guess the number and variety of U.S. space systems that would follow, or the telling impact they would have on civilian and military activities and even on the manner in which we view our home planet, earth. Only dreamers talked about the extensive constellations of communications satellites that now bring live television into homes around the world; or photoreconnaissance platforms overhead (revealed officially to the American public by President Carter in 1978), which verify arms-control agreements and collect intelligence imagery with startling detail; or meteorological satellites capable of providing synoptic photographs to which weathermen can key their daily forecasts; or the thunderous elegance of a Space Shuttle as it is launched into the depths of space, only to glide back quietly to an aircraft-like landing for piggyback flight and re-use. By 1980, the biggest tourist attraction in Washington had become the National Air and Space Museum—not the White House or U.S. Capitol.

There is no doubt that the second quarter-century of the American space program can produce dazzling technological advances comparable in quality and novelty to those noted above. Space technology, most definitely, is America's strong suit. As President Reagan reaffirmed in his July 4th, 1982, speech after the fourth Columbia landing that ended preoperational testing of the Space Shuttle, the United States has made a firm national commitment to remain the world leader in space technology. In some sense, then, the technical

The editors appreciate the courtesy and permission of the National Defense University, for which Dr. Smernoff wrote a different version of this chapter.

side of the American space program is easiest to tackle, notwithstanding the problems and cost overruns that beleaguered the shuttle (and every other serious development program) and the
competing priorities and bureaucratic conflicts that laced media
reports.

What the U.S. space program has been missing are compelling
answers to the essential and central questions of Where, What, and
Why. Where are we headed? What important national goals should
we be pursuing in our space program? And why are they of such
critical significance? Do we have a workable and coherent national
strategy for "getting from here to there," with strategic milestones
and goals that must be achieved along the way?

One of the critical tasks of political leadership in the United
States has been to mobilize the American people behind goals that lie
clearly in the national interest. The second quarter-century of the
American space program presents such important and intriguing
opportunities for meeting key national needs that we would be
extraordinarily remiss to ignore or reject them. Yet, national policy in
certain areas either does not exist or is contrary to the kind of bold
and clearly articulated guidance needed to take advantage of these
opportunities for exploiting outer space. Consequently, it is not
surprising that coherent and practical strategies are totally lacking
for pursuing goals in space that virtually everyone, if given the
chance, might agree are both important and feasible to achieve.

Meeting such strategic goals in space, however, will demand
much more than development of the appropriate space technology,
and merely *technical* solutions to the problems associated with these
aims are neither feasible nor desirable. Bold and forward-looking
two-track strategies will be required to blend the relevant political
components, such as arms-control diplomacy, with promising technological advances, such as space-based laser weapons.

Accordingly, one must explore the assumptions and hypotheses
that are linked with this central theme. One can then develop the
rudiments of a national security strategy for moving boldly into the
second quarter-century of the space age that blends competition and
cooperation, technical nerve and political imagination, physical
strength and moral courage. This period takes us forward into the
long-range future, through the year 2000 into the new millennium,
with all of its chiliastic overtones.

NET ASSESSMENT OF U.S. AND SOVIET SPACE PROGRAMS

A review of space history suggests strongly that the United States
holds a clear and compelling edge in demonstrated space technol-

ogy, frequent publications concerning Soviet space achievements
notwithstanding. Specific cases in point are easy to find. Whereas
American satellites carrying infrared sensors constitute the primary
means of providing warning of ballistic missile attacks to the National
Command Authority and have been operational since the early
1970s, as of 1981 the Soviet Union had deployed no effective early-
warning system in space—and not for lack of trying.[1] Russian cosmonauts may have spent more time in long-duration space missions
than American astronauts, but the Soviet space program never completed its development of a large Saturn-class launch vehicle
(reported to have failed catastrophically in several tests beginning in
the late 1960s) and never landed men on the moon. While this large
Soviet space booster reportedly "will have the capability to
launch ... even larger and more capable laser weapons" into orbit,[2] it
is generically more than one dozen years overdue. The 120–250
thousand-kilogram size of the large manned space platform under
development by NASA for possible launch in the next 7–10 years
suggests that the Soviet Union may be hard-pressed to keep pace
with ambitious American plans in this area, in which the Russians
have been thought to have a unique advantage over the U.S. space
program.

Admittedly, space spending in the Soviet Union does appear to
be growing more rapidly than overall defense spending. Highly
publicized Soviet statements regarding the desired demilitarization
of space contradict the consistently heavy military emphasis of the
Soviet space program, which currently expends about $17–18 billion
per year, compared with the annual U.S. level of about $14 billion for
FY 1983.[3] Such comparisons can be deceptive, however, since the
Soviet Union launches annually from four to five times as many
spacecraft as the United States, dozens of which are short-lived
photoreconnaissance birds.[4] Analysts believe that fully one-third of
the Soviet total is spent on spacecraft placed into orbit. Moreover,
substantial U.S. spending on classified programs may not be
included in total U.S. space outlays.

During the past several years, the pace of American spending on
military activities in space has accelerated sharply, with real growth
rates approaching 20 percent per year. In FY 1982, DoD spending
on space programs exceeded NASA's budget for the first time since
1960 as U.S. military forces became increasingly dependent upon
space capabilities to accomplish many basic support functions, such
as precise navigation, long-haul communications, meteorology, and
surveillance. The sharp acceleration of U.S. space spending led by
DoD programs suggests that the Soviet Union may be playing catch-
up, both qualitatively and quantitatively, in the near future, and that

the American space lead will widen, perhaps markedly, by the late 1980s. Recent establishment of the Air Force Space Command will reinforce the trend toward rapid growth of U.S. military activities in space.[5]

WHAT THE UNITED STATES SHOULD DO WITH ITS LEAD IN SPACE

Given the clear U.S. lead in space technology and the emerging U.S. edge in space spending over the Soviet Union, how can and should these definite advantages be exploited to serve U.S. national interests and goals? Five generic options have been identified, three of which can be quickly rejected.[6] Briefly, these basic options are:

1. *Do nothing*, for fear of destroying the "sanctuary" of space.
2. *Negotiate*, to prevent an arms race in space.
3. *Prepare* reactively, to deny the Soviet Union any major advantage.
4. *Compete* vigorously, to achieve U.S. superiority in space.
5. *Blend technology and politics*, to exploit the clear U.S. edge in space during an "age of obligatory arms control" and thereby achieve strategic goals more in keeping with deeply rooted American values than mutual assured destruction (MAD) forms of nuclear deterrence.

This section will examine these policy alternatives; since the first three can be discussed and rejected quickly as nonviable options, the "compete" and "blend" options will receive more attention.

Do Nothing

Quite clearly, this option has been overtaken by events, decisions, and steeply rising budgetary trends. The United States has moved into space for military purposes with increasing vigor, and for good reason: space systems can be potent force multipliers.[7] There are unique advantages to be gained from basing increasingly powerful communication, navigation, meteorological, warning, surveillance, and other equipment (eventually including nonnuclear weapons) on space platforms that have global and synoptic coverage. As a high-level defense official stated recently:

> Hopes for demilitarization are only realistic in areas with no military worth; space is emphatically not one of these.

> While there are undoubtedly well-intentioned people who
> decry what they regard as the "militarization" of a pristine
> frontier, history teaches us that each time a new medium is
> opened to man it is exploited to gain a military advantage.
> The course of world affairs has repeatedly been altered by
> the nation which first grasped the advantages offered by
> developing the military potential of the newest medium.[8]

In a more pragmatic tone, Colin Gray writes that "in a global war it
would be no more feasible to retain space as a privileged sanctuary
than it would be to preclude military action in any other geographical dimension.... Space cannot be isolated from the earth with
reference to armed conflict."[9]

Perhaps, in the absence of a large and growing Soviet threat to
U.S. vital interests, the option of doing nothing about military
activities in space would appear more desirable. The rather Hobbes-
ian nature of the existing international scene has made this option
infeasible as well as undesirable. It is inconsistent with the American
"can-do" style of technological development to think that doing
nothing in military space could ever be a practical alternative,
especially given our unambiguous edge in this key arena and the
obvious parallel of airpower development.

Negotiate

During the Carter administration, three rounds of U.S.-Soviet
talks were held during 1978–79 on the matter of developing arms-
control constraints for antisatellite (ASAT) weapon systems. The
guiding policy for these negotiations was summarized as follows:

> The United States finds itself under increasing pressure
> to field an antisatellite capability of its own in response to
> Soviet activities in this area. By exercising mutual restraint,
> the United States and the Soviet Union have an opportunity
> at this early juncture to stop an unhealthy arms competition
> in space before the competition develops a momentum of its
> own.... While the United States seeks verifiable, com-
> prehensive limits on antisatellite capabilities and use, in the
> absence of such an agreement, the United States will vig-
> orously pursue development of its own capabilities.[10]

Although this expressed preference for arms control designed to
preserve space as a sanctuary is widely acknowledged, the practical
feasibility of negotiating an even-handed and verifiable agreement
banning ASAT capabilities appears virtually nil. After all, superpower arms control has suffered generally from the severe erosion of

political relations following the Soviet invasion of Afghanistan in late 1979 and the subsequent demise of SALT II, not to speak of the "yellow rain" and Bulgarian connection problems. There will always be well-intentioned groups believing that the strategic arms race must not be extended into outer space and that time is running out for banning the testing and deployment of antisatellite weapons.[11]

Prepare

Once doing nothing and unadulterated arms control have been dismissed as serious policy options for guiding U.S. military activities in space, one is faced with the "reactive" option of hedging against Soviet technological surprises by increasing our own activities through an emphasis on moderately aggressive research and development programs. To a large degree, this alternative is most consistent with Air Force thinking up to several years ago. Now there is a clear shift toward more vigorous exploitation of space, as the new blue-suit Space Command—perhaps the organizational precursor to a future U.S. Space Force—becomes fully operational and the steep upward ramp of DoD space spending produces greater policy interest in this area.

Primarily reactive moves are out of keeping with the characteristic American pursuit of action-oriented solutions to pressing problems, once the essential nature of any new frontier situation has been clearly understood. The U.S. Space Shuttle was not developed during the 1970s simply to deny major political and military advantages to the Soviet Union or to preserve the U.S. lead in applied space technology. It was developed because enough American leaders understood that the exploration and exploitation of space are of sufficient strategic significance, and that more routine (and, one hopes, cost-effective) transportation systems for launches into near-earth orbit would be required before fuller use of space systems could be possible. Perhaps, in the absence of a Soviet threat perceived to be growing in both scope and intensity, a purely reactive space policy would be in the cards. Since there is an ever-stronger consensus that military space programs are much too important to be shaped solely as responses to Soviet actions and decisions, this policy option, like the first two, is not a viable choice. Furthermore, America traditionally has wanted to control its own destiny, especially in frontier settings.

Compete

The strategic vision of a technologically dynamic America, seizing the ultimate high frontier (and high ground) of space to acquire clear-cut space superiority and provide unambiguous politico-military advantages to the United States, has captured the minds of many in recent years.[12] Post-Sputnik literature reflects the underlying feeling that the United States must obtain control of space first, and the sooner the better. As we bask in the national afterglow of the first five Space Shuttle missions during 1981–82, it is hard to dispute the increasingly prevalent view that, as the world's preeminent spacefaring nation, the United States must exploit its inherent technical and political advantages to achieve a clear and durable position of space superiority—unilaterally, without attempting to use diplomatic or other kinds of cooperative "crutches." In a very fundamental sense, space has become a critical new arena for the American people, now that scientific research has become the leading edge of America's frontier tradition:

> A major world power such as the United States has to pioneer in those areas of life which are historically relevant and crucial. To the extent that ours is a scientific age, the failure of the United States to push beyond existing frontiers—and space offers a very dramatic challenge—would mean the loss of a major psychological motivation for innovation.[13]

Indeed, national resolve to reach beyond the ordinary is perhaps the essence of our topic, and it has several extremely important implications. On one hand, many would agree with Lt. Gen. Kelly Burke's recent statement that space weapons "have a transcendental flavor, a little like gunpowder. We ignore them at our peril."[14] Hence the thrust to use space as a war-fighting medium, beyond its historical supporting role, comes naturally. On the other hand, there is little doubt that Americans are searching actively for what Fred Iklé (now Under Secretary of Defense for Policy) has termed "a new path into the twenty-first century" insofar as strategic thinking is concerned.[15]

There is little doubt that the United States could achieve durable space superiority, assuming that the Soviet Union would not rock the boat by undertaking preemptive attacks on, say, laser-bearing spacecraft thought to have BMD capabilities which the United States might deploy in the 1990s and beyond.[16] Advanced space technology such as space-based laser weaponry is opening attractive opportunities for constructing effective layered defensive systems capable of destroying attacking strategic bombers and missiles.[17] Accordingly, space-related systems eventually could provide for the "common defense" in quite a direct manner, beyond the beleaguered concept of nuclear deterrence. This alone would constitute sufficient motivation for aggressive U.S. competition in the fourth arena of space.

Rather than focusing upon business as usual, making only evolutionary improvements in existing functions, the United States must continue to develop qualitatively new functions, such as spaceborne ocean and air surveillance systems and lasers, to take full advantage of space for meeting critical national needs. This point is even more valid now that the surprisingly rapid spread of the antinuclear movement in the United States has created a host of seemingly intractable problems for sustaining the so-called defense consensus. Many Americans feel increasingly uncomfortable about the mutual-hostage relationship between the United States and the Soviet Union. Others, in massive ignorance of current strategic realities, tend to assume that the United States is defensible and defended, at least in part, at the present time.

Blend Technology and Politics

It is precisely for these reasons, transcending the more obvious politico-military and technical imperatives for moving into space much more aggressively, that the fifth option has become so essential: in contemporary terms, we have moved into "the age of obligatory arms control."[18] Whereas the a priori negotiability of practical agreements that could have substantial influence on reshaping the nuclear mutual-hostage relationship is certainly very difficult to estimate, arms control has become an important part of the political scene. Although the future of formal arms-control limitations is in severe doubt, increasingly powerful domestic and European groupings embrace control ideals as necessary concomitants of growing defense expenditures, in keeping with the now-traditional *two-track-*approach.

This fifth space-policy option is a deliberate attempt to blend the physical power of advanced U.S. military technology—especially the two key technologies of microelectronics and lasers, which are being applied to emerging and new space systems[19]—with the political and psychological power of bilateral arms-control diplomacy. The essential policy objective is to shift the balance of strategic military power from a clear emphasis on nuclear offense toward nonnuclear defense, grounded in weapons of self-protection. To be sure, the technical prospects seem brightest for nonnuclear defensive weapons when concepts are synthesized using space-based laser systems, aided by various C^3I systems (many of which would themselves be based in space)[20] and other defensive layers, such as exo/endoatmospheric nonnuclear kill-vehicle systems and advanced sensors under active development in the large and growing Army BMD program.

In his San Francisco speech to the editors of UPI announcing the Johnson administration's Sentinel ABM deployment decision, Secretary of Defense Robert McNamara stated that:

> it is important to understand that none of the [ABM] systems at the present or foreseeable state of the art would provide an impenetrable shield over the United States. Were such a shield possible, we would certainly want it— and we would certainly build it.... If we could build and deploy a genuinely impenetrable shield over the United States, we would be willing to spend not $40 billion [in 1967 dollars] but any reasonable multiple of that amount that was necessary. The money in itself is not the problem; the penetrability of the proposed shield is the problem.[21]

Thus, defensive emphasis would be preferable to the existing mutual nuclear-hostage relationship between the superpowers.[22] The problem does not seem to be money but leakage! If a perfect "astrodome" could be developed and built to protect the United States from "all" nuclear weapons deliverable by traditional means (not counting covert/clandestine emplacement by proverbial oxcart), and if everyone agreed that this were possible, defensive emphasis could clearly carry the day. Unfortunately, perfectionist demands for zero leakage will always remain unfulfilled, and it goes without saying that the best is the enemy of good enough.

Apprehensions about unacceptable leakage in a future nation-wide defensive shield could be diminished considerably if the overall size of the Soviet nuclear threat were reduced greatly. Indeed, deep cuts could reduce the thousands of existing strategic nuclear-delivery vehicles to hundreds on each side of the balance. The BMD problem could thereby become much less demanding, and the chances for building affordable defenses to protect cities with acceptably low leakage rates would become correspondingly larger. The rub would be to sustain the political credibility of nuclear deterrence during an extended transition toward a defensive emphasis or, even beyond, to a stage of last-resort deterrence of large-scale central war only, through the threat of using whatever nuclear weapons are left after deep arms-control cuts.

This, then, is the pragmatic reason for justifying the critical significance of arms control. In his Eureka speech of May 1982, on the occasion of his fiftieth college reunion, President Reagan affirmed his goal of achieving deep reductions in strategic offensive forces (SOF) through negotiated arms-control agreements. It is now widely believed that finding a home for the MX ICBM (with multiple-protective shelters, fixed silos, and, subsequently, closely spaced or densepak basing modes having been considered to no avail) will create negotiating leverage and provide Soviet leaders with clear incentives to make deep cuts in their strategic offensive forces, and particularly in their heavy MIRVed ICBMs, such as the SS-18s.[23]

THE BOTTOM LINE: NEW GOALS AND STRATEGIES FOR DEFENSIVE EMPHASIS

Where are we going in space during the 1980s and beyond, in pursuit of what goals, and why? The answers to these basic questions are unclear, largely because Americans tend to explore and exploit new frontiers by doing rather than by thinking. It is within a fluid and somewhat confusing strategic context that the core questions of where, what, and why—in connection with the U.S. military space program—must be addressed. If Americans are to exploit space for sound reasons, then new and more appropriate goals must be set before authentic strategic approaches can be conceived and implemented to reach them. As implied in the previous section, space promises to facilitate a transition in emphasis from nuclear offense toward nonnuclear defense. Advanced systems (such as mosaic sensors and space lasers) will play a critical role in allowing the United States to defend against external threats without relying utterly upon nuclear deterrence, an aging strategy of declining political credibility. Though the United States cannot (and should not) pursue unilateral approaches to nuclear arms control, any strong American thrust toward serious arms control with the Soviet Union will complement the even stronger American thrust into space. The combination could produce a new strategic context in which national security—for both the United States and the Soviet Union—can be placed on a much sounder, safer, and more sustainable basis over the long haul.

The launch of Sputnik by a Soviet ICBM in 1957 heralded the emergence both of the space age and of long-range ballistic missiles capable of delivering nuclear warheads to targets across the planet. Now, in the early 1980s, American entry into the second quarter-century of the space age is beginning with sharply accelerated spending, important organizational changes, and numerous references to the advent of beamed weapons in space. The latter will have very long lethal reach and "transcendental flavor"; the most mature type is the high-energy laser that, ironically, is similar (in aerodynamic operation) to the powerful rocket engines that propel ICBMs and Space Shuttles. Given this history, it is important that Americans continue to explore and exploit the high frontier of space by doing *and* thinking.

Accordingly, new strategic goals must be developed to reflect the need to make a timely transit from nuclear offensive toward defensive emphasis. In the spirit of exploiting the traditional U.S. edge in military technology, it is fortunate that such a strategic transition can be based largely upon advanced space technology, with microelectronics, lasers, and other basic research and development areas leading the way toward increasingly powerful mosaic sensors and beamed weapons overhead. Realistic understanding of what such an ambitious transition will involve, however, implies that arms control, as well as technology, must play a central role.

Too often, Americans have relied on blind faith in technology, under the mistaken assumption that technical solutions can resolve virtually all major issues facing the United States. The primacy of human factors in international politics means that there is no purely technical (competitive) solution to the problem of defending America against nuclear attack. Conversely, there is no purely political (cooperative) solution for doing so. Workable approaches will contain a blend of both technical and political components, competitive and cooperative elements, working together. For this fundamental reason, "proper" American entry into the second quarter-century of the space age is of extraordinary importance.

The "compete" option for achieving unilateral space superiority could (and probably should) be employed by the United States as effective bargaining leverage for pursuing arms-control objectives such as deep SOF cuts, in order to reach the more preferable "blend" path. If prospects for serious arms control become even bleaker than they currently are, the stage would be set for unilateral pursuit of space supremacy, which would serve the United States well if an unremitting, all-out arms competition with the Soviet Union became inevitable.

FUTURE DIRECTIONS

Rather than provide a normative list of specific technological thrusts that might be planned and programmed, with highly uncertain estimates of costs and schedules, the concluding section of this chapter will attempt to indicate important goals and directions for the American space program during the next twenty-five years. In this regard, it is extremely useful to recognize that developing technology for its own sake is not the proper policy for guiding this or any other program with high national priority. While technology clearly is the organizational essence of the U.S. Air Force, which will continue to play the leading institutional role in military space activities (unless a U.S. Space Force is established soon after Space Command becomes a unified command), human and political factors are critical to both defining and achieving important goals.

Indications are clear that the United States is moving toward space superiority in the 1990s and beyond; 20 percent real annual growth in DoD space spending, formation of the new Space Command, and widespread attention to the brightening prospects for MAD-busting space laser weapons support this conclusion. Our past track record suggests that the United States can achieve a relatively durable form of space superiority, just as we have sought and sustained naval, air, and tehnological superiority in the past, each of which now appears to be getting ragged at the edges. The surprising implication is that achievement of U.S. space superiority would help greatly to restore each of these traditional forms of military superiority to their old levels. It is this general potential that gives military activities in space their authentic meaning as "force multipliers" in the strategic sense of that phrase.

Two examples are useful to illustrate this point. Infrared and radar ocean/air surveillance satellites which may become operational by the early 1990s could place Soviet surface ships and high-altitude aircraft at risk from missiles and other long-range weapons.[24] First-generation space laser weapon systems that might become available somewhat later, but probably before the end of the century, could place many types of missiles and aircraft (not to say spacecraft) at risk. Together, these advanced sensors and weapons could produce the kind of space superiority that would restore naval and air superiority to the United States in a manner that exploits traditional American advantages, but without spending tens of billions of dollars on ever-smaller numbers of expensive, complex, and vulnerable ships and aircraft.

This kind of emphasis on space could produce a modern U.S. advantage in spacepower that dovetails with and enhances the traditional American advantages in seapower and airpower, giving rise to three great fleets: one sailing on and especially under the blue-water oceans; another orbiting earth in the black depths of space; and the third flying (as stealthily as possible) in the coastal seas of space, the atmosphere. Technological superiority would enable each of these fleets to maintain a qualitative edge over adversaries. The purpose of attaining clear-cut space superiority would be two-fold.

First, there is no doubt that eventually the United States must move beyond NATO in its politico-military emphasis. Steps toward establishing a central command for dealing with Persian Gulf and other nonstandard crises and increasing American unwillingness to spend many tens of billions of dollars each year to sustain our large and visible troop presence in Europe and Asia constitute clear signs that we will move beyond NATO eventually, and perhaps sooner than we think. In this context, a relatively persuasive case can be made for turning back to our natural advantage in seapower.[25] A similar case can be made for complementing traditional forms of seapower with modern spacepower as the keystone of a new U.S. strategy for defending America as an island continent (but *not* as a "Fortress America") having vital interests around the globe.

Just as important a strategic goal as moving beyond NATO is the gradual achievement of nuclear deemphasis, during which process the now-dominant role of nuclear weapons would be substantially diminished through a judicious combination of tehnology and politics. Hence the second critical task for emerging U.S. space superiority is to exert effective bargaining leverage on the Soviet Union so that deep cuts in SOF levels can be made (and made to stick), and the strategic balance can be moved firmly toward defensive emphasis, away from its historical emphasis on nuclear MADness. In effect, the United States would be applying its strong technological leverage in space to encourage a superpower competition in nonnuclear *defensive* weapons, thereby forcing a concomitant reduction in spending on, and policy attention paid to, the nuclear component of the competition. For this the entire international community would be much better off in the long run. If strategic competition were moved into space within a context of deep SOF reductions, arms-control diplomacy could suppress the offense-defense arms race that defensive hardware would otherwise trigger.

Hence the answers to our original questions have brought us to the point of beginning to understand what the future holds for U.S. military activities in space. Military use of space is much more than simply a "force multiplier"—it is a potential restorer of traditional forms of U.S. miitary superiority. Military use of space will not be a quick fix for resolving the prolem of nuclear war, once and for all, but it could go a long way toward reducing the awesome role that nuclear weapons and the unprecedented threat of nuclear holocaust have played in postwar history. If spacefaring Americans develop and build large-scale space structures for collecting and beaming solar energy down to earth, such solar-power satellites would in the distant future join the growing constellations of communication, navigation, surveillance, meteorological, and other spacecraft that ply earth-centered orbits. But most of all, a forceful and thoughtful blend of space technology and arms-control politics could prove to be of lasting significance for the long-range security of the United States.

NOTES

1. U.S. Congress, *FY 1982 Department of Defense Program for Research, Development, and Acquisition,* statement by William J. Perry, Under Secretary of Defense for Research and Engineering. 97th Cong., 1st sess., January 20, 1981, pp. II-10.

2. U.S. Department of Defense, *Soviet Military Power,* September 1981, pp. 76–79.

3. "Soviets Outspending U.S. on Space by $3-4 Billion," *Aviation Week & Space Technology,* July 19, 1982, p. 28.

4. Stockholm International Peace Research Institute, *Outer Space— Battlefield of the Future?* (London: Taylor & Francis Ltd., 1978), especially chapter 3, "Reconnaissance Satellites."

5. Edward C. Aldridge, Jr., Under Secretary of the Air Force, "Space Command: Defense in the Fourth Medium," *Defense 83,* January 1983.

6. Four of the five basic military space options were initially defined and discussed by Lt. Col. Dino A. Lorenzini and Maj. Charles L. Fox in "2001: A U.S. Space Force," *Naval War College Review,* March–April 1981.

7. See Richard L. Garwin, "Effective Military Technology for the 1980s," *International Security,* Fall 1976.

8. Ronald Stivers, Assistant Under Secretary of Defense for Policy, Speech to AIAA meeting, May 26, 1982.

9. Colin Gray, "The Military Uses of Space to the Year 2000," paper presented to the Seventh International Arms Control Symposium, Philadelphia, 6–8 May 1982, pp. 3–4.

10. White House Press Release, June 20, 1978. Also see Donald L. Hafner, "Averting a Brobdingnagian Skeet Shoot: Arms Control Measures for Antisatellite Weapons," *International Security,* Winter 1980–81; and David A. Andelman, "Space Wars," *Foreign Policy,* Fall 1981.

11. See *Common Security: A Blueprint for Survival,* by the Independent Commission on Disarmament and Security Issues, chaired by Olof Palme (New York: Simon and Schuster, 1982), pp. 154–55.

12. See especially the Lorenzini-Fox article in *Naval War College Review* and *High Frontier: A New National Strategy,* coordinated by Lt. Gen. Daniel O. Graham (ret.), 1982, as well as the fine paper by Lt. Col. Barry Watts and Maj. Lance Lord, "Beyond the Missile Age: How to Think about Military Competition in Space," in *Military Space Doctrine: The Great Frontier,* a book of readings for the U.S. Air Force Academy's Military Space Doctrine Symposium, April 1–3, 1981, vol. 4.

13. Zbigniew Brzezinski, *Between Two Ages: America's Role in the Technetronic Era* (New York: Viking Press, 1970), p. 247.

14. James Canan, *War in Space* (New York: Harper & Row, 1982), p. 179.

15. Fred Charles Iklé, "Can Nuclear Deterrence Last Out the Century?" *Foreign Affairs,* January 1973, p. 285. His complete line is: "While luck has been with us so far, strategic thinking must and can find a new path into the twenty-first century."

16. This scenario was posed by Richard L. Garwin ("Effective Nuclear Technology," p. 73): "nuclear-armed interceptors would be used to attack the imagined laser-bearing satellites as they were being readied to orbit over a period of months." Ballistic missile defense (BMD) is usually construed as

equivalent to antiballistic missile (ABM) systems, which are now severely constrained by the U.S.-Soviet ABM Treaty of 1972.

17. Barry J. Smernoff, "The Strategic Value of Space-Based Laser Weapons," *Air University Review*, March–April 1982.

18. William V. O'Brien, *The Conduct of Just and Limited War* (New York: Praeger, 1981), p. 130.

19. The Organization of the Joint Chiefs of Staff, *United States Military Posture for FY 1983*, p. 64. In its discussion of technological leadership, this document states that "lasers are perhaps second only to microelectronics in their promise of impact on military systems." Indeed, the laser is the only major weapon-system component based on a new scientific phenomenon that has beeen introduced since the development of nuclear weapons during World War II; see Alexander H. Flax, "Military Aerospace to 2000," *Astronautics and Aeronautics*, May 1980, p. 33.

20. C³I is the standard acronym for command, control, communications, and intelligence.

21. *Department of State Bulletin*, October 9, 1967.

22. For a current statement of the proposition that "we are fated to live in a MAD world," see Spurgeon M. Keeny, Jr., and Wolfgang K. H. Panofsky, "MAD Versus NUTS: Can Doctrine or Weaponry Remedy the Mutual Hostage Relationship of the Superpowers?" *Foreign Affairs*, Winter 1981–82.

23. The Soviet Union has always emphasized strategic defense more than the United States, suggesting that it may more easily "tilt" toward a world of defensive emphasis. See Col. William J. Barlow, "Soviet Damage-Denial: Strategy, Systems, SALT, and Solution," *Air University Review*, September–October 1981.

24. William J. Perry and Cynthia A. Roberts, "Winning through Sophistication: How to Meet the Soviet Military Challenge," *Technology Review*, July 1982; and William J. Perry, "Technological Prospects," in *Rethinking the U.S. Strategic Posture*, edited by Barry M. Blechman (Cambridge, Mass.: Ballinger, 1982).

Skeptics contend that billions of dollars spent on small numbers of costly and complex satellites would be *equally* bad, with Soviet ASAT weapons operational and advanced ones under development. Indeed, they are *right*— and it will be the responsibility of the R&D managers and operators of new military space systems to establish and meet realistic goals for large robust networks of inexpensive and stealthy (hence more survivable) satellites.

25. Jeffrey Record, "Beyond NATO: New Military Directions for the United States," in *U.S. Strategy at the Crossroads*, Institute for Foreign Policy Analysis, July 1982. Also see Michael Vlahos, *America: Images of Empire*, SAIS Occasional Papers in International Affairs (Washington, D.C.: Johns Hopkins Foreign Policy Institute/SAIS, August 1982) for the case that America and Europe are in the initial stages of slow disengagement, and that the former must develop efficient modes of power projection to protect its new interests and allies.

2

Geographical Parameters for Military Doctrine in Space and the Defense of the Space-Based Enterprise

MARC E. VAUCHER

THE ECONOMIC BASIS FOR SPACE INDUSTRY AND DEFENSE NEEDS

The success of the Space Shuttle program heralds a new age of increased activity in space. The reusable nature and large cargo capacity of the shuttle provide a range of new options for the exploitation of space. Already, available cargo space has been booked through 1985. Shuttle "customers" will include private industry, foreign governments, the Department of Defense, and civic groups, as well as the traditional NASA experiment packages.[1] Once again, a new technology will drastically change the way industrial man operates and plans for the future.

Permanent manned stations in orbit and large space structures, such as factories and solar-power satellites, as well as the mining of the moon's resources and even the asteroids are today a step closer to reality. NASA has plans for the first factories in space, serviced by the shuttle.[2] The potential for economic benefits from space is tremendous, because of the near absence of gravity and the availability of a high-quality vacuum in space.

These qualities of space have important implications for a wide range of modern manufacturing processes. Experiments conducted aboard Apollo, Skylab, and the Apollo-Soyuz missions have confirmed the expectation that space will prove a valuable area for new applications in electronics and metallurgic solidification techniques. Certain exotic high-strength metal alloys, used by aerospace and defense industries, are nearly impossible to produce on earth because of gravitational settling as the metals cool. Zero-g manufacturing could lead to the perfection of new metals and the casting of perfect spheres for ball bearings and other industrial products. High-quality silicon chips and other electronic components can be constructed in the near vacuum of space much more easily than is presently possible on earth.[3] Manufacture of pharmaceuticals is another area of great promise for space manufacturing.

As America's investment in space, both public and private, continues to grow, the importance of space-based assets will become a matter of concern to military planners. Already space has proved its unique importance to America's defense. Today, three-quarters of all Defense Department command, control, communication, and intelligence (C[3]I) relies on a space-based component at some point.[4] Surveillance satellites supply real-time reconnaissance data on a global basis. Navigation and weather satellites have proved their effectiveness in aiding military operations. Both superpowers are rapidly expanding their military roles in space from use of passive systems to active weapons deployment. The development of killer satellites, orbiting weapons platforms, laser and particle beam weapons, and manned military space vehicles is being pursued.[5] With the Air Force having already reserved one-third of all planned shuttle cargos (this may well increase in the near future), the sophistication of space-based defense systems will expand during the 1980s.

The expansion of activities in space will require formulation of guidelines for the proper use of the new technologies and the resulting benefits. Among the most important of these guidelines will be the formulation of military doctrine for space. The new space industries will generate their own defense requirements, which must be considered in addition to the defense needs of strictly military installations. While the establishment of an international regime to demilitarize space could protect commercial assets, the present political realities do not allow much confidence in declaratory measures. It seems unlikely that the commercial exploitation of space can be separated from political and miltary issues. Even if demilitarization were agreed upon, however, the need for a military doctrine would remain. Such a doctrine must take into account both the value of space assets to national political and economic goals and the unique physical properties and geography of space.

This chapter will review the elements that must guide the formulation of a military doctrine for space and will concentrate on the policy implications of the geographical and physical realities that will control the use of any foreseeable weapons system. Though Air Force Aerospace Doctrine Manual 1-6 identifies the political and technological basis for Air Force doctrine, the manual does not address the impact of the physical realities of space on doctrine.[6]

THE GEOGRAPHICAL REGIONS OF SPACE

In space, as on earth, "geography" is an important factor. While, at first glance, outer space may seem to be an undifferentiated void, in fact it can be divided into distinct geographical regions (see figure 2.1). These regions are: (1) near earth orbit, extending from the earth's surface to (and including) the valuable geosynchronous orbit, 22,300 miles out; (2) cislunar space, extending from geosynchronous orbit to the orbit of the moon and including the important Lagrange libration points; and (3) translunar space, extending from an orbit beyond the moon, where the gravitational effect of the sun becomes greater than that of the earth to the edge of the solar system.[7] Each of these three regions can be considered a separate zone of operation, having distinct characteristics that will influence military doctrine.

Before considering each, it is necessary to explain the concept of "gravity wells" in space. Gravitation gives shape to apparently feature-less space. Every body in the solar system has its gravity well, the area

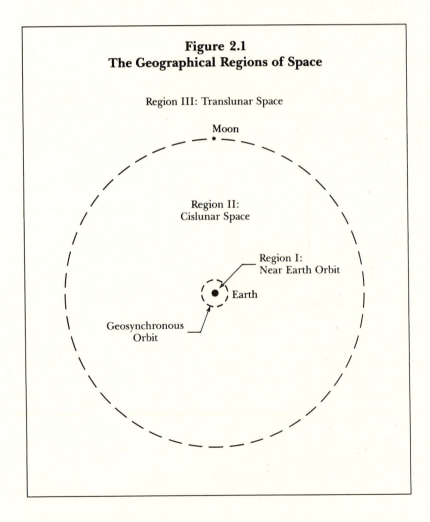

Figure 2.1
The Geographical Regions of Space

Region III: Translunar Space

Moon

Region II:
Cislunar Space

Region I:
Near Earth Orbit

Earth

Geosynchronous
Orbit

around the mass in which the force of its gravity is of major significance. The more massive the body, the deeper the well and the more
force must be used to escape from its surface. The earth's well is
twenty-two times deeper than the moon's (see figure 2.2).[8] Hence it
takes considerably less energy to move from the moon's surface to
geosynchronous orbit than it does to reach that orbit from the earth,
despite the much shorter distance. In space what becomes important
is the change in velocity (known as Delta V) required to move from
one point in space to another. Delta V determines the cost of space
transportation, and hence is a relatively more important factor than
simple distances between points.[9] It will often prove less expensive to
move a great distance following a low Delta V trajectory than to travel
a short one, such as climbing out of earth's massive gravity well at a
high Delta V cost. It is this fact that will determine the economics of
space industry, because lunar resources will be cheaper to transport
to earth orbit than will ground-based materials.

It seems clear that an economic incentive exists for private
enterprise to move into space, following the paths of least economic
resistance. A number of private firms have reserved space on the
shuttle to conduct their own industrial experiments. In addition, the
European Space Agency's Spacelab, built to fly aboard the shuttle,
will also conduct many experiments to determine the feasibility of
various manufacturing ideas. Ideally, large "pallets" or platforms
could be set in orbit to contain manufacturing facilities and could be
regularly serviced by the shuttle. The industrialization of space will
be well under way before the end of this decade.

A look at exactly what materials are available in space will make
clear the feasibility of large-scale manufacturing above the earth.
Samples brought back from the Apollo landing show that lunar soil
contains large concentrations of such valuable construction material
as silicon, aluminum, titanium, iron, and manganese. Also oxygen
(more important as a component of rocket fuel than for use as air)
makes up approximately 60 percent by weight of the lunar soil.[10]
These materials could be used to build large space structures in orbit.
Hence, space industry will turn to the moon as a source of raw
materials because of its small gravity well and low Delta V costs.

The gravity well has strategic importance, because movement is
less costly and easier near the top of the well than at any lower point
on its sides.[11] The top of the gravity well will be the "high ground" of
space.[12] The importance of this fact for military doctrine will recur in
the discussions of the geography of space.

Region 1, near earth orbit, is the only region of space today that
is heavily utilized. It includes the area of operations of all commercial
and military satellites. There are two important areas within this

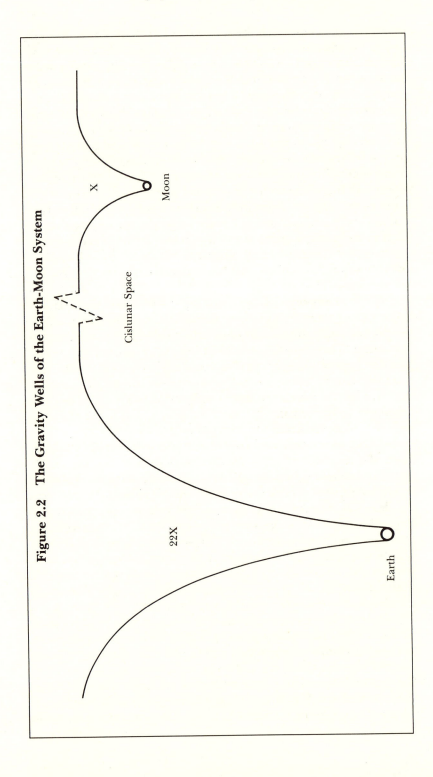

Figure 2.2   The Gravity Wells of the Earth-Moon System

region. The first is low earth orbit at about 300 miles in altitude. This is within the present operational range of the shuttle, and the first large structures will be deployed here.[13] Low earth orbit is quickly and easily accessible from earth at a high cost in fuel, but it is an unstable orbit; objects placed there will eventually fall toward earth and burn up unless fuel is expended to maintain their orbit. It is therefore useful only for short-term operations.

The second area of region 1 is geosynchronous orbit, and equatorial orbit some 22,300 miles high, which is unique in that an object placed there will remain stationary relative to a point on earth. Once there, an object will remain in place indefinitely at little cost in fuel. It is perfect as a site for large structures, which would be very costly to maintain over long periods in a lower orbit. It is near the top of the earth's gravity well, making it a likely spot for space factories receiving lunar resources.[14] Its geostationary character has already made this a crowded orbit, filled with communication and resource-sensing satellites.

The most important aspects of near earth orbit are the high Delta V costs for transportation because of the effect of the gravity well and its clear advantages over ground sites for many military operations. The utility of satellites in orbit for C^3I, remote sensing, weather forecasting, reconnaissance, and navigation is now well accepted. From a military standpoint the defense of these assets in region 1 will be determined by their proximity to earth and the physics of Delta V requirements in the gravity well.[15] Movement in region 1, although relatively fast and over short distances, will be costly. The ability to maintain a presence in geosynchronous orbit at the top of the well will be crucial for timely defense.

Turning to region 2, cislunar space, a new set of physical characteristics emerges. Encompassing the entire earth-moon system, cislunar space lies at the top of the gravity wells for that system. It is the new high ground, characterized by low Delta V requirements to travel great distances (see figure 2.3).[16] Note the difference in Delta V required to move from the moon to geosynchronous orbit and from the earth to low earth orbit. Transportation costs will be relatively minor, while the effects of distance and time for travel will be much greater than in region 1.

Cislunar space also commands all access routes to the moon. The development of space industry utilizing lunar resources will lead to the commercial occupation of certain strategic points in cislunar space. These are called the Lagrange libration points, named after the eighteenth-century French mathematician who first postulated their existence (see figure 2.4). He stated that five points exist in space where the gravitational effects of the earth and moon would cancel

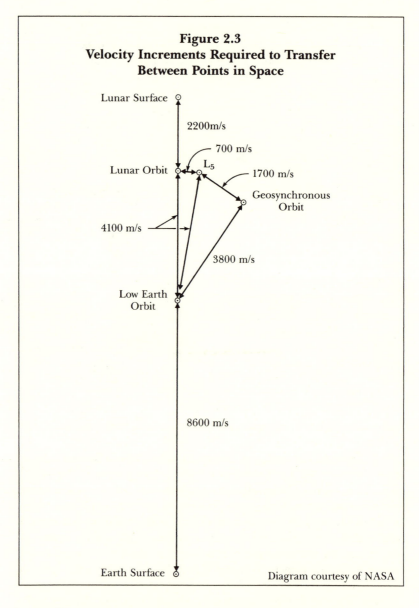

Figure 2.3
Velocity Increments Required to Transfer
Between Points in Space

Lunar Surface

2200m/s

700 m/s

L₅

Lunar Orbit

1700 m/s

Geosynchronous
Orbit

4100 m/s

3800 m/s

Low Earth
Orbit

8600 m/s

Earth Surface

Diagram courtesy of NASA

each other out, and an object placed there would remain permanently stable. In fact, because of the perturbing effects of the sun, orbits around only two of these, the "Trojan" libration points L_4 and L_5, are truly stable.[17]

The military and commercial importance of the Lagrange points is immense. The low Delta V trajectories of cislunar space

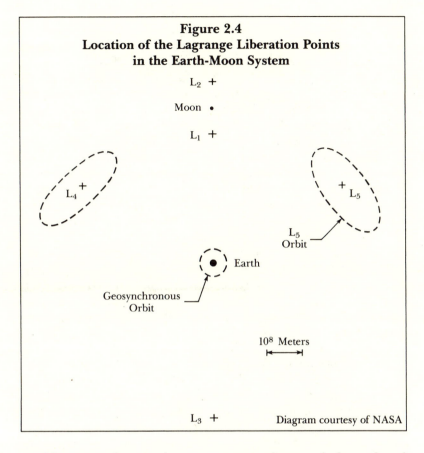

Figure 2.4
Location of the Lagrange Liberation Points
in the Earth-Moon System

L_2 +

Moon •

L_1 +

L_4 +

L_5 +

L_5 Orbit

Earth

Geosynchronous Orbit

10^8 Meters

L_3 +   Diagram courtesy of NASA

would serve as the stepping stones to supply space industry based either in geosynchronous orbit or at the Trojan points.[18] The Trojan points are logical places to put large space structures; such as factories, colonies, or military bases. They sit at the top of the gravity well of cislunar space. Structures placed there will remain permanently in place, and they command the access routes to all cislunar space. In effect, control of the Trojan points means control of the entire earth-moon system.[19] Region 3, translunar space, can be divided into two functional areas. The first comprises the inner solar system, extending out from the orbit of the moon to the asteroid belt. The second is the outer solar system, from the asteroids to the orbit of the farthest planet. No immediate uses are foreseen for this second area. Serious consideration, however, has been given to the first area. Mining of the asteroids for the support of space industry may be an effective economic proposition, since again low Delta V trajectories make it cheaper to move an asteroid to L_5 or geosynchronous orbit than to bring an equivalent amount of material up from earth.[20] This is not simply idle dreaming. The asteroids represent a gigantic reserve of mineral wealth, cheaper to use at geosynchronous orbit than earth resources once the industrial infrastructure is in place.

The two major kinds of asteroids, nickel-iron and carbonaceous chondrite, contain a wealth of material. Nickel-iron asteroids are essentially pure, high-grade stainless steel, with 5 percent or more nickel. It has been estimated that a single asteroid one mile in diameter (of which there are hundreds) equals 33 billion tons of steel, enough to meet U.S. needs for the next two hundred years.[21] The movement of only two or three such asteroids for use at a factory in geosynchronous orbit would have a tremendous economic impact. The carbonaceous chondrites contain high proportions of silica, carbon, and hydrogen, as well as iron. These could be used to meet the needs of space habitats and industry.[22]

Although it is of little practical importance today, translunar space nevertheless holds the promise of economic riches in the medium term, locked in the asteroids, the Galilean moons, and the Jovian atmosphere. The establishment of mining facilities and eventually colonies in these remote areas will expand the scope of defense requirments.

Analysis of the characteristics of translunar space requires a heliocentric orientation that defines paths for exploration and commercial investment based on the gravity well of the sun. Also required is an appreciation for the vast distances involved, which will be the greatest single factor facing economic and military planners. The effects of gravity wells around bodies such as the moon, Mars, Jupiter and its moons will be of local significance, but the development of mining industries in deep space will be affected more by distance than by gravity wells which can be bypassed. Space-based industry will follow the paths through translunar space conforming with the lowest Delta V requirements. These paths are called Hohmann Transfer Orbits, which define the trajectory between two orbits of lowest Delta V and hence lowest cost (see figure 2.5).[23] These orbits are longer and slower than high Delta V routes, but for mineral shipments the key factor is the cost of shipment. As long as a steady supply of resources can be assured, it matters little whether the trip takes six weeks or six months.[24] Hence, Hohmann Transfer Orbits will serve to define the "space lanes" in translunar space, and doctrine will have to account for the defense of these routes.

MILITARY USES OF THE REGIONS OF SPACE

Having reviewed the characteristics of the major regions of space, it is now necessary to look at the military uses of those regions.

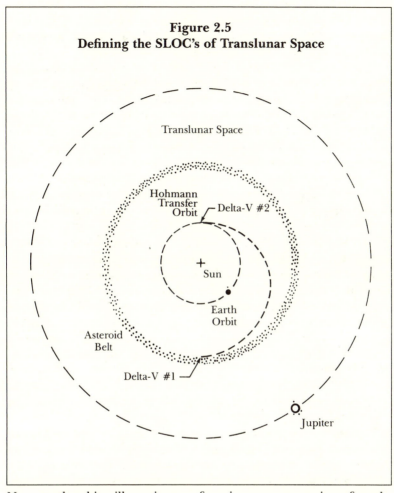

Figure 2.5
Defining the SLOC's of Translunar Space

Translunar Space

Hohmann
Transfer
Orbit ⌐ Delta-V #2

+
Sun

Earth
Orbit

Asteroid
Belt

Delta-V #1

Jupiter

Near earth orbit will continue to function as an extension of earth-based systems. Well-defined military roles already exist for the support of ground forces by satellites. As space-based assets move from these traditional, passive roles to new active ones, and especially as weapons platforms for ASAT and ABM defense and manned military vehicles are developed, the importance of the gravity well will be apparent. The need to place weapons systems and manned stations near the top of the well will make the ability to control geo-synchronous orbit vital.[25] It will be the most important area of near earth orbit.

In cislunar space the establishment of bases at strategic points, or the ability to control those points in some form, will be the overriding military concern. One requirement might be the ability to defend a lunar mining operation. Such an operation would encompass a base and its attendant mass driver, used to hurl lunar soil into space. Another station might be located at L_2 to retrieve the soil and send it on to a factory at L_5 or in geosynchronous orbit.[26] The most effective means to defend this network and control all of cislunar space would be to establish a base at one of the Trojan points. The use of manned or unmanned patrol craft based at L_4 or L_5 could effectively extend an umbrella of protection reaching from the lunar surface to geosynchronous orbit. The Trojan points, with their inherently low Delta V positions in the earth-moon system, will be the high ground of cislunar space.[27]

Translunar space, in the long term, will require the development of a deep space fleet capable of patrolling the space lanes and supplying far-flung bases. In many ways, power projection in deep space will reflect the geopolitical theories of Alfred Mahan. The nation that has the ability to control the space lanes will control the economic resources of bases in the asteroid belt and the Jovian system. In translunar space, Mahan's Sea Power will be the nation that can patrol the space lanes and protect its extended base structure. Control of the space lanes will require control of bases on certain asteroids, as well as control of, or at least the ability to utilize, lunar and Trojan bases in cislunar space. Hohmann Transfer Orbits will define the mechanics of trade and will shape military doctrine for its protection.

IMPLICATIONS FOR MILITARY DOCTRINE

Military doctrine will be constrained by "geopolitical" (or, perhaps more properly, "cosmopolitical") factors such as location, distance, Delta V, and the economics of space industry, and any doctrine must be formulated with these factors in mind. In the near term space will be used for the defense and support of ground-based forces. Passive systems will give way to active defense systems to protect space-based links for C^3I and other uses. New ASAT and AMB/BMD technologies and offensive space-based systems for use against targets both on the ground and in space are likely to be developed. The present heavy push to develop lasers and particle beam weapons for deployment in space will continue. By the early 1990s, near earth orbit will contain a variety of defense systems.[28]

In the longer term, the expansion of industrial activity in space will lead to commercial investments and trade. The defense of these assets will become a major concern of military planners. In response to the growing need for space-based defense systems, a unified space force may be established distinct from the other branches of the armed forces. Senators Malcolm Wallop of Wyoming and Harrison Schmitt of New Mexico have called for the establishment of such a force to control and coordinate military space activities.[29]

The duties and goals of such a future space force could include defense of the national interest in space, the security of space industry, maintenance of order in space, control and defense of the space lanes, and the ability to wage all-out war, if necessary. The list is not exhaustive, but it gives an idea of how a space force might fulfill the traditional defense roles of any armed service.

Formulating doctrine for space should help determine which technologies are most useful to pursue. This can be achieved only once the basic parameters for man's activities in space are understood. Military doctrine should vary according to the characteristic needs of each region of space.

In region 1 the emphasis of doctrine will be to insure the free access of industry and the military to the vital geosynchronous orbit. This orbit is already crowded. As of mid-1977, there were more than one hundred unmanned satellites located in geosynchronous orbit.[30] Orbital crowding and the possibility of frequency interference caused by beam overlapping will require that these numerous small satellites be replaced in the late 1980s with large, multipurpose platforms that will be militarily vulnerable. Facilities located in geosynchronous orbit, however, will be more secure from earth-launched offensive operations because of the time required for vehicles to climb the gravity well. Various location and detection systems sited in near earth orbit may be used to identify potential threats with sufficient early-warning time to permit counteraction.[31] Control of geosynchronous orbit will be vital to protect these systems.

Effectively, control of geosynchronous orbit means control of all near earth space. Its position at the top of the gravity well makes it imperative that this new high ground not be unilaterally controlled by an enemy power. Deployment of cheap reusable shuttles and orbital transfer vehicles is a prerequisite for the building and supplying of manned or unmanned weapons systems in orbit. The vulnerability of space assets to ground-based and later space-based attack will increase drastically in the next few years. Strategically, the ability to deploy weapons systems from geosynchronous orbit will be the single most important factor of operations in near earth orbit.

In cislunar space, the most vital doctrinal requirement will be the establishment of bases at the Trojan libration points to command the access routes of the earth-moon system. It will also be important to command lunar geosynchronous orbit because of its strategic position for any lunar base. The ability to patrol the entire earth-moon system to insure freedom of access to lunar resources and protection of space industry will be a basic concern. The new high ground will now be the Trojan libration points. Their inherently low Delta V trajectories to all other points in cislunar space make it vital that they be either demilitarized or multilaterally controlled. Unilateral military control of these points would effectively close cislunar space to any other power.[32]

In translunar space distance will become the major determinant of operations. The great distances will result in serious communications time lags. The effect will be to promote increasing independence of far-flung bases and patrols. In many ways, parallels with the settlement of the early American West come to mind. In both cases local settlements are cut off for long periods of time from direct government control. In the West, Army bases, which were required to patrol large tracts of territory, often constituted the only effective government influence. In the asteroid belt and beyond, the situation may well be similar, with only sporadic government patrols from widely scattered bases to keep order over what will undoubtedly be a very hardy and independent breed of miners. Effective government control in this area will require military outposts to maintain government authority in areas beyond the asteroid belt.

Hohmann Transfer Orbits will help determine the routes used to traverse space. Patrols to prevent piracy or tampering with cargoes may be necessary. Should war begin, the great distances involved would preclude rapid resupply or reinforcement.[33] Beyond the necessity to maintain a deep space fleet to support far-flung bases and project power throughout the solar system, the requirements of doctrine in the very long term are difficult to project. Should the asteroids and Jovian system prove to be as economically attractive as they now appear, local colonies may develop into power centers in their own right.[34] Such speculation, however, is best left until the economic feasibility of space colonies can be established.

A DOCTRINE FOR SPACE

Distance, Delta V, and the regional configuration of space are likely to shape future defense doctrine. Evolving technologies will provide the means for implementing this doctrine. In the near term, space doctrine will be an extension of concepts relating to earth-based power configurations, first in support of ground forces, and later in support of space assets. Before the end of this decade, doctrine must accommodate space-based industry, as well. In the formulation of a doctrine to provide the most efficient use of military resources, the economics of space industry will dictate the means for its defense. Stable points in orbit, low Delta V trajectories, and the importance of space resources will all determine the elements of doctrine.

In the long term, doctrine is likely to be concerned less with earth-based power relationships than with the possibility of new power centers arising in space. The economic fortunes to be made from space resources may give rise to a new class of people living in space. They may come to identify more with their own needs in space than with the traditional earth-bound rivalries. It seems only reasonable to assume that historical patterns of nation building will continue in space. Once economic independence is attained by a colony, cultural and eventually political independence is likely to follow. Doctrine in the long term will have to adapt to take account of the shift from traditional earth-based power rivalries. It is not clear that the earth powers will always hold the upper hand in this struggle. After all, the colonists will hold the high ground.

NOTES

1. R. Powers, *Shuttle: The World's First Spaceship* (Harrisburg, Pa.: Stackpole Books, 1979), pp. 144–47.

2. J. Grey, "Implications of the Shuttle: Our Business in Space," *Technology Review*, October 1981, pp. 40–42.

3. G. H. Stine, *The Third Industrial Revolution* (New York: Ace Books, 1975), pp. 141–42.

4. M. Vaucher, "Exploiting the New Frontier," *Harvard International Review*, April–May 1981, p. 30.

5. C. A. Robinson, "Beam Weapons Technology Expanding," *Aviation Week and Space Technology*, May 25, 1981, p. 40.

6. Air Force Manual 1-6, Aerospace Doctrine, *Military Space Doctrine*, Pentagon, XOXID, 1981.

7. G. H. Stine, "Defending the Third Industrial Revolution," in R. Bretnor, ed., *The Future at War*, vol. 1, *Thor's Hammer* (New York: Ace Books, 1979), p. 40.

8. C. Holbrow and R. Johnson, eds., *Space Settlements: A Design Study* (Washington, D.C.: Science and Technology Information Office, NASA, 1977), p. 9.

9. M. J. Gaffey and T. B. McCord, "Mining Outer Space," *Technology Review*, June 1977, p. 54.

10. Z. Kopal, *The Moon in the Post-Apollo Era* (Boston: D. Reidel, 1974), p. 161.

11. Stine, *Future at War*, p. 35.

12. Ibid.

13. Grey, "Implications of the Shuttle," p. 41.

14. Vaucher, "Exploiting the New Frontier," pp. 4–5.

15. Stine, *Future at War*, pp. 35–36.

16. Holbrow and Johnson, *Space Settlements*, pp. 9–10.

17. T. A. Heppenheimer, *Colonies in Space* (Harrisburg, Pa.: Stackpole Books, 1977), p. 144.

18. Ibid., pp. 142–47.

19. Stine, *Future at War*, pp. 45–46.

20. G. H. Stine, *The Space Enterprise* (New York: Ace Books, 1980), p. 115.

21. Ibid., p. 118.

22. N. Calder, *Spaceships of the Mind* (London: British Broadcasting Corp., 1978) pp. 73–74.

23. Gaffey and McCord, "Mining Outer Space," pp. 52, 54.

24. Stine, *Space Enterprise*, pp. 119–20.

25. Stine, *Future at War*, p. 42.

26. Heppenheimer, *Colonies in Space*, pp. 106, 112–18.

27. Vaucher, "Exploiting the New Frontier," p. 5.

28. Robinson, "Beam Weapons," pp. 40–41.

29. Ibid., p. 43.

30. Stine, *Future at War*, p. 42.

31. Ibid.

32. Ibid., p. 45.

33. Calder, *Spaceships*, p. 113.

34. Ibid., p. 108.

3

The Soviet Approach to Space: Personalities and Military Doctrine

URI RA'ANAN

This chapter does not concern itself with the details of the evolution of the Soviet space program, which is dealt with extensively in appendix 2, or of the technological developments that have been reflected by Soviet military efforts in space, which are discussed in chapters 4 and 5. It is devoted to an examination of the personalities and institutions, as well as the military doctrine, that influence the Soviet approach to space.

Immediately after L. I. Brezhnev's death, Soviet publications placed considerable emphasis upon his contribution to Soviet achievements in space. *Pravda*, in an official obituary on November 12, 1982, emphasized that "Brezhnev paid much attention to the problems of scientific and technical progress ... and the space exploration effort." Moscow radio, in its domestic broadcasts on the same day, pointed out that "leading scientific figures, workers of scientific institutes and design offices are passing by [the coffin]. They pay tribute of deep respect to L. I. Brezhnev for his inestimable contribution to the scientific-technical progress of the country, the creation of a mighty material and technical base of developed socialism, and the *mastery of space*" (my emphasis).

Andropov, on the other hand, in his speech to the special plenary meeting of the Central Committee, seemed anxious to tone down the attribution of space achievements to Brezhnev personally when he said that "exploration of outer space" was among the "great landmarks" of "*the Soviet people* and of L. I. Brezhnev" (my emphasis).

It is significant, however, that at the funeral itself it was left to Defense Minister Ustinov to deal with this issue, when he stressed that "the building of developed socialism in the USSR and the greatest social, economic, scientific, and technical achievements of our homeland are associated with the name of Leonid Brezhnev. He devoted much effort and energy to *the development of missile and space technology*" (my emphasis). Neither Andropov, nor, even stranger, the chairman of the Soviet Academy of Science, A. P. Aleksandrov, both of whom spoke on the same occasion, mentioned the space effort. Aleksandrov would have been the obvious person to stress the *civilian* aspects of space achievements, whereas leaving the monopoly on this topic to Ustinov amounted to emphasizing the *military* side alone.

A careful survey of the personalities of the Brezhnev era whose names are associated with the Soviet space effort leaves very much the same impression. The space spectaculars of the period received a great deal of publicity, and the presence of the various participants in the welcoming committees greeting the returning heroes of space was duly noted in the Soviet media, as were the signatories of obituaries of leading figures in the space sciences. Analysis of such documents focuses attention particularly upon seven personalities in the leadership of the Party and the state, whose participation is noted with remarkable frequency:

1. I. F. Dmitriyev, "head of a section of the Central Committee"
2. A. I. Blatov, "aide to Leonid Brezhnev"
3. L. V. Smirnov, "Deputy Chairman of the Council of Ministers"
4. N. I. Savinkin, "head of a section of the Central Committee"
5. Ye. M. Tyazhel'nikov, "head of a section of the Central Committee"
6. M. V. Zimyanin, "Secretary of the Central Committee"
7. B. N. Pastukhov, "First Secretary of the All-Union Komsomol"

These names, if fully and properly identified, should put an end to the fruitless speculation as to whether military or civilian aspects predominate in the Soviet space program:

1. The Central Committee "section" to which Mr. Dmitriyev is linked so vaguely, in fact happens to be the Defense-Industry Department of the Central Committee, which he directs.

2. Mr. Blatov indeed was an "aide" to the General Secretary of the Party, Brezhnev, but more interestingly he was the member of Brezhnev's personal chancellery who, it seems, represented the "Gensek" on the Soviet Defense Council, the peacetime equivalent of the "GKO" that led Soviet war efforts during 1941–1945.

3. Mr. Smirnov actually is chairman of the Military-Industrial Commission under the Soviet Council of Ministers.

4. Mr. Savinkin, in fact, is the chief of the Administrative Organs Department of the Central Committee, which enjoys a supervisory role over various security agencies (including the Prokurator's office) and rides herd over the "Nomenklatura" (the list from which promotions and replacements are drawn), as well as being represented on the Soviet Defense Council.

5. Mr. Tyazhel'nikov was the chief of the Propaganda Depart-

ment of the Central Committee. (He was recently transferred to a lesser post.)

6. Mr. Zimyanin is Tyazhel'nikov's superior, the Secretary who has a supervisory role over ideology, science, education, culture, and propaganda.

7. Mr. Pastukhov was in charge of the agency that traditionally has supplied the cadres for the KGB, namely, the Komsomol. (Recently, he was demoted.)

It is not far-fetched, therefore, to assume that the Soviet space effort is run predominantly by persons with a direct role in military-industrial and security affairs and that the "civilians" involved are drawn primarily from the propaganda arms of the regime, which have a particular interest in playing up the space spectaculars, especially those that involve "joint" ventures between the Soviet Union and personnel from other countries.

It would seem reasonable, therefore, to explore how space fits in the overall Soviet defense effort and, particularly, what role it plays in Soviet military doctrine. With regard to the parameters of the latter, however, it is essential to realize that the leadership of the Soviet Union takes a very broad view. The late Marshal A. A. Grechko, one-time Soviet defense minister, in 1975 defined the Soviet approach to military doctrine as follows:

> The concept of doctrine, in its broad definition, encompasses teaching, a scientific or philosophical theory, and a system of guiding principles and views. Accordingly, military doctrine is understood to be an officially accepted system of views in a given state and in its Armed Forces on the nature of war and methods of conducting it and on preparation of the country and army for war.
>
> Military doctrine, at the very least, answers the following basic questions:
>
> —what enemy will have to be faced in a possible war?
> —what is the nature of the war in which the state and its armed forces will have to take part; what goal and missions might they be faced with in this war?
> —what armed forces are needed to complete the assigned missions, and in what direction must military development be carried out?
> —how are preparations for war to be implemented?
> —what methods must be used to wage war?
> . . . all the basic provisions of military doctrine stem from actually existing conditions, and above all from domestic and foreign policy, the socio-political and

economic system, level of production, status of means
for conducting war, and the geographic position both
of one's own state and that of the probable enemy.
... The theoretical basis of Soviet military doctrine consists of the following: Marxism-Leninism, military science, and, to a certain degree, *branches of* social, *natural,
and technical sciences related to the preparation and waging
of armed struggle* as well as to other forms of struggle
(economic, ideological, and diplomatic). Military doctrine in its turn has a reverse influence on military-
theoretical thought. (my emphasis)[1]

This is the general context for the particular attention devoted
by Marshal Grechko to "scientific-technological progress." He
stresses that "the scientific-technological revolution [has] led to a
qualitative change in ... material means of waging war," since "contemporary science is undergoing a phase where there is a fundamental break with outmoded theses and methods of research." He
continues:

A most important result of the scientific-technological revolution in our time is mankind's practical development of the
discoveries and achievements in the field of physical-mathe-
matical sciences, nuclear physics, solid-state physics, electronics, radiophysics, cybernetics, metallurgy, and many
other spheres. The adoption of the latest achievements of
science and technology in the economy played a decisive
role in the development of power engineering, especially
atomic energy, *in the exploration of space*, and in the creation
of new materials, highly complex machines and mechanisms, devices, and means of mechanization, automation,
and control, etc. [my emphasis]
In essence, the scientific-technological revolution now
serves as a most important arena of struggle between two
opposing socioeconomic systems ....
[We have] to use the results of scientific-technological
progress in the interests of strengthening the Motherland's
defensive capability .... This objective necessity for steadily
increasing the military might of the socialist state serves as
the political basis for revolutionary transformation in the
Soviet Armed Forces ....
All conditions have been created in the Soviet Union to
direct the efforts of scientists in a planned and purposeful
manner toward resolution of the most important, key long-
range, theoretical and practical problems having vital

importance ... for defense ....

[We have to] consolidate the foremost positions held by
Soviet science in the most important branches of knowledge
and to assume a *leading position in world science* ....

The rapid development of science and technology produced revolutionary changes in military affairs and had a
determining influence on the weaponry and organization
of the Armed Forces, on the methods of conducting combat
operations and ... of training and education of personnel ....

Classified issues of the military journal *Voyennaya mysl'*, in discussing the operational utilization of recent technological achievements, pay particular attention to developments that *"promote
achieving the element of surprise."* In this context, goals that are stressed
particularly include:

—destruction of hostile reconnaissance means, since under
present-day conditions destruction of electronic intelligence-gathering devices is of particular importance;
—fire neutralization and active jamming of the enemy's
communications system, leading to reduced enemy
capabilities for exchange of information, troop warning,
and control.[2]

In another issue of the same journal, especial emphasis was
placed upon the specific applications of these concepts to space
systems:

Aware of the present importance of electronics in space,
[some countries] are engaged in programs to develop hardware and methods of conducting electronic countermeasures in space. The purpose is to make radar detection
of spacecraft more difficult, and to reduce the effectiveness
of weapons employed in antispacecraft, antimissile, antiaircraft defense systems, and space weapons systems. ...
Spacecraft in flight can be concealed by antiradar camouflage and jamming. ... Radioelectronic devices of a defense
system against space weapons can be jammed by automatic
jamming transmitters carried on board satellites. ... It is
proposed that spacecraft radioelectronic equipment be
jammed by means of ground installations or satellite-borne
equipment. There is the possibility of utilizing powerful
electromagnetic radiation obtained from a laser in order to
put out of commission radioelectronic equipment carried
by spacecraft.[3]

The appearance of fairly detailed material concerning military aspects of space-related technology in classified Soviet journals during the 1970s is of particular interest. Thanks to the monumental scholarly work of Dr. Harriet Fast Scott in juxtaposing the three editions of *Soviet Military Strategy*, by Marshal V. D. Sokolovskiy et al., we know that reasonably overt (if brief) discussions of Soviet military activities and plans concerning space, published in the earlier editions, disappeared from the 1968 version or were transferred from chapters dealing with the Soviet military program to the section addressing U.S. space activities. It is evident, therefore, that the change resulted not from any decision to diminish this aspect of the Soviet military buildup, but rather from its increasingly topical (state-of-the-art) status. Soviet censors apparently deemed it advisable to make such programs disappear from view, at least as far as non-classified publications were concerned. Dr. Scott has drawn attention, in this connection, to the Soviet conviction that "the creation of a weapon that is new in principle and secretly nurtured in scientific research bureaus and constructors' collectives can in a short time sharply change the relationship of forces. The *surprise* appearance of one or another type of weapon is advancing as an essential factor, especially in contemporary circumstances."[4]

Another reason for taciturnity regarding military uses of space in the 1968 third edition of the Sokolovskiy volume was the January 27, 1967, Soviet-U.S.-British signature of the Treaty on Principles Governing the Activities of States in the Exploration and Use of Outer Space, which, in Article IV, sharply restricted potential military activities in space and on "celestial bodies."

Whereas the earlier editions of *Soviet Military Strategy* had considered military exploitation of space in the chapter "Methods of Conducting Warfare," under the heading "Problems of Using Space for Military Purposes," the 1968 edition transferred such discussions to a chapter called "Military Strategy of Imperialist States and Their Preparation of New Wars."

The result was a curiously contradictory document which, at one and the same time, conformed with the demands of secrecy by attributing to the United States both doctrinal and operational developments that applied, in fact, to the Soviet Union (an oblique way of keeping one's cadres up to date), while simultaneously making sufficient general references to Soviet scientific and technological capabilities to reassure the uninformed rank-and-file. Moreover, there are two apparently countervailing factors that make this publication of the late 1960s relevant to contemporary analysis of the role of space in Soviet military doctrine: while it is true that the requirements of surprise and secrecy, as well as the 1967 treaty, made for the longest postponement possible of any overt acknowledgment of the details of Soviet military capabilites in space, an entirely different timetable applied to statements of doctrine (even if attributed in unclassified material to the adversary). As stated very appropriately in *Soviet Military Strategy*, "military theory must outstrip the development of the means for armed conflict, actively influence their development, and, at the proper time, determine the changes in the methods of conducting armed conflict" (p. 275). This means, of course, that doctrinal statements could predate not only deployment, but even the research and development stage, of space systems. For that reason, space doctrine enunciated well over a decade ago is likely to be in force to this very day.

In fact, the 1968 edition of *Soviet Military Strategy* contains a new statement on this topic (albeit attributed to the United States) which, in terms of its very presentation and language is unmistakably *Soviet* doctrine, as a comparison with Marshal Grechko's 1975 publication of other aspects of Soviet military doctrine, quoted earlier in this chapter, indicates rather clearly. According to one significant pronouncement, plans exist

> to use the great achievements of modern science and technology in the mastery of space for ... military purposes.... The military mastery of space ... is proceeding in three basic directions:
>   —toward creating space weapon systems that will assure high combat operations effectiveness for all services of the armed forces;
>   —toward creating space systems that will prohibit the other countries from probing and mastering space (means of antispace defense);
>   —toward developing strategic offensive space systems to conduct armed conflict in space and to strike earth targets from space. [pp. 84–85]

These, then, would appear to be the broad outlines of Soviet military doctrine on space; some additional confirmation and elaboration may be distilled from (1) overt statements on Soviet space plans and activities that were omitted from the 1968 edition (for reasons of discretion explained earlier), (2) statements added in the 1968 edition (whether attributed to the Soviet Union or the United States), and (3) statements appearing in all three editions.

> (1) Certain military theoreticians believe that ... [stalemate] could be overcome by using outer space for military purposes where it would be possible to attain a [favorable]

balance of power. [Omitted from 1968 edition, p. 274][5]

The USSR has achieved important successes in the mastery of space. . . . In this regard Soviet military strategy takes into account the need for studying questions on the use of outer space and aerospace vehicles to strengthen the defense of the socialist countries. . . . It would be a mistake to allow the imperialist camp to achieve superiority in this field. We must oppose the imperialists with more effective means and methods for the use of space for defense purposes. [Omitted from 1968 edition, p. 303]

The concept of "geographic expanse" of war in the future will require a substantial supplementation inasmuch as military operations may embrace outer space. [Omitted from 1968 edition, p. 205]

[Because the adversary has] devoted great attention to a study of the possibilities of carrying out military actions in space and through space, Soviet military strategy cannot ignore this fact and must also study the possibilities opening up in the sphere of military action. [Omitted from 1968 edition, p. 386]

The rapid development of spacecraft and specifically of artificial earth satellites, which can be launched for the most diverse purposes, even as vehicles for nuclear weapons, has put a new problem on the agenda, that of defense against space devices—PKO. It is still early to predict what line will be taken in the solution of this problem, but as surely as an offensive one is created, a defensive one will be too. [Omitted from 1968 edition, p. 251]

(2) It must be assumed that in the near future radical corrections will be . . . introduced . . . as a result of the incorporation of various cosmic means. All of this in turn conditions the nature of a future war, the methods of waging it, and the principles of organization of the armed forces. [Added in 1968 edition, p. 48]

(3) It is quite evident that the Soviet Union has left the United States far behind in the mastery of space. [Appears in all editions, p. 45]

The modern concept of a theater of military operations may include the entire territory of a belligerent or coalition, whole continents, large bodies of water, and extensive regions of the atmosphere, including space. [Appears in all editions, p. 13]

Space means, including various devices, are by their very

nature strategic weapons, or serve to assure the successful use of other strategic weapons in wartime. [Appears in all editions, p. 84]

An extremely important type of strategic operations is the protection of territory of the country from nuclear attacks by the enemy, using PVO (antiair), PRO (antimissile), and PKO (antispace defense). [Appears in all editions, pp. 284–85]

The material presented here would appear to permit two general conclusions. First, the Soviet space program today is supervised predominantly by Party and state personnel in charge of military industry or security. The supervisors also include experts in propaganda exploitation of space spectaculars. Second, unclassified Soviet documentation up to the late 1960s and restricted material going into the 1970s reflect military doctrine concerning the development both of the capabilities and of the appropriate force structures and combat modalities to (a) create space weapons systems ancillary to the existing military services; (b) neutralize space systems (including reconnaissance and communications systems) of other countries; and (c) develop strategic offensive space systems, both to conduct warfare in space itself and to attack targets on the planetary surface. In this general context, particular emphasis is placed upon (d) achievement of suprise, through destroying the adversary's capacity to engage in electronic intelligence-gathering and through jamming of his communications system, stressing the space aspects of these objectives; and (e) diminution of the vulnerability of the Soviet space systems and the enhancement of the vulnerability of adversary space weapons systems and antispace defense systems (the latter, or PKO system being emphasized as particularly desirable for the Soviet Union to achieve).

In the light of the factors presented here, it would appear that such developments as the deployment of a Soviet ASAT system are the tip of the iceberg of a long-term Soviet military space effort, envisaged and planned first in the 1960s and embodied in Soviet military doctrine at that early stage. That is not to say that nonmilitary components of the Soviet space program are absent or that they are insignificant. Indeed, those aspects, as well as fuller details of Soviet military technology, are discussed at appropriate length elsewhere in this volume.

NOTES

1. *The Armed Forces of the Soviet State*, 2nd ed., Voennoe Izdatel'stvo Ministerstva Oborony SSSR, Moscow, 1975.

2. Col. Dr. L. Kuleszynski, "Some Problems of Surprise in Warfare," *Voyennaya mysl'*, no. 5, May 1971.

3. Maj. Gen. Engr.-Tech. Serv. A. Paliy, "The Status of and Some Trends in the Development of Radioelectronic Warfare," *Voyennaya mysl'*, no. 12, Dec. 1971. Many of the available publications date back to the 1970s, but it was not unusual for technologies to be mentioned that the Soviet Union had not yet fully developed or deployed.

4. V. D. Sokolovskiy, *Soviet Military Strategy*, 3rd Ed., ed. Harriet Fast Scott (New York: Crane, Russak, 1975), p. 48. (Originally published in *Voyenizdat*, Moscow, 1968.)

5. The pages cited as the sources of the quotations listed refer to Harriet Scott's work (above).

2

Space As a High Frontier for Strategic Defense

4

Space and ICBM Defense: U.S. and Soviet Programs, with Special Emphasis on Boost Phase and Midcourse Ballistic Missile Defense

WALLACE E. KIRKPATRICK

Although planning for strategic defense has attracted attention thoughout the defense community, a clear consensus on the role of strategic defense in the context of the emerging strategic force structure has not yet developed. Strategic defense, or ballistic missile defense as it is more commonly referred to in the United States, could become an important fulcrum in the strategic policy arena and hence in East-West relations during the next twenty years. U.S. decisions on ballistic missile defense during the 1980s may prove to be among the most important national security topics debated in the decade. Directed energy systems, the principal application of which is defensive, offer the potential for dramatic improvements in national security and world stability.

The great debates, frustration, and uncertainty about the future of current systems center on details, albeit important ones, about individual weapon system programs, which underpin a national strategy that relies primarily on offensive weapons or deterrents. The offense-dominated strategy has provided increasing strategic instability, and a return to a balance between offensive and defensive systems is warranted.

The recent movement to "freeze" the level of nuclear weapons is only a symptom of a deeply imbedded, rapidly growing ailment stemming from the increasing population of nuclear weapons. The only effective treatment is a move toward a postnuclear era in which the role of nuclear systems is diminished. The manifestations of the symptom will increase until political accommodations can be reached that permit meaningful reductions in the number of nuclear weapons. It is certain that such agreements will not be concluded easily or rapidly. Nuclear weapons are such powerful political and military instruments that national leaders will find it difficult to discard them. The high stakes justify caution in serious deliberations on reductions of strategic nuclear arms. If, however, the political and military value of nuclear weapons could be reduced, the irresistible urge to retain them could be mitigated. A return to active strategic defense can play a positive role in limiting the value of nuclear systems.

The combination of past technological limitations and political goals has denied both the United States and the Soviet Union the means to reduce the value of offensive nuclear weapons through the use of active strategic defense. The technological base for such systems in the decades of the 1950s and 1960s was embryonic, and the ability of either the United States or the Soviet Union to develop ballistic missile defense (BMD) systems with enduring effectiveness was at least debatable. At the same time, the political environment facilitated a new set of experiments in international relations: detente and arms control. Great expectations were expressed by Western political leaders and strategic analysts about the prospects of "capping" the growth in nuclear systems. Regrettably, the high expectations have gradually faded, and today the political leaders and strategic analysts of the West must grapple with the aftermath of disappointment. They must find new approaches to protect the national security interests of the United States and the Western Alliance. Major segments of the body politic, in both the United States and throughout Western Europe, are concerned and alarmed about the trend of continuing growth in the number of nuclear weapons and increasing uncertainty of future arms-control initiatives. The birth of the "freeze nuclear weapons" movement conveys a clear message: continued increases in nuclear weapons are unacceptable. The present political and technical landscape provides an ideal opportunity to rethink the role of strategic defense.

STRATEGY

From the inception of the nuclear era, U.S. strategic policy has generally been based on the theory of mutual vulnerability. This strategy has borne a variety of labels; recently, the concept of mutual assured destruction (MAD) has given way to the concept of the Countervailing Strategy, established by Presidential Directive 59 in 1980. While MAD has yielded place to the Countervailing Strategy, the underlying theory of deterrence has not changed. The concept of mutual vulnerability was officially codified in the Anti-Ballistic Missile (ABM) Treaty of 1972, which severely limits the use of BMD.

The great ABM debate in the United States in 1967–69 centered on two discrete issues: (1) the workability of the ABM system, and (2) the strategic role of BMD. BMD was argued to be destabilizing, and mutual vulnerability of the United States and the Soviet Union was said to provide the greatest degree of deterrence. Development, testing, and deployment of the U.S. ABM system proved the system's technical feasibility and resolved the first issue, although some argued that its long-term effectiveness against more sophisticated threats was questionable. The ABM Treaty of 1972 (and subsequent protocol) and unilateral dismantling of the U.S. ABM system codified the attitude that defense is destabilizing.

The unrelenting pace of Soviet development and deployment of strategic weapons, and the consequent vulnerability of the U.S. land-based ICBM systems, now seriously casts doubt upon the wisdom and adequacy of deterrence by mutual vulnerability and undercuts the argument that ABM is destabilizing. The unprecedented pace of Soviet ICBM deployment places the U.S. land-based ICBM force at an unacceptable level of vulnerability to a Soviet first strike. The abandonment of active strategic defense is the single most significant contributor to the emerging vulnerability of the U.S. land-based ICBM force, and the most effective means of removing the vulnerability is to protect the ICBM force with strategic defense systems.

The resurgence of interest in BMD can be attributed principally to a rejection of past images of Soviet military and political motivations. Past miscalculations about Soviet behavior have provided a false sense of national security in the United States which has, in turn, provided the Soviets with time to overcome U.S. domination in the strategic nuclear arena. Strategic analysts know all too well of the erosion of the U.S. position. Any credible theory of deterrence must include survivable strategic nuclear offensive weapons.

Active defense of strategic "hardened" assets is technically and economically feasible, but population defense is not. The ICBM silos are hardened to withstand nuclear blast effects. Hostile enemy nuclear warheads may therefore be intercepted only a few thousand feet from the defended silos. Other critical elements of the strategic forces, such as command, control, and communications systems and the national command authority, are also hardened, although to lower levels than the ICBM silos. Defense of strategic forces does not require perfect intercept of all the hostile warheads; a small number of warheads can be absorbed while still ensuring a sufficient number of survivable nuclear weapons to preserve deterrence.

Defense of the population (cities, industry, and so forth) is not considered to be technically or economically feasible at the present time, since population centers cannot be "hardened" and no hostile warhead "leakage" would be acceptable. The development of space-based systems, however, could facilitate area defense systems.

Return to a strategy of active strategic defense would require modification of, or unilateral withdrawal from, the ABM Treaty. The sensitivity of the arms-control community to the suggestion can be understood but not condoned. The nation must decide on its foreign policy and defense policies, and devise strategies and doctrine, including arms control, appropriate to such policies. Conceptually, changes in existing arms-control agreements should be no more sensitive than other bold diplomatic initiatives or the movement of military forces as world situations change. Military forces and arms-control policies are means of achieving national foreign policy objectives in a constantly changing world.

THE ROLE OF STRATEGIC DEFENSE IN THE REAGAN PROGRAM

President Reagan announced on 2 October 1981, a comprehensive plan for revitalizing the strategic deterrent, to end the relative decline of U.S. strategic capabilities and place the United States in a position to reshape the U.S.-Soviet competition in the years ahead. The central elements of the Reagan administration strategic program include communications and control systems, the bomber program, sea-based forces, a step-by-step approach to land-based missile modernization, and strategic defense. The Reagan plan rejected the Multiple Protective Shelter (MPS) basing mode for MX because of the belief that any ground-based scheme ultimately would require ballistic missile defense for survivability. In assessing the role of BMD, the administration concluded that it was not ready to commit itself to existing ballistic missile defense concepts. Uncertainty about cost, technical capability, treaty ramifications, and Soviet countermoves were cited as the reasons for the administration's reservations about BMD.

BMD, however, is potentially relevant to all five areas of the administration's strategic programs. A December 1984 timetable was outlined for selection of one or more of the options. Subsequent negotiations between Senator John Tower (R-Texas), chairman of the Senate Armed Services Committee, and the secretary of defense added a defended deceptive basing option and advanced the decision timetable to July 1983. The Senate Armed Services Committee deleted MX procurement funds in the amount of $2.6 billion from the FY 1983 defense budget and requested that the administration select a permanent basing mode for MX.

The administration is committed to additional research and development relating to space-based missile defense and active defense of land-based missiles. Within the context of the Reagan administration, the relevant BMD-related issues are: adequacy of defense systems, cost, arms control, and the effects on alliance relationships. Strategic policy and doctrinal issues should be treated explicitly, for it is these issues that provide the policy framework for resolving the four central issues.

While future BMD developments seem likely to produce a space-based system, four criteria should guide development efforts. First, the long-term role of BMD must be assessed in the context of strategic policy; this assessment should focus on BMD contributions to stability and deterrence. The central issue is whether the deployment of BMD could reasonably reduce the chances of nuclear war. Second, BMD systems must present workable, long-term solutions in the context of the emerging strategic environment. Third, arms-control policies should reflect national objectives related to BMD. Fourth, BMD programs must be capable of accomplishing the selected strategic and arms-control objectives. Unless policy initiatives rely on these criteria, the prospects for a return to active strategic defense seem sharply limited.

EMERGING FORCES THAT INFLUENCE A RETURN TO ACTIVE STRATEGIC DEFENSE

Dissatisfaction with SALT

There has been a slow and agonizing realization that U.S. SALT objectives have not been achieved. The dissatisfaction came into focus during the Senate review of the SALT II Treaty. Many aspects of the SALT II Treaty worried responsible and objective analysts. The unrelenting pace of Soviet development and deployment of strategic nuclear systems, the increasing vulnerability of the U.S. land-based ICBM force, and the increasingly clear Soviet intention to seek strategic superiority combined to reduce the appeal of arms control as a guarantor of national security.

Survivability of the U.S. Land-based ICBM Force

There is widespread agreement that the Minuteman ICBM force will become unacceptably vulnerable by the mid-1980s. The planned U.S. response to assure a survivable ICBM is the deployment of MX, but the search for a survivable basing mode continues.

The SALT II Treaty would have expired in 1985 if it had been ratified. Without limitations on the warhead levels of Soviet offensive systems, the MX program may not adequately guarantee the survivability of the U.S. land-based ICBM force. The START negotiations will focus on such limitations, but the results to be achieved are extremely uncertain. An extension of the SALT II force levels beyond

1985 would degrade the Soviet position relative to the United States. The consequence of such a future agreement, from the Soviet perspective, would be a change from a position of assured vulnerability to assured survivability of the U.S. ICBM force.

An MX deployment coupled with an active defense may ultimately be necessary to assure survivability of the U.S. ICBM force, even at launcher/warhead levels contained in the SALT II Treaty (the only limits currently being observed). BMD could also change the nature of the competition from quantitative to qualitative.

Decreasing Distinction between Strategic and Tactical Weapons

The initial efforts at negotiating arms-control agreements focused on strategic weapons. Definition and classification of strategic weapons was fairly easy for the United States; it was much more difficult for the Soviet Union because of the ability of forward-based systems in Western Europe to strike the heartland of Soviet territory. The introduction of the extended range Pershing II and nuclear armed cruise missiles in Western Europe can only enhance Soviet arguments that forward-based systems should be counted as strategic weapons. Conversely, the classification of the Soviet Backfire Bomber as a theater weapon has caused some concern in the U.S. deployment of the SS-20, has further blurred the distinction between strategic and tactical systems, and has led to discussion of an antitactical ballistic missile system for NATO.

Such an antitactical ballistic missile (ATBM) system would necessarily adopt some ABM technology, thereby causing a future blurring in the distinction between tactical and strategic defense systems. While ABM technology transfer is constrained by the ABM Treaty, deployment of ATBM systems is not. Verification that ATBM systems do not possess capabilities against strategic systems (ICBM and SLBM) would be extremely difficult.

Modernization in China

China's opening of relations with the West is integral to its long-term modernization program, which includes the Chinese military. The West is opening its military and technological vaults to China, and in the next decade or so the Chinese are likely to forge a military force, including strategic missiles, that will have a greater influence upon Soviet military behavior than in the past. The Soviets will be compelled to respond with strategic defense systems, which will further complicate preservation of the present ABM Treaty. While Western analysts tend to downplay the military threat posed by China to the Soviet Union, the deployment of at least fifty Soviet divisions along the Chinese border reflects Moscow's view of the military potential of its neighbor. Long-term U.S. strategy and force structure should at least note the implications of an emerging China on East-West relations.

Technology

Significant advances have been made in technology needed for terminal and exoatmospheric defense systems. Potentially revolutionary technology for directed energy weapons, currently in an embryonic state, is progressing at a steady rate. The movement of BMD toward applications in space is a clearly identifiable trend.

Dramatic improvements in "conventional" BMD technology include small, inexpensive radars, commercial data processors, and single-stage interceptors. Nonnuclear kill capability for conventional terminal defense systems operating at low altitudes in the dense atmosphere is being pursued vigorously; it appears that the nonnuclear kill technology for terminal defense systems may mature in the mid- to late 1980s. Systems based on this technology could become a reality in the 1990s.

An important new class of technology, called long wavelength infrared (LWIR) optics, is undergoing experimental field tests. This exoatmospheric technology is extremely attractive because it can provide the basis for systems that detect, acquire, and discriminate warheads from decoys, and then guide an interceptor. Long wavelength infrared technology extends the reach of BMD interceptors to the midcourse area of the ICBM trajectory, thus increasing the time available to identify and intercept hostile warheads from a minute or two in a conventional terminal defense system to between fifteen and twenty minutes. In addition, LWIR permits "viewing" the threat at ranges as great as 2,000 miles and allows use of two different methods—radar and LWIR optics—for discriminating the warhead from decoys, tank clutter, and other objects, thereby making penetration of the BMD system technologically very difficult. Finally, the new technology facilitates intercepting hostile targets outside the atmosphere with nonnuclear BMD warheads and provides the capability to deny the attacker several strategies, such as highly structured attacks, precursor nuclear attacks, and use of electronic countermeasures. The LWIR optics technology also offers potential applications to other miitary needs, including tactical warning and assessment programs.

New and revolutionary research in high-energy laser and particle beam technologies is progressing in theoretical, laboratory, and experimental development. These technologies offer the potential for directed energy systems. High-energy laser technology generally is considered to be the more practical system, though particle beam technology should not be ruled out.

Continuous progress has been made in laser technology since the first laser was invented in 1960. The greatest potential application of such high-energy laser technology in directed energy weapons is in active defense systems. The applications could include disabling or destroying passive or hostile satellites and defending against advanced sensors, tactical aircraft, guided munitions, tactical ballistic missiles, or intercontinental ballistic missiles.

Lasers can disable or destroy cruise missiles if the beam is put on the target; the extremely low altitude at which cruise missiles operate (a few tens of feet), however, presents unique detection and engagement problems. A lookdown-shootdown capability could be provided by putting a high-energy laser in an aircraft, but such a system could produce unacceptable collateral ground damage.

Features and applications of laser technology. High-energy laser directed energy weapons systems offer several unique and attractive features and a variety of potential applications. Laser beams travel at the speed of light, reducing or eliminating the requirement to "lead" the target. The speed and precision of a laser weapon would permit it to disable or destroy single enemy targets selectively in the midst of a host of friendly vehicles.

For each "shot" of the laser, relatively small amounts of fuel are used to generate the beam. There is, therefore, the potential of storing a large number of shots in each laser system. Finally, since the beam is directed by mirrors, the laser weapon has the potential to move rapidly from target to target over a wide field of view. Consequently, a laser weapon could handle a large number of targets even if the targets were coming from all directions.

To achieve an effective weapons system, development efforts must address those characteristics of high-energy laser weapons that tend to limit the capabilities of such weapons. For example, a successful laser weapon engagement occurs when the beam burns through the target surface and destroys the warhead or other vital component. While the energy is delivered instantaneously, the laser must dwell for a short time on the target to destroy it. Jitter of the focused spot on the target smears the energy of the beam over a large effective spot, increasing the time required to destroy the target. Thus the beam control subsystem must hold the beam steady on the target.

Fire control for laser weapons will have to be especially capable. A laser must be pointed with great accuracy, and therefore the fire control subsystem must be highly accurate in telling the beam control subsystem where to point. In addition, to realize the firepower potential of a laser weapon, the fire control must be quick to recognize that the target being engaged has been damaged sufficiently, so that the laser weapon can then move to the next target.

A final example of a characteristic that tends to limit laser capabilities is the effect the atmosphere has on the laser beam. The atmosphere absorbs some of the energy being propagated, causes the beam to "bloom" or defocus, and adds jitter to the beam. The severity of the atmospheric effects varies among the various laser frequencies and under different atmospheric conditions.

Interactions between the high-power beam and the atmosphere effectively increase the spot size of the beam on the target, lowering the intensity of the beam and increasing the amount of time the beam must be held on the target. Of course, in bad weather or in the presence of clouds or aerosols such as smoke, more of the energy in the laser beam is absorbed, thus limiting the range of the laser weapon. Space-based systems would not encounter such effects, since they would operate in the vacuum of space. Space-based systems would face other problems associated with deployment of systems in space, however, such as size, weight, lifetime, and reliability.

There are many potential applications for which high-energy weapons systems appear attractive, including the defense of satellites, aircraft, ships, and ground-based targets against guided projectiles, hostile aircraft, and missile threats. There is also a wide variation in the performance requirements of high-energy laser systems, depending on the "mission" they are performing. Current U.S. technology could support the least difficult high-energy weapon system requirements, such as antisensor systems, and the technology could probably be scaled to provide weapons systems capable of other potential applications, such as disabling hostile satellites. Defense against intercontinental-range ballistic missiles is extremely difficult, however, and further development is necessary to provide such systems.

Test results to date. In the course of development efforts to date, laser weapon testbeds, using technology developed in the Department of Defense high-energy laser program, have scored first for the United States in engaging moving targets. The first such success was in 1973 when the Air Force used a high-energy gas-dynamic laser of moderate power and an ongimbal telescope to shoot down a winged drone on the Sandia Optical Range at Kirtland Air Force Base, New Mexico. In 1976, the Army, using a high-energy electric laser of modest power, successfully destroyed winged and helicopter drones at Redstone Arsenal, Alabama. The most recent tests were in March 1978 when the Navy, using a chemical-laser of moderate power developed by the Defense Advanced Research Projects Agency and a

Navy pointer tracker, successfully engaged and destroyed a TOW antitank missile.

The major objectives of these experiments have been to obtain experience and insight into the problems of integrating a laser of moderately high power with a pointing and tracking device and maintaining the laser beam on the selected aimpoint. The successful destruction of moving targets provided dramatic proof of the successful attainment of these technology goals.

Current and planned program. The DARPA and the military services are proceeding with a number of technology demonstration programs to provide the technological foundation for prototype weapons systems development programs that could be initiated in the late 1980s.

The DARPA high-energy laser program is concentrated in three technical areas: laser devices, optics and mirrors, and pointing and tracking. The pointing and tracking experiment will be conducted in space; the other technology demonstration programs will be ground tested. While encompassing the three critical technology areas of laser weapons, these efforts are not integrated and therefore will not provide a complete understanding of the total system.

The testbed for the Air Force is the Airborne Laser Laboratory, a highly instrumented NKC-135 aircraft. The Air Force is investigating the integration and operation of a high-energy laser system in a dynamic airborne environment and the propagation of the laser beam from an airborne vehicle to an airborne target. Potential applications include aircraft defense against hostile aircraft, air-to-air and ground-to-air missiles and disablement or destruction of hostile satellites.

The Army is in an early phase of examining the feasibility of laser weapon concepts for defense against weapons that use optical sensors and against aircraft, and for other air defense scenarios typical of the Army battlefield. A modestly funded technology development program is under way, which could provide the technological foundation for defense against guided munitions, low-altitude defense against tactical aircraft (helicopters and fixed-wing), and defense against high-altitude, high-performance aircraft. Conspicuously absent is the evaluation of a laser system capable of destroying tactical ballistic missiles, such as the Soviet SS-20, which poses a serious threat to NATO forces.

The Navy is developing plans for a test series in the 1980s at the Department of Defense High-Energy Laser National Test Range, being built at the White Sands Missile Range (WSMR) in New Mexico. The principal application of interest to the navy will be ship defense against guided munitions, aircraft, and missiles.

Army and Air Force tests are also planned at WSMR laser test facilities.

Program funding. The cumulative Department of Defense funding for high-energy lasers through fiscal year 1982 exceeds $1.97 billion. Another $.5 to $1 billion may be required before an adequate technology base is developed to support the most difficult high-energy laser system applications. The costs of developing laser weapons will be high, but the potential military value of the technology justifies the investment.

CONCLUSION

A return to active strategic defense can be a positive, balanced, and widely supported policy choice. In a sense, return to active strategic defense and the development and deployment of space-based ballistic missile defense systems seems inevitable. First, the technology will be developed to support such weapons. In little more than two decades, the technology development of lasers has been most impressive. Second, the principal application of directed energy weapons is for defensive systems. These weapons are unlikely to replace bullets, tanks, artillery, missiles, or bombs, either conventional, chemical, or nuclear, as offensive instruments of war. They also offer enormous advantages over systems of current technology in "defensive" applications. Third, the political and military advantages conferred by these weapons will make their deployment irresistible, notwithstanding the ABM Treaty or other arms-control accords. Rarely do technological developments offer the potential for such revolutionary shifts in the national security posture of the superpowers. Fourth, such systems can mitigate the military power of nuclear weapons, thereby making meaningful reductions more palatable to world leaders. Space-based BMD can be the development that moves us into the postnuclear era. The Soviet leadership has paid a high price for its present military capability; they will not willingly negotiate away their military advantages. Space-based BMD can diminish the value of nuclear weapons, thereby contributing a strong and practical rationale for negotiations to reduce the immense nuclear arsenals of the United States and the Soviet Union.

Movement to a postnuclear era is both desirable and inevitable. The issue is whether—and how—the transition will be planned.

5

Antisatellite Weaponry and Possible Defense Technologies against Killer Satellites

CLARENCE A. ROBINSON, JR.

Space systems can perform many missions more efficiently than earthbound systems. Effective military operations on the modern battlefield increasingly depend on spaceborne surveillance, warning, and communications and on meteorological and navigation support provided by satellites.

The Soviet Union is well aware of the military utility of operating in space and has committed sizeable resources toward a significant space presence. Over the last decade, Soviet space launches exceeded in substantial number those of the United States; the majority of these launches were made for military purposes. The Soviets are supporting an active man-in-space program, and they have deployed and continue to test an operational antisatellite capability.

Unless the United States can negotiate a treaty that effectively controls antisatellite weapons, the development of the necessary systems to respond to an attack on U.S. space systems is extremely important. The United States depends heavily on its spacecraft and is becoming even more dependent as these assets gain the potential to provide survivable warning and strategic communications and weapon targeting. These capabilities are particularly important at a time when the Soviet intercontinental ballistic missile force has made the U.S. land-based missile force vulnerable to first strike.

There is widespread recognition that space systems may be suitable early targets in any warfare scenario, not only because they will be available, but also because they will range in value from being of little military significance to being extremely important. In testifying to the Congress on the Fiscal Year 1983 budget request for space activities, Robert S. Cooper, director of the Advanced Research Projects Agency, said that Soviet deployment of an operational antisatellite system demonstrates an understanding of that situation and provides an additional rationale for Defense Department consideration of the role of space weapons. Cooper added that the United States must develop the means to deter an enemy attack with anti-satellite weapons against military spacecraft. If deterrence fails, the United States must protect its spacecraft, if necessary, by using active satellite defense weapons.

SOVIET MILITARY SPACE INITIATIVES

Soviet space activities continued in 1981 with the launch of 98 space missions carrying 126 payloads; the United States launched only 18 missions. High-level Defense Department officials expect this trend to continue through the 1980s with the advent of new systems and capabilities. Over the last several years, the Soviets have launched about ten times as much payload as the United States. While only one-third of U.S. spacecraft are used for military applications, the Soviet ratio is about three-fourths for military use only, with another 15 percent for shared military and civilian systems. Since October 1968, the Soviet Union has flown 20 hunter-killer satellite intercept tests against Russian target spacecraft. In 16 of these tests the intercept distance was close enough for the mission to be ruled a success. During these tests, Soviet killer satellites are placed into orbits that allow them to approach targets under guidance system control, flying by a specific target at a relative velocity of 400 meters per second. The conventional warhead detonates at close range, sending a shower of shrapnel into the target at high velocity. In all of the tests of these antisatellite weapons conducted by the Soviet Union, the interceptor vehicle has closed on the target within one or two orbits to demonstrate a quick reaction capability.

Hunter-killer satellites launched on SS-9 boosters constitute the primary threat to U.S. space-based systems because of the rapid response of the weapon system. U.S. intelligence has learned that SS-9 boosters carrying antisatellite payloads can be wheeled from shelters at the Tyuratan launch site and erected for launch in less than ninety minutes. Observation of this capability gave the first indication that the Soviets had perfected a quick-reaction system that could attack U.S. spacecraft without lengthy warning.

The intercept altitudes for the killer satellites are believed to range from 160 to 1,500 kilometers; the apogee could be increased with a larger booster. The quick reaction capability built into the Soviet antisatellite system permits them to react much like an air defense fighter group. Flying an intercept in only one or two revolutions of earth allows a much shorter period for the United States to determine that a target spacecraft is being chased or for ground stations to track the killer spacecraft. The chase and intercept could take place out of communications view of the United States, making it difficult to confirm the attack. For this reason, the North American Aerospace Defense Command has established a space defense operations center at Cheyenne Mountain to provide a focal point for all U.S. spacecraft and to report the status of these space assets. In addition, U.S. spacecraft are likely to be equipped with flight data recorders and sensors to detect electromagnetic radiation or electronic jamming received during passes over the Soviet Union.

The Soviet Union has startled U.S. Defense Department space experts with what intelligence community officials believe to be a feasibility demonstration of a new type of antisatellite or defense satellite (ASAT/DSAT) battle station. This new system is improving the Soviet Union's capability for space warfare. The space-based antisatellite system is equipped with clusters of interceptor vehicles that could destroy U.S. spacecraft. It has been identified as Kosmos 1267, docked to Salyut 6, since 19 June 1981, ostensibly as a test of enlarging the space station's capability. The 30,000-pound Kosmos 1267 demonstrated extensive maneuvering capability after launch from Tyuratam on 24 April 1981. The Defense Department is concerned that future operational spacecraft like Kosmos 1267 will be employed to threaten U.S. missile early warning and communications spacecraft operating at geosynchronous altitude. The Soviet Union's success in docking this antisatellite weapon platform with Salyut 6 demonstrates that the Soviet Union may be able to use a manned Salyut to conduct attacks on U.S. spacecraft or to protect Soviet satellites against a retaliatory attack by the United States. In recent Congressional testimony, General Lew Allen, Jr., Air Force chief of staff, told the Senate that the Soviet Union does not have an operational orbital antisatellite system. However, while a single system—such as Kosmos 1267—would pose no real threat to U.S. military space systems, full-scale deployment of the system would be threatening, particularly if coupled with the ground-based killer satellite system or future directed energy weapons.

The initial role of directed energy weapons—particle beam and high-energy laser devices—would be for satellite destruction, but these weapons could eventually be used against ballistic missiles, high-flying aircraft, fleets at sea, and air defenses. Operational directed energy weapons based in space would not only provide control of the high ground in space but could control warfare on earth as well.

THE U.S. RESPONSE

The U.S. response to Soviet space weapons development has been to pursue technology for two separate systems: a conventional air-to-space heat-seeking miniature homing vehicle fired from an F-15 aircraft; and directed energy weapons, especially high-energy chemical lasers. The U.S. Air Force is still approximately a year away from the first developmental test of the Vought Corporation miniature homing vehicle antisatellite system. An operational capability is at least two years away for this direct ascent weapon system, which will use long wavelength infrared sensors to home on a spacecraft target. The weapon is not designed to go into orbit, but to engage all Soviet spacecraft operating in low earth orbit up to approximately three hundred nautical miles. Though a limited operational capability is two years away, a longer period will be needed for production of sufficient numbers of the weapon to provide the full inventory required to present a credible deterrent to hostile acts against U.S. spacecraft.

The Defense Department's Advanced Research Projects Agency (DARPA) is heading the technology development effort to provide a space-based laser weapons system for antisatellite roles and for possible use against ballistic missile targets. The Air Force is involved in a joint program with DARPA, turning service attention toward the weapons system aspects of space-based laser weaponry, while DARPA continues to develop the technology. Another major Pentagon effort is under way to determine effective countermeasures that could be developed to resist laser weapons. Applications of a wide variety of technology are being examined to provide countermeasures for the United States and to determine the effective levels of Soviet hardening against potential U.S. lasers.

There is no debate that the Soviet-directed energy program is a massive national effort and that the Soviet Union's high-energy laser development program is from three to five times larger than the U.S. effort in this area. During the hearing on the 1983 Defense Department budget request, legislators heard testimony that the Soviet Union will be able to launch a space-based laser platform by the mid-1980s and by about 1990, can have operational a large, permanently manned orbital space complex capable of effectively attacking ground, sea, and airborne targets from space. Despite this testimony, the U.S. response has been restrained, while the scientific community debates whether such weapons could alter the balance of power or provide a solution to the problems presented by the nuclear "balance of terror."

The rapid Soviet development of antisatellite weapons should come as no surprise to serious students of the Soviet military. As early as 1964, a division of the air defense branch of the Soviet military was described by the Soviets as intended for destroying the enemy's cosmic means of fighting. This branch of the Soviet armed forces has also improved the military potential of the Soviet manned space flight program. The Defense Department expects to see a continued high rate of development by the Soviet Union through the 1980s and the advent of new systems and capabilities, including a new space booster in the Saturn 5 class and large permanently manned space stations and complexes.

The key to this Soviet space station activity is a massive new booster estimated to have approximately a 400,000-pound payload capability (the U.S. Saturn 5 has a payload capability of 250,000 pounds). The Defense Department believes that a space station launched by this new Soviet booster could support up to twelve cosmonauts and could carry high-energy weapons.

U.S. INITIATIVES AND ALTERNATIVES

The United States is moving to develop the capability to obtain free access to space through enhancing reliable and responsive launch systems and protection of spacecraft. The plan calls for making U.S. space systems—satellites and ground processing stations—more survivable. Programs are also funded to improve surveillance, communications, and navigation capabilities of space systems, to procure backup satellites, and to remove dependency on overseas ground stations.

Spacecraft are also being deployed that can conduct multiple missions with longer orbital life. The Air Force is deploying more sophisticated satellites, developing a new space launch capability, and aggressively pursuing advanced, space-related technology. The Air Force is also working on a new consolidated space operations center to manage space missions for the Defense Department. A satellite test center will provide mutual emergency backup for mission essential functions, should either the consolidated space operations center or the test center experience an outage.

One passive defense measure that has been undertaken by the United States is the upgrading and installation of new radars on Guam, the Philippine Islands, and Kwajalein Atoll to form a barrier through which Soviet spacecraft must pass after launch. This radar barrier will allow earlier identification than does the present system, which uses radars in the Eastern Test Range.

Moving to supersynchronous orbit is considered one of the best options available to the United States to provide survivability for satellites. Spacecraft will be operated at the higher altitude, and will therefore have more time to react to attack, in the next five to ten years.

Most current spacecraft are able, to some extent, to maneuver in orbit and can use this capability to dodge an attack. The United

States will add maneuverability to its satellites to enable them to evade an attack without warning. Maneuverable spacecraft compound the tracking problem for an enemy because spacecraft do not appear in the same position for the period required for accurate tracking. Maneuvering, however, cannot be accomplished if that tactic interferes with the basic mission of the satellite.

Another tactic for spacecraft survival is the use of duplicate nonoperating satellites placed in orbit along with operational primary satellites. The duplicates remain dormant until signaled to replace a destroyed or damaged spacecraft. Yet another concept involves small, inexpensive spacecraft placed on boosters and hidden in Minuteman silos. These smaller spacecraft are configured for specific missions and can be placed in orbit as temporary replacements for larger, more capable satellites destroyed during hostilities. The replacement spacecraft are configured only to operate for an interim period during a crisis. As an alternative, one or more launch tubes on each fleet ballistic missile submarine could be equipped with a replacement spacecraft. The emergence of the Space Shuttle makes spacecraft that are stored in orbit somewhat more attractive than replacement ground- or sea-based spacecraft, but some combination of both may result.

Spacecraft are also being hardened to both nuclear and thermal effects, and technology will now enable a single type of material to be used for protection against both nuclear and thermal effects. The United States has also made great strides in developing antijamming techniques for its spacecraft.

The General Accounting Office has recommended that development of chemical infrared high-energy laser technology be accelerated, in accordance with a program outlined by DARPA. The DARPA Triad program is designed to develop and test separately the three major subsystems of a laser weapon: the device to generate the beam, known as the Alpha program; the large optics demonstration experiment (LODE); and Talon Gold, the acquisition, pointing, and tracking technology for a space-based laser. The GAO report states that laser technology has reached a point at which the military utility is relatively clear, but that technical uncertainties remain. The study calls for funds to meet objectives efficiently, explaining that existing technology can now support a program to demonstrate the feasibility of a space-based laser. The GAO proposes doubling the funding for the joint USAF/DARPA laser program to speed up a feasibility demonstration in orbit, concluding that vital data required for systems integration cannot be obtained until such a feasibility demonstration is accomplished. At the current pace of the DARPA effort and the USAF space-based laser plan, a demonstration will not occur until the late 1980s. Differences over the levels of Soviet laser hardening are fueling the debate within Congress, the Defense Department, and scientific laboratories over the appropriate direction and pace of U.S. laser efforts.

Although space-based lasers can have a major impact on the strategic situation they cannot prevent ballistic missile damage to the United States. Any commitment to an active defense for the United States should include all forms of several different systems. The Army's layered defense concept could be applied and integrated with space-based lasers. In this approach, long-range multiwarhead interceptors would engage incoming warheads several hundred miles from the target, and low-altitude (LoAD) terminal defense would engage those remaining. The space-based laser would constitute a third, high-altitude layer to engage targets during the boost phase, negating the advantages of multiple independently targetable reentry vehicles, decoys, and chaff. This would alleviate the discrimination and tracking problems of the lower defensive layers.

Laser weapons in space could defend themselves against conventional nonnuclear interceptors and nuclear warheads. In the latest DARPA space-based laser battle station system concept, twenty-four laser weapons would be placed in orbits 1,200 kilometers above earth in three polar rings of eight stations each. The lasers would operate in the mid-infrared wavelength and could not readily penetrate cloud cover; therefore, primary targets—Soviet ballistic missiles—would be destroyed high in the atmosphere, before the booster burns out at approximately four minutes after launch.

To keep the number of battle stations reasonable, the maximum range of each laser would be on the order of 5,000 kilometers. The lasers themselves could be used for surveillance, acquisition, pointing, and tracking. Optical equipment is more precise and can work at wavelengths 10,000 times shorter than radar. Passive acquisition can be used since ballistic missiles generate large amounts of heat, which can be detected by the battle station. For these reasons, the entire system of radars necessary for conventional defense can be replaced by the optical detectors on the battle stations.

The term "laser battle station" is an appropriate one to describe these spacecraft. They would be the first combat satellites; because they would be subject to attack, the battle stations would be designed to survive, even against nuclear warheads.

In space the nuclear device is not as awesome as it is in close proximity to earth. About three-fourths of the energy of a nuclear warhead is emitted as X-rays, which are absorbed in very small amounts of material. Within the atmosphere, X-rays are absorbed in only a few feet of air. This absorption results in the massive fireball and the shock and blast waves that characterize nuclear bursts in the atmosphere. The atmosphere absorbs the X-rays in space, and this radiation can be absorbed in a thin layer of the surface of a space vehicle. Gamma rays and neutrons will penetrate the spacecraft, but these emissions affect only certain items, such as electronics equipment, which can be shielded by layers of material.

The proper design of a chemical laser battle station could permit it to exist relatively close to nuclear bursts in space, according to a DARPA study, which also found that the necessary design techniques resemble those used for reentry vehicles carrying nuclear warheads. Surviving the detonation in space of a one-megaton nuclear warhead at a range of only from ten to twenty kilometers seems feasible, according to the DARPA study. The battle stations could operate with "keep-out zones" surrounding them and destroy anything that comes within that range. Thus explosive charges placed in small satellites will not be permitted near the battle stations.

The DARPA study adds that attacks by miniature homing vehicles would probably be difficult to mount, since homing vehicles depend on optical sensors for guidance. It seems likely that the homing vehicle's warhead could be destroyed by lasers at close ranges, or that the optical guidance system would be blinded at long ranges by laser radiation, causing the homing vehicle to miss the station entirely. Nuclear-armed interceptors could also be blinded, but their destructive power is so large that simply programming the vehicle to proceed on course when the sensors are blinded could pose a serious threat to the battle station. An ability to manuever the station during attack would reduce this hazard.

The battle station must be designed so that it cannot be blinded by a nuclear blast. To accomplish this, sensors could be stored in shielded wells and make observations through reflecting mirrors. Since X-rays are not reflected by mirrors, the sensors would be safe.

There is no way to protect thermal control coatings on the outside of the battle stations, and therefore thermal control of the units will probably have to be achieved by louvers. In addition, solar cells would almost certainly be destroyed, but extra solar cells in arrays could be carried in shielded containers and deployed after attack. Vast expertise exists today on construction of extremely lightweight extendable solar arrays. More precise pointing and tracking and heavier shielding could be used on battle stations if other nations were to deploy larger, more powerful lasers against chemical laser battle stations.

As technology matures, the best counter to a laser battle station may be another laser battle station. In that event, the contest will become a traditional race of technology against numbers like the races involving tanks, aircraft, ships, and ballistic missiles. It will be an expensive race, but it will be compelling to enter, to lead, and to win.

6

Space System Survivability:
Strategic Alternatives for the 1990s

ROBERT B. GIFFEN

America's military dependence on our space assets may perhaps not be as great as is feared by some, nor may these systems be quite as vulnerable as is suspected. However, while the United States forges ahead in the development of sophisticated space systems to support our national security, the deployment of these systems must be consistent with our overall military strategy.

Space-based systems are critical to the effective employment of U.S. military forces throughout the spectrum of conflict. Communication satellite systems provide vital links between all military forces by ensuring uninterrupted communications, command, and control (C^3) ties both to strategic and tactical forces. Space-based sensors serve as an integral part of the U.S. early warning and attack assessment network. Intelligence collection relies overwhelmingly on space-based assets. Overhead space systems provide data to assure verification of treaty compliance. Tactical exploitation of our space-based systems serves as a force multiplier to our tactical and strategic forces. In short, the armed services depend on space systems to implement their tasks and attain their objectives.

Because these space systems are critical to national security, they must be enabled to survive long enough to do their work. Some systems, for example, may be required to function only during limited (conventional) conflict, whereas others may need to continue operating during total nuclear war. As clarified and restated by Presidential Directive 59, the focus of our national military strategy is on flexible response and countervailing tactics. The emphasis today is on an enduring, survivable capability with the capacity, if need be, to conduct nuclear war for several months. Space systems constitute an integral part of this strategy; these systems, therefore, must be designed to survive at the same level as the forces they support.

Although much has been made of the slogan "exploiting space

for peaceful purposes," neither U.S. national policy nor international agreements on the use of outer space prohibit the exploitation of space for military purposes. President Carter made it clear in Presidential Directive 37, National Space Policy, that the United States has the inherent right both to use space to support national objectives and to protect and defend all U.S. assets in space. Current international agreements place only minor limitations on the military use of space. Specifically, the Outer Space Treaty of 1967 prohibits deploying weapons of mass destruction in space and restricts the use of the moon and other celestial bodies exclusively to peaceful purposes. Moreover, the Anti-Ballistic Missile (ABM) Treaty (which contains specific provision for its own termination) prohibits the use of space-based antiballistic missile systems. The United States, therefore, can take steps to ensure the survivability of its space assets, including deployment of defensive systems, without changing current national space policy or violating any international agreements.

HOW TO DEFEAT A SPACE SYSTEM

The ultimate goal of defeating any space system is to prevent the product of that system from reaching the user by neutralizing either the space segment, the ground segment, or the communications, command, and control link between the two segments. In planning the method of attack, two factors are critical to a successful strategy. First, the attack strategy should be efficient. (It might not make sense, for example, to target a geosynchronous communications satellite system with several large antisatellite boosters if that system can be jammed electronically.) Second, that strategy ought not to enhance the risk of escalating the level of conflict. For example, during a limited conventional conflict, a direct attack on the command and control facility of a tactical reconnaissance satellite may result in a totally different response by the adversary than a more subtle laser attack against the satellite's optical sensors. The practical result is the same; yet, the latter approach is much less risky. To sum up, the attacker should plan to defeat a space system in the cheapest way without risking unexpected escalation.

Given this context, one may focus on the methods of defeating the space segment, the ground segment, and the C^3 link between these two components, and proceed to discuss the effectiveness of each threat during different levels of conflict.

NEGATING THE SPACE SEGMENT

Knocking out the satellite obviously constitutes the most straightforward way of defeating a space system. Before one can attack satellites directly or "spoof" their systems, however, one must have a space targeting system that can locate satellites and identify the probable mission of each.

Few realize the difficulty of keeping track of satellites in space. The problem is to sort out the few hundred active payloads from the 4,500 trackable objects, all of whose orbits are to varying degrees changing because of maneuvers, drag, and small perturbations. The North American Air Defense System (NORAD) makes about 30,000 observations each day with radar and optical trackers located throughout the world and tries to fit these observations to known objects through use of complex computer algorithms. The Soviet Union has a similar system. The tracking problem is complicated further because active satellites frequently make unannounced maneuvers, are launched without prior notification, and are difficult to distinguish from debris and inactive satellites. The higher the altitude of a satellite, the more difficult it is to track. Geosynchronous satellites, for example, are not routinely tracked by radar because they are out of the range of most surveillance radars. These satellites are normally tracked optically, a process constrained by weather and lighting conditions. As a result, the higher a satellite, the more difficult it is to target. Only when a satellite has been identified and continuously tracked can it be targeted.

Spoofing is a subtle, effective means of defeating a satellite. Spoofing means either controlling an enemy satellite directly or making the satellite—or the ground controller managing the satellite systems—believe that an on-board system needs to be controlled when actually it does not. For example, if the correct frequencies, codes, and transmission sequences to control the maneuver engines of an enemy reconnaissance satellite are known, then a hostile transmission to fire the engines will cause the satellite to become disoriented, lost, or to burn all its fuel. The advantage of spoofing an enemy satellite derives from the probability that the enemy may never know what happened. Even if he suspects foul play, he may have difficulty proving it.

Direct attack by a variety of ASAT weapons is the surest way of killing a satellite but also the most expensive. Direct attack includes employing directed energy weapons, orbital interceptors, and space mines.

Ground-Based Directed Energy Weapons

Directed energy weapons use either coherent light energy (laser) or particle beam energy to radiate and damage the target satellite. Both these weapon systems require enormous amounts of power and accurate pointing systems to keep the beam on target.

Range is limited because of atmospheric dispersion and attenuation of the beam. The advantage of these weapons is that, once developed, they will be able instantaneously to damage or interfere with any low earth orbit satellite passing over their position. Laser weapons will probably be effective against satellite sensors and solar panels, while particle beam weapons have the potential to destroy systems internal to the satellite. Both weapons demand precise targeting information and extremely accurate pointing systems to find and then illuminate their target.

Orbital Interceptors

Using conventional, nuclear, or impact warheads, orbital interceptors kill a satellite by direct attack. Manned interceptors can knock out a reconnaissance satellite simply by spray-painting the optical sensors or by turning off critical systems. Nonnuclear orbital interception can be accomplished either by sending the U.S. Miniature Homing Vehicle (MHV), for instance, in direct ascent or by maneuvering interceptors already in orbit, such as the Soviet killer satellites. In either case, precise targeting information is needed prior to initiating the attack, so that the interceptor may come close enough to the target to allow the terminal guidance system to take over and complete the intercept. Nuclear interceptors, unlike those just mentioned, have a large kill radius—on the order of hundreds of kilometers—and can be targeted at a point in space. In space, nuclear warheads kill by radiation and electromagnetic pulse rather than by blast effect. The disadvantages of using nuclear warheads are possible interference with or destruction of nearby friendly satellites and unintended escalation in case of a conventional conflict.

Orbital interception is a complex and expensive process, requiring an accurate surveillance network to provide precise targeting information and a sophisticated launch vehicle with enough booster capability to place the nonnuclear warhead on target. In addition, a complex terminal guidance system is necessary to complete the intercept. In short, orbital interception is neither easy nor cheap.

Space-Based Directed Energy Weapons

Multiple-shot laser or particle beam weapons mounted on a satellite platform pose a unique threat. With no atmospheric dispersion or attenuation, these weapons could have sufficient range to disable most satellites and would have a built-in defense against orbital interception. Power requirements, pointing accuracy, and targeting information still present significant challenges, but such a weapon, particularly if manned, would be formidable.

Space Mines

Satellites at geosynchronous altitude are particularly vulnerable to space mines. The concept calls for the launch of a mine, either nuclear or conventional, into geosynchronous orbit next to the targeted satellite. This mine then stays dormant in the vicinity of that satellite (within 1,000 kilometers) until attack time. At that time the mine is switched on, and it locks on to the target satellite, maneuvers within lethal range, and explodes.

Figure 6.1 shows the vulnerability of the four popular military orbits to satellite threats. Spoofing is relatively easy to counter; the remaining threats, however, are more difficult to defeat. It is important to remember that these threats involve complex, high-technology weapons systems that are expensive to develop and deploy.

ATTACKING THE GROUND SEGMENT

The objective of attacking the ground segment is to incapacitate either the command and control ground station or the user's communication ground station. Negating either of these links in the space system chain will stop the user from obtaining the product.

Figure 6.1
Summary of Vulnerability of Military Orbits

Threat	Orbit			
	Leo	Semisynch	Molniya	Geosynch
Spoofing	C	C	C	C
Ground-based directed energy	C*	—	—	—
Space-based directed energy	P	P	P	P
Orbital interceptor	C	C	C	C
Space mine	—	—	—	C

*Only current threat is low-power laser capable of damaging optical sensors on Leo satellites.

KEY: C Current threat, either demonstrated or within current capability
P Potential threat before the year 2000
— No threat, either current or potential

The attack can be subtle (in the form of sabotage) or direct (as in the case of terrorist, conventional, or nuclear action). In either case, the ground station must be geographically accessible and must be critical to the continuing operation of the space system. A mobile ground station, for example, may not be accessible. A satellite system that can operate autonomously for long periods without command and control may be unaffected by loss of its command and control ground station.

Most fixed ground stations are dependent upon central support systems for continuous operation. In many cases, sabotaging one of these support functions is relatively simple; in fact, it may be difficult to detect as an overt act. Since many satellite systems are dependent on nearly realtime command and control for continued operation, any interruption of this link could degrade satellite operation and ultimately lead to the loss of the satellite. Sabotage can therefore be an effective method for degrading or negating an enemy's space capabilities prior to actual outbreak of hostilities. Sabotage is particularly attractive because it is cheap and, when operating against a free and open society (such as the United States), relatively easy to accomplish.

Depending upon the level of conflict, direct terrorist, conventional, or nuclear attack can be effective in defeating any space system that relies on a fixed ground station for its operation. Terrorist attacks can be particularly effective because they can be disguised to avoid being identified as the acts of a particular state and can thus avoid international confrontation. Conventional attacks are most likely during limited theater conflicts against stations located in that theater. Nuclear attacks would be most effective against homeland stations immediately prior to a global nuclear war.

JAMMING THE COMMAND, CONTROL, OR COMMUNICATIONS LINK

One of the most effective means of defeating a space system is to jam or block the communications link between either the satellite and the user or the satellite and the ground command and control station. Electromagnetic interference, exoatmospheric nuclear detonation, and elimination of communications relay satellites are all effective methods of blocking communications.

The principle of electromagnetic jamming is to saturate the airways with electronic noise at the same bandwidth that the enemy is using to communicate. This same technique has been used for decades to block undesired propaganda broadcasts. The higher the frequency, the more directed the communications broadcast becomes and the more difficult it is to jam. Essentially, as the frequency goes up, the beam becomes narrower, forcing the jammer to move closer to the receiver or transmitter. A trawler located a few miles offshore next to a major satellite control facility or a remote telemetry site, for example, could be very effective in jamming communications from several satellites. The advantages of electromagnetic jamming are its potential effectiveness and its low cost and risk.

High-altitude (above 40 kilometers) nuclear bursts have the effect of jamming satellite communications by absorption or scintillation of the broadcast frequency. This effect can last from seconds to hours depending on the frequency transmitted. The higher the frequency, the shorter the duration of the interruption. A single detonation can have widespread effects: for example, a one-megaton detonation at 100 kilometers above the central United States can block UHF communications for almost thirty minutes over the entire country. Even though such a burst would appear to be no more than a momentary flash, it is unlikely that it would go undetected and would therefore risk escalation to nuclear war.

If a space system relies on a communications satellite to relay communications to either the user or the command and control ground station, then that satellite becomes a critical node whose loss would effectively defeat the space system. If a communications satellite or satellite system serves as the relay for several other space systems, then it becomes a high priority target and should be defeated as discussed earlier.

Another way to look at threats to space systems is to analyze each threat during the period prior to a global nuclear exchange when all home-based space assets are still intact. Under these conditions, all the threats discussed earlier are active threats; however, after the initial exchange of nuclear weapons, the picture changes significantly, because the position of enemy satellites is no longer known, the targeting network having been lost. Jamming, detonating prepositioned space mines, or launching surviving nuclear warheads targeted against points in space corresponding to the last known enemy satellite positions would be the only practical antisatellite tactics under such conditions. Any enemy satellites launched or activated after the initial nuclear exchange will be difficult to defeat, because their existence will probably go undetected.

MEETING THE THREAT

No known space system is invulnerable; however, a range of options exists to minimize system vulnerability. The advantages and disadvantages of each tactic depend upon the mission of the space system and the projected level of conflict. The merits of each tactic must be analyzed separately to see how well each meets the threats discussed above.

Doing Nothing

Doing nothing to protect space systems would appear foolish, at first sight. Yet this might be an appropriate option for selected space systems that do not have a vital wartime function under certain scenarios. For example, a high-resolution reconnaissance space system may no longer be necessary after the outbreak of global nuclear war. A government might decide, moreover, that ensuring survivability of certain capabilities in space may not be as cost-effective as doing without or finding some other means to perform the same function. The basic tenet of such an approach is a willingness to lose the capability provided by the space system. In the case of reconnaissance satellites, an alternative capability might be provided by high-altitude reconnaissnce aircraft, since violation of airspace would no longer be a restriction during global war. The key to this option is identifying expendable assets and planning accordingly.

Deterrence

Deterrence as a strategy calls for the protection of space-based assets by placing enemy systems at risk. Maintaining any deterrent space defense posture has two fundamental prerequisites. First, the enemy must place an equivalent value and reliance on his space systems, and second, a real capability to negate his systems must exist. Deterrence is a cheap way to make space systems "survivable." It does have serious pitfalls, however. Deterrence is not infallible: a rapid development in enemy capability can create a "window of vulnerability" through which the adversary can defeat one's systems, while neutralizing retaliatory options. Deterrence based on threatening other assets may be unconvincing and difficult to implement and may result in unplanned escalation.

A deterrent space posture presents a unique problem: detecting enemy interference. It would be difficult to maintain credible deterrence if the causes of sudden failure of one's satellites could not be ascertained. To foil a clever enemy, sensors capable of detecting adversary interference—impacts, laser illumination, nuclear detonation, and other aggressive acts—would have to be installed on all military space platforms.

A deterrent space defense tactic constitutes a real option, provided the enemy believes that potential losses, as a consequence of any actions on his part, would far exceed any gains he could achieve.

In short, a deterrent tactic in space must be founded on real capability, not on rhetoric.

Negotiation

As a space survivability measure, arms-control negotiation can serve two purposes: it can put a cap on the number of enemy assets; and it can specifically prohibit any interference with space assets. Negotiating arms limitations may be effective in limiting a potential arms race in space by stunting the growth of ASAT weapons, but it cannot guarantee survivability. The main drawback of relying on negotiation is the difficulty of verifying compliance with arms agreements. Converting a directed energy antiaircraft weapon to an ASAT weapon, or a low-altitude orbital interceptor to a high-altitude one, is not difficult technically and could create a serious imbalance. Nor does negotiation make ground stations less vulnerable. During hostilities, of course, arms-limitation agreements would become meaningless.

Negotiating an agreement not to interfere with one another's space assets prevents the enemy from practicing interference techniques during peacetime. The result may have real value, since any interference would immediately flash a warning signal that the enemy may be initiating an attack. Without such an agreement, the enemy could interfere incrementally, masking his aggressive intentions to some extent, since no precise definitions would be in effect, while at the same time decreasing the effectiveness of the other party's routine space systems, especially intelligence satellites.

Any negotiated arms limitation must be based on a position of equivalent strength. An agreement limiting ASAT development, for example, would be of little use if one side had no ASAT capability.

Hardening

Hardening is a method for making the ground segment, the space segment, or the C^3 link less vulnerable to physical attack. Hardening can do little to defend against a nuclear onslaught, but it can eliminate or reduce the success probability of a "cheap shot." Total survivability cannot be guaranteed, of course, but the price can be raised for an adversary attempting to suppress our systems.

Because they need exposed C^3 antennas, permanent ground stations will always be vulnerable to direct nuclear or conventional attack. Preventing electromagnetic pulse (EMP) coupling from high-altitude nuclear bursts and minimizing vulnerability to sabotage and terrorist attack are two ways of hardening the ground segment.

High-altitude nuclear bursts generate an electromagnetic pulse that can couple into unprotected circuits and cause either circuit upset or burnout. Incorporating faraday-cage, filter, surge-arrestor, waveguide-cutoff, and fiber-optic technology in ground site design can provide significant protection againt this threat, but such measures are costly. Hardening new facilities to meet global EMP protection standards raises the total installation cost by 10 percent. Retrofitting current sites is even more expensive, and maintenance to insure the integrity of EMP protection requires additional funds.

Susceptibility to sabotage and terrorist attack can be minimized by proper site location and design and by increasing physical security. Locating ground stations away from urban areas and in terrain easy to defend can eliminate cheap shots. Increased physical security will make sabotage and terrorism more difficult. The best way to defend against both sabotage and terrorism is to eliminate critical operational nodes within the ground station by employing redundant and backup systems to preclude single-string vulnerability. Although satellites will always be vulnerable to direct nuclear attack, hardening can reduce the vulnerability to orbital interceptors, laser illumination, and nuclear radiation effects.

The key to defeating an orbital interceptor is first to recognize an attack. Once the attack is identified, the objective becomes to defeat the terminal guidance system of the vehicle in question, which may be of the radar, infrared, or optical type. Radar guidance can be jammed, and infrared can be fooled using decoy heat sources. Optical guidance systems can be defeated with stealth technology. The main problem is that once the system is designed to defeat a given terminal guidance threat, the enemy can change that frequency, wavelength sensitivity, or design of the terminal guidance and render the countermeasures obsolete. Retrofit of an orbiting satellite is difficult. The problems involved in obtaining adequate warning of impending interception and in employing long-lived countermeasures make such measures against orbital interception unlikely candidates for increasing survivability.

Reducing the vulnerability of a satellite to laser illumination can be effected by shielding soft components, such as solar panels, and by shuttering or filtering optical and infrared sensors. The more powerful the laser, the more shielding is necessary, and the more expensive the spacecraft beomes; shielding, however, does increase survivability. Shielding against particle beam weapons, on the other hand, is not effective beause the particle beam penetrates shielding easily and causes molecular damage to components within the satellite. Some protection against directed energy weapons may be afforded by spinning the satellite when it comes under attack, thereby spreading out the effect of the energy beam. Such action, of course, would degrade the mission performance of many satellites.

Radiation from nuclear detonations causes EMP and trapped electron effects that reduce spacecraft life by creating noise in sensors and by destroying electronic components. These effects can be mitigated by hardening electronic components, shielding sensitive parts, and designing the system to withstand increased radiation. All of these concepts are within the state of the art and, when employed, reduce the probability that the enemy may achieve multiple kills with a single nuclear burst. Antijamming measures can enhance the survivability of the C^3 link by overcoming electromagnetic countermeasures and exoatmospheric nuclear detonation. Transmitting at Extremely High Frequency (EHF) narrows the transmission beam to such an extent that a jammer has to be practically in the line of sight between the transmitter and receiver. Using EHF also decreases the debilitating effects of nuclear scintillation and absorption from minutes to seconds. Using even higher frequency communications yields similar results, for jamming must interrupt the beam physically to block the signal. Automated fast frequency hopping can also make jamming more difficult, but it is not as effective as transmission at EHF or higher frequencies. All these measures require great expenditures both for design and building of new transmitters and receivers and for retrofitting literally thousands of existing transmitters and receivers. Encrypting command and control transmissions can defeat enemy efforts to spoof satellites. Encryption is relatively inexpensive to employ and, with today's technology, can be highly effective against spoofing.

Mobility and Maneuver

Employing mobile ground stations and satellites with increased maneuvering capability can greatly improve the survivability of both the ground and space segments.

Assuming their locations remain covert, mobile ground stations essentially counter the threat of sabotage, terrorist attack, and direct conventional or nuclear attack. The problems involved in making both user and command and control ground stations mobile depend on the mission of the space system. The worst case is a low-altitude reconnaissance satellite that requires both frequent command and control and a great deal of processing to convert reconnaissance information into usable form. In this case, the mobile command and control station would have to be manned by highly trained personnel, possess extensive computer hardware and software capability, and have sophisticated means of communication both with the user and the satellite. A mobile user ground station would have similar requirements to process the data. Although these capabilities are within the current state of the art, they are expensive and require considerable manpower.

The higher the satellite, the easier it is to control and the simpler it is to make the satellite's ground station mobile. Likewise, the simpler the satellite mission, the easier it is to make the user stations mobile. A high-altitude weather surveillance satellite, for example, needs little command and control or data processing to maintain orbit or send weather pictures directly to mobile user terminals.

Adding a maneuver capability to satellites decreases their vulnerability to orbital interception, particularly if the satellite is in a medium-altitude orbit or higher. Although maneuvering of low-orbit satellites complicates the enemy's targeting problem, such satellites could still be intercepted if there were not sufficient warning to initiate a maneuver. Intercepting satellites in higher orbits demands a much longer time of flight, thus providing more warning and more time to maneuver out of range of the interceptors terminal guidance system.

The disadvantages of adding maneuver capability to satellites are that payload weight must be sacrificed to permit additional fuel to be carried, and that satellites are frequently unable to perform their missions during maneuvers. Satellites requiring precise pointing or position information would show degraded performance during maneuvers. Moreover, maneuvering offers little protection from attack by directed energy weapons.

Maneuver capability does little to counter the threat of space mines targeted against geosynchronous satellites, since the mines would be colocated with the targets, and little warning time would be available to maneuver out of range. The best defense against a space mine is to avoid using geosynchronous orbits for satellites performing wartime missions. This defense is quite costly because the unique advantages of geosynchronous orbits would be lost. To provide approximately the same coverage as three geosynchronous communications satellites, eight satellites in Molniya orbits (or four, to provide the same coverage just in the northern hemisphere) would have to be used. Although mines placed in orbits other than geosynchronous would still constitute a threat, the act of placing them there would immediately telegraph enemy intentions. A geosynchronous orbit has only one unique orbital plane with an exact altitude of 35,800 kilometers; placing a payload next to another satellite in this orbit can be justified easily by mission requirements alone. Putting a similar satellite in a Molniya orbit, however, cannot be justified, because there is literally an infinite number of other orbits that would satisfy the same mission requirements.

Another alternative is to place satellites in orbits at altitudes higher than geosynchronous. As in the Molniya orbit, satellites in these higher orbits are less vulnerable to space mines and also difficult to intercept by direct attack. First, the time of flight for interception would be great—on the order of a day—which would provide adequate warning of attack; and, second, these satellites would be hard to track accurately and, therefore, difficult to target. Satellites placed in these higher orbits, say at 100,000 kilometers, could be stored at such high altitudes until needed and then maneuvered down during wartime.

Autonomy

The objective of developing autonomy in satellites is to eliminate vulnerable and expensive fixed ground stations and provide more direct interface with the users. The more functions a satellite can perform on board to provide its own command and control and data processing, the less dependent it becomes on support from ground stations. Incorporating redundant, fault-tolerant processors and housekeeping software on board the satellite reduces external command and control requirements. Such a satellite would perform its own health management, positioning, and command sequencing. Adding on-board data processing can also enable the satellite to interact directly with its user. The initial investment required to develop autonomous systems is significant, but the long-term potential exists for reducing system cost and increasing system survivability.

Proliferation and Deception

The fundamental principle behind the tactic of proliferation and deception is to complicate the enemy's targeting problem: proliferation gives him too many targets to kill and deception prevents him from finding targets. These methods can be employed both for ground stations and satellites.

Making satellites more autonomous (and therefore less dependent on ground stations) and using using advanced microelectronics technology provide an opportunity to employ simpler, more compact ground stations. Eliminating critical single-node segments of the ground network by using mobile, redundant ground stations, each of which can control more than one satellite system, will significantly decrease space system vulnerability. Adding deceptive tactics, such as using decoy ground stations and hiding mobile ground stations, will further complicate the enemy's targeting problem and increase space system survivability. The disadvantages of employing a mobile, redundant ground network are additional expense, increased manning requirements, and the need for a coordinated centralized control.

Orbiting many small, simple payloads and piggy-backing payloads on other satellite platforms are two means of proliferating the space segment. Many missions, including some surveillance, communications, and reconnaissance functions, can be accomplished by relatively simple, small payloads. A single launch vehicle can place several of these payloads in orbit as individual satellites or the payloads can be connected to the support systems of large satellites and therefore be scattered among several different large platforms. In either case the net effect is to proliferate potential targets, and thus force the enemy to expend more resources to kill the space segment of a satellite system.

Combining proliferation with deception has the potential of making the space segment practically invulnerable. (A few payloads can be hidden in space for example, by minimizing both the radar and optical return and using only cross-link communications to relay information to and from ground stations.) Two payloads, one a normal satellite and one an "invisible" satellite, can be launched into geosynchronous orbit with a single launch vehicle. When the destination orbit is reached, the two payloads could be separated covertly, and communciations would occur only through the announced payload. The enemy might never know that the other payload is there. An alternative approach would be to launch many small, single-mission payloads using one multipayload launch vehicle. Interspersed with these payloads would be decoys having the same physical characteristics as the functional payloads. All payloads could use small kick motors to disperse randomly their orbits. The functional payloads would remain dormant in orbit until activated when required during hostilities. If all payloads either are identical in size, shape, and mass properties or are each randomly different, the enemy might be unable to determine functional payloads from decoys. Upon activation, satellites could be maneuvered to orbits appropriate to their mission requirements.

Proliferation and deception are valid survivability strategies only for relatively simple, low-cost payloads. Complex, high-resolution reconnaissance satellites, for example, would be prohibitively expensive to proliferate, as would large multichannel communications satellites. This strategy would be suitable, however, for simple communications relay, nuclear detection, and tactical reconnaissance missions.

Reconstitution

Reconstituting essential space assets after hostilities begin may be the only method of ensuring that critical systems survive. Space systems requiring large, complex satellites not suitable for prolifera-

Figure 6.2
Ground Segment Threat and Defense

Threat	Primary Defense	Contributing Defense
Sabotage	Physical security Mobility	Satellite autonomy Proliferation
Terrorist attack	Mobility	Satellite autonomy Proliferation
Coventional attack	Mobility	Satellite autonomy
Nuclear attack	Mobility Harden against EMP	Satellite autonomy

tion may require backup satellites stored on prepositioned launch vehicles, ready to replace satellites lost to enemy action. Missiles in hardened silos, mobile launchers, or missile-launching submarines offer launch-on-demand capability to reconstitute space assets. The problems encountered with this strategy limit its use to those missions considered absolutely vital. The cost of developing backup satellites capable of long-term storage and the need to reserve launch vehicles for this purpose make this an expensive approach. Such a strategy also may require sacrificing missile silos or submarine launch tubes normally used for strategic weapons because of limitations imposed on the total number of these launch facilities by strategic arms-limitation agreements. Though the problems and cost of providing reconstitutable space assets are significant, it may still be the best strategy for guaranteeing survivability of space assets.

The "Invulnerable" Space System

Fixed ground stations can best be defended by hardening against sabotage and nuclear attack and by incorporating EMP countermeasures to decrease the vulnerability of the overall ground segment. The key strategy, however, is redundant mobile ground stations. Ultimately, satellite autonomy decreases dependence on the ground segment and increases the survivability of the total space system. (See figure 6.2.)

Figure 6.3 shows selected defenses for each threat to the space segment of a satellite system. This comparison and previous discussion indicate that the optimum combination of tactics would include the use of maneuverable satellites, hardened against spoofing and laser illumination, using medium-altitude or higher orbits; avoiding geosynchronous orbits; and, when possible, the use of proliferation

Figure 6.3

Space Segment Threat and Defense

Threat	Primary Defense	Contributing Defense
Spoofing	Hardening	Autonomy
Ground laser	Hardening Higher orbits	Proliferation and deception
Ground particle beam	Higher orbits	Proliferation and deception
Orbital interceptor (conventional)	Higher orbits Maneuvers	Proliferation and deception
Orbital interceptor (nuclear)	Very high orbits Maneuvers	Proliferation and deception
Space laser	None	Proliferation and deception
Space particle beam	None	Proliferation and deception
Space mine	Avoid geosynchronous orbit	Proliferation and deception

and deception to avoid enemy detection and tracking. Further protection against threats can be provided by reconstitutable satellites prepositioned on dedicated, survivable launch systems.

Use of EHF and higher frequencies is one of the best ways to decrease the vulnerability of the C^3 link to electromagnetic interference and exoatmospheric detonations (see figure 6.4). Satellite autonomy and mobile ground stations also render enemy interference more difficult. Moreover, eliminating or protecting single critical nodes, such as relay satellites, also adds to the survivability of the C^3 link.

By using a combination of the strategies discussed in this section, a high degree of survivability can be achieved. The key elements are deciding what must survive and requiring that survivability be a part of every space program.

MATCHING SURVIVABILITY TO REQUIREMENTS

The first and most important step in developing a comprehensive survivability strategy is deciding which assets must survive, for how long, and against what threat. Only after completing this process

Figure 6.4
C³ Link Threat and Defense

Threat	Primary Defense	Contributing Defense
Electromagnetic interference	EHF and higher frequencies	Satellite autonomy Mobile ground stations
Nuclear detonation	EHF and higher frequencies	Satellite autonomy Mobile ground stations
Loss of relay satellite	Proliferation (elimination of single critical node)	(See figure 6.3)

of matching survivability strategies to actual requirements can one integrate the strategies discussed in the previous section into a comprehensive survivability plan.

DECIDING WHAT MUST SURVIVE

Anticipating wartime mission requirements for space systems across the spectrum of conflict is the most important task in formulating survivability strategy, and also the most difficult. By looking briefly at the issues involved in the missions of communication, navigation, surveillance, and reconnaissance, however, the complex questions and processes involved in determining space system requirements can be understood better.

To determine military communications requirements, strategic communications—those required by the National Command Authority (NCA) to maintain the continuity of government and connectivity with strategic forces—and tactical communications—those required by theater and task force commanders for the command and control of their tactical forces—must be considered. Questions to be answered include: Which space communications systems must survive to launch retaliatory bomber, missile, and submarine attacks? Must all of these assets survive a first strike? How are surviving strategic forces directed to launch a second strike? How does the NCA receive damage assessments and second-strike targeting information? Can a naval task force operate without space-based communications? Do local wing and battalion commanders or ships' captains rely on space-based communications to operate effectively in limited theater war? and Can the Rapid Deployment Joint Task Force operate without space communications?

Similar questions arise in determining the survivability of space-based navigation systems. Do strategic bomber forces need these systems to find and destroy their targets? Should space-based navigation systems that enhance ICBM guidance systems be survivable? Can strategic submarine forces function effectively without navigation satellites to update their positions prior to launching their missiles? Navigation satellites offer the potential to increase significantly the combat effectiveness of tactical forces; what effect do such satellites have on the successful employment of these tactical air, land, and sea forces? Space-based navigation platforms can serve as force multipliers for both strategic and tactical forces; the importance of this effect should determine the level of survivability needed for these systems.

SURVEILLANCE

Two space surveillance missions—missile launch warning and nuclear detonation detection—are critical to U.S. national security. Yet, do their respective space systems need to be survivable across the entire spectrum of conflict? What detection capabilities are needed to execute an effective second strike? What kind of weather information is necessary to support strategic nuclear forces? Do tactical commanders need the same type of information to conduct a theater war? Surveillance from space is vital to warn of impending attack and to provide accurate weather information, but where, when, and for how long this capability must survive are complex questions.

The requirements of strategic reconnaissance systems are significantly different from those of military reconnaissance in wartime. For example, a high-resolution photo reconnaissance satellite may require camera resolutions of about one foot to obtain valid intelligence information, while a tactical photo-reconnaissance satellite used to follow enemy troop movements or to count tanks and aircraft certainly will have reduced resolution requirements. Some pertinent questons are: How long must strategic reconnaissance resources survive? What reconnaissance capability do theater and field commanders require at different levels of conflict? and Do tactical commanders need satellite reconnaissance data in real time? All these issues must be addressed before resources are expended on survivability measures for reconnaissance space systems.

Once these questions are answered, suitable tactics must be selected to make each system—communications, surveillance, navigation, or reconnaissance—survivable. More important, the use of space systems in all exercises and war games must be restricted to include only those assets that will survive.

MAKING THE SYSTEM SURVIVE

To make a space system survive, the benefits of each tactic must be integrated into an overall plan that will meet the survivability requirements at the least cost. One reasonable starting point is developing and deploying one's own antisatellite capability. Only with such a symmetry of capabilities can we maintain a credible deterrent posture and also enter into meaningful negotiation to limit further weapons development in space. Once this capability is in place, negotiations can seek specific agreements prohibiting interference with space systems and limiting further development of weapons in space. As in any arms limitation agreement, compliance must be verifiable.

Next, programs for hardening, mobility, maneuver, autonomy, and orbit selection techniques must be adopted to increase survivability by minimizing the possibility of the enemy defeating the space system at low cost. Both the satellite system and permanent ground stations must be hardened to some level against the EMP effects of proximate nuclear detonations so as to eliminate the enemy's capability to defeat multiple targets with a single nuclear weapon. Antijamming techniques—fast frequency hopping and EHF and higher frequency technology—should be used on vital C^3 links. Where possible, the system should use mobile ground stations. Satellite orbits should be high enough to keep satellites out of the range of ground-based directed energy weapons and to provide adequate warning of orbital interception. Satellites in these higher orbits must have maneuver capability to evade direct attack. To defeat the threat of space mines, essential satellites must avoid the geosynchronous orbit. Future satellite systems should decrease dependence on ground stations by using on-board, autonomous command and control systems. Obviously, trade-offs are involved in incorporating all these techniques into a single space system. The objective is to look at the entire system, find the vulnerable links, and strengthen these links incrementally by adding appropriate survivability measures.

After exploiting these measures, the next step to increase space system survivability consists of using proliferation, deception, and reconstitution to ensure continuing capability throughout all levels of conflict. If the payloads of a particular space system are relatively simple and numerous, as they are in communications and navigation satellite systems, then the unique features of the Space Shuttle can be used to proliferate and camouflage these payloads. For example, to insure communications with strategic forces through all levels of conflict, the Space Shuttle could be used to deploy a system of proliferated small communications satellites, which would remain stored in orbit until needed, to send out emergency action messages to strategic ICBM, bomber, and naval forces. The Space Shuttle could carry several of these small satellites into orbit on a single launch. Astronauts could check the satellites while still in the payload bay and then activate small kick motors to send each satellite into a different orbit. Interspersed with each group of real satellites would be several decoy payloads. Seventy-five such payloads—including twenty-five actual communications satellites and fifty decoys—randomly placed in orbits between 500 and 600 kilometers would make this communications capability practically invulnerable to orbital interception; and, if deceptively deployed, the satellites might be impossible to catalogue and track properly, thereby defeating the threat of directed energy weapons. Adding pop-off shrouds to each payload would provide additional protection against laser illumination and foil attempts to discern real payloads from decoys by optical means.

The disadvantages of such a proliferation strategy are not insignificant. Such a scheme will be economically feasible only for simple payloads in low earth orbit. Although the Space Shuttle will have extra space to accommodate small payloads, the problems of integrating these payloads so as to be compatible with the primary shuttle payload are complex. Electromagnetic interference between payloads, outgassing of harmful materials, and maneuvering requirements are just a few of the factors to be considered in deploying mixed payloads with the shuttle. The shuttle offers such an advantage in launch capability, however, that these problems should not be allowed to hinder the full military exploitation of this system. Of course, if proliferation and deception tactics are used to make the space segment survivable, then a similar effort must be extended to the supporting ground stations. Proliferating these stations, keeping locations covert, and using mobile stations where possible will add the same level of protection to the ground segment. Likewise, the C^3 link must use multiple satellite cross-link and antijamming techniques to ensure that the entire space system has the same level of survivability.

For space systems unsuitable for proliferation and deception, particularly those requiring a few complex satellites, reconstitution is the only method for increasing survivability. These satellites will be prepositioned on hardened launch vehicles for deployment after the initial assets have been lost. The primary disadvantage of this tactic is expense. Launch vehicles must be dedicated solely to a particular payload, and payloads must be constantly checked and monitored to insure that they will function after launch. Other problems include insuring that the launch system is hardened properly or deployed deceptively to survive attack and maintaining the command and control network necessary to launch the vehicle and operate the satellite when in orbit. Reconstitution is, however, the only way to guarantee continuity of operations for certain crucial space missions.

The first step in developing an effective survivability strategy is deciding which space-based capabilities must survive to support strategic and tactical forces thoughout the spectrum of conflict. After this decision has been made, an overall survivability plan must be developed for each space system. Most important, this plan must be enforced strictly during all stages of design, development, and deployment of the space system.

PAYING THE PRICE

Determining survivability requirements and choosing the right strategies to meet these requirements are no simple tasks, but neither is as difficult as implementing the strategy chosen. At this point, more than twenty government agencies are involved to some degree in establishing requirements for space systems. The problem of persuading these agencies to share developmental costs is difficult enough; devising a method of sharing survivability costs is even more difficult.

Making space systems survivable also involves trade-offs between survivability and primary mission capability. Maneuver capability, hardening against laser illumination and EMP, and installing sensors to detect attack all take valuable weight and space that could otherwise be used to increase mission capability. Satellite program managers are faced constantly with the dilemma of choosing between satisfying the user by obtaining every possible ounce of capability from a system and making that system survivable enough to implement the mission for which it was designed. Survivability adds nothing at all to capability in a peacetime environment and is frequently the first to suffer during program budget cuts or cost overruns.

The recent emphasis on the resurgence of U.S. naval power presents an interesting parallel to the issue of survivability of space systems; the naval Carrier Battle Group (CBG), the mainstay of naval power, is a useful example. The mission of the CBG is threefold: to show U.S. presence, to maintain control of the sea, and to project power to any area of the globe. The primary offensive capability to perform these missions is provided by the aircraft aboard the aircraft carrier, the heart of the CBG. Typically, this carrier is armed with from twenty to thirty attack aircraft, fifteen fighter aircraft, two photo-reconnaissance aircraft, and twenty support aircraft for air refueling, electronic countermeasures, and antisubmarine warfare. Thus a typical carrier has between approximately thirty-five and forty-five actual warfighting aircraft. From one to three supply ships are also necessary to provide the carrier and its aircraft with fuel, ammunition, and food. The threats to this wartime capability come from attacking enemy aircraft, surface ships, and submarines. To protect the carrier against these threats, the typical CBG has from three to five guided missile cruisers or destroyers, from three to five frigates or destroyers, one Towed Array Sonar System frigate, and one or two attack submarines. These eight to thirteen escort ships exist primarily to protect the carrier against enemy attack. In short, to make the carrier, with its thirty-five offensive aircraft, survivable in a wartime environment we deploy a Carrier Battle Group of a total of from ten to seventeen ships.

Similar examples exist for other forces. A prime illustration is the Airborne Warning and Control System (AWACS) aircraft, which has to be protected by up to twenty-four fighter aircraft. Likewise, huge resources are allocated to protect our strategic missile forces. The current debate on the basing configuration of the MX missile focuses not primarily on the weapon itself, but rather on the best way to ensure its survivability.

The point of these analogies is that the Carrier Battle Group, the AWACS, and strategic missile forces are national security requirements to which the necessary resources have been committed to ensure survivability, at many times the cost of the basic system. The same rationale must apply to those space systems that are essential to American national security and whose survivability can be enhanced at lower cost than the other systems mentioned.

Spending billions in space makes little sense if the assets are unusable in wartime. The president, through the National Security Council structure, should formulate a national space policy directing the Department of Defense to create a single executive agent for space within DoD. This executive agent would be responsible for ensuring that every U.S. space system used for national security incorporates appropriate survivability measures to match its wartime requirements. Further, the same national space policy would hold the Office of Management and Budget (OMB) accountable for guaranteeing that survivability funds are provided throughout the life of each space program. Finally, Congress should endorse this policy as a national priority and, through its control of the purse, make sure that it remains such a priority.

To sum up, to ensure space survivability, the DoD executive agent for Space must (1) define the requirements of space system survivability for each of the appropriate levels of conflict; (2) select the appropriate strategies to meet these requirements; and (3) with the support of the OMB and the Congress, fund each program to implement selected strategies and ensure that these funds remain intact.

7

Space: A Sanctuary, the High Ground, or a Military Theater?

JOSEPH E. JUSTIN

Debates in the public press and by military analysts concerning both the U.S. space program and increased military spending have brought public attention to a critical question: What should be the U.S. strategy for the military use of space in the 1980s? Should space be a demilitarized sanctuary, a place for enhancement of terrestrial military forces, or a new military theater in its own right? Three schools of thought can be delineated which represent the major alternative approaches to space policies and goals available to the United States. These include: (1) space as a sanctuary from which weapons are excluded; (2) space as a "high ground" from which U.S. interests are defended; and (3) space as a distinct environment, or theater, for military operations. This chapter outlines the implications of each school for the following issues: the Soviet space threat; the doctrinal view of the U.S. military role in space; the Space Shuttle, manned space flight, and expendable launchers; the development of space survivability and warfare programs; the diplomatic and arms-control negotiations for space; and the creation of military space organizations.[1] Each school of thought contains elements that could be combined to develop a national security policy for the use of space.

MILITARY SCHOOLS OF THOUGHT AND SPACE ISSUES

Space As a Demilitarized Sanctuary

Two of the three schools provide for some military activities in space but disagree on the nature and extent of these activities. The

---

The views and opinions expressed are those of the author and should not be construed to reflect any endorsement or confirmation by the Department of Defense, the Department of the Air Force, or any other agency of the federal government.

Figure 7.1
Military Space Schools of Thought and Issues

Schools of Thought

Issues	Space As a Sanctuary	Space As the High Ground	Space As a Theater
Threat	Space race	Soviet space threat to terrestrial forces	Soviet space threat
Military role	Space demilitarization	Force enhancement	Space war: fighting and winning
Space shuttle	Civilian shuttle	Shuttle and expendable launchers	Military shuttle and man and woman in space
Resources	Freeze on ASAT systems and space weapons	Satellite autonomy and survivability	Space weapons
Arms control	ASAT negotiations	Existing agreements	Existing agreements
Organization	Open civilian—closed military	Present space command	Unified space command

third is fundamentally opposed to any military weapons in space (see figure 7.1). The "space in sanctuary" school believes space should not be used as a military instrument of policy[2] and that the United States should at a minimum honor its present international agreements on the free use of space, the right of self-defense, and a prohibition on the means of mass destruction, particularly the 1967 Treaty on the Principles Governing the Activities of States in the Exploration and Use of Outer Space.[3] Furthermore, the United States should be actively involved in the resolution of such issues as claims of orbital sovereignty, rights of remote sensing and open dissemination, allocation of radio frequencies, nuclear power sources in space, and the use of the moon.

To the sanctuary group, two main areas of concern are antisatellite negotiations and the 1972 Anti-Ballistic Missile (ABM) treaty regarding limitations on ABM systems and noninterference with technical means of verification. They argue that the Soviet Union has indicated an interest in cooperation[4] and that the Soviet threat lies in the distant future and can be minimized by encouraging better cooperation and restraints. The sanctuary group maintains that the threat in space may be less from the Soviet Union than from the danger of a prospective arms race. According to the sanctuary group, because the Soviet Union is currently technologically inferior to the United States, it may be better to negotiate to limit the technology race now, before it is too late. According to this group, the United States should unilaterally freeze any plans for space testing and deployment of an ASAT system, any possible geosynchronous (high-orbit) ASAT system, or any space-based directed energy system. The United States should reopen negotiations with the Soviet Union to freeze its systems and to dismantle its present ASAT system.[5] To this group, space should be utilized only for exploration and for the advancement of mankind. They believe that the shuttle is an important program and should not be used for military weapons and that, if space systems are truly essential for national security, they should be separate from the civilian programs.

Space As the High Ground of the Aerospace Medium

The group called here the "high-ground" group believes that space should be used to enhance terrestrial forces as an essential element of national security.

This high-ground group maintains that General Thomas D. White, the chief of staff of the Air Force from 1957 to 1961, was correct when he stated that air and space are inseparable parts of aerospace[6] and form an integral element of national security. To them, there is no distinct or natural operational limit between air and space. According to General Alton D. Slay (USAF, Ret.), former commander of Air Force Systems Command, "It is a place—an environment, an arena of considerable operational mission import, but certainly not a 'mission,' per se, any more than the atmosphere, or the ocean, or the land is a mission."[7] In other words, space's real military mission is related to terrestrial security operations.

In the view of this school, the use of space to enhance military terrestrial forces is essential to national security. About $100 billion has already been spent, with current spending about evenly divided between civilian and military programs. In the 1980 fiscal year the requested total space budget was up 12 percent to $7.9 billion.[8] The two most vital military roles in space are warning and surveillance. Space photo-reconnaissance systems have been particularly important to security.[9] Space systems also provide over 70 percent of the overseas communications of the U.S. military and enhance the utility of these forces. During the 1975 Mayaguez incident, for example, space systems aided in President Ford's direct communication with the commander of the landing party and in the relocation of the helicopters' inflight refueling area, necessitated by bad weather in the original location as revealed by weather satellites.[10]

The Soviet Union is challenging the U.S. use of space. Each year the Soviet Union launches at least seventy-five missions, while the United States launches between fifteen and twenty. At least 70 percent of Soviet missions are purely military.[11] The Soviet Union is threatening to deny free passage in space with tests of a killer satellite system, although reportedly this system may be used only against low-orbit satellites.[12] Further, lasers and directed energy weapons will eventually pose a threat.[13]

Space's harsh environment and the difficulty of maintaining satellites can be minimized by technology and the shuttle. The high-ground group argues that the shuttle should be supported in part because of the military need for low-cost transportation into space. The Department of Defense has put over $1 billion into the shuttle development and has budgeted another $2 billion to complete it.[14] The Air Force has budgeted over $1 billion per year for shuttle operational support during the mid-1980s. Although it is the first step, the shuttle program and schedule must be balanced against the advantages of expendable launchers and overall military space needs. This school argues that the need for low-cost transportation is the key to the balance. They argue that the United States needs increased launch capabilities for larger satellites, spares, proliferation of systems, decoys, and highly maneuverable systems. For these requirements, expendable space systems have many advantages and should be maintained along with the shuttle.

In assessing the role of military personnel and a permanent presence in space, this group argues that we should carefully consider what benefit these programs would provide to the United States. According to General Slay, "To put military people in space just because it's something we can do is not my idea of a judicious expenditure of our scarce resources."[15] In other words, military personnel should be used in space only if their presence enhances system effectiveness.

Because this group holds that space systems should be based upon the need for enhancement of terrestrial forces, it feels that the Global Positioning System is justified because it provides accurate velocity and position information. Terrestrial forces can use such a capability to drop bombs accurately, to fire weapons, or to command the battle. Other important programs are the Defense Satellite Communication System (DSCS III), the Air Force Satellite Communication (AFSATCOM) system, the Defense Meteorological Satellite Program (DMSP), the programmed deployment of mobile ground terminals for our early warning satellites, the deployment of the Integrated Operational Nuclear Detonation Detection System (IONDOS) with the Global Positioning System, and the MILSTAR program, which will provide a survivable means of global two-way military communications.[16] To this group, such futuristic systems as directed energy systems should be carefully reviewed. If these "Star Wars" systems prove feasible, they may be of interest, but the school of thought in question wonders whether they can be afforded and how they will help combat troops. According to this group, priority should be given to programs for improved satellite autonomy and survivability.

The high-ground group believes that proposed new arms-control agreements for space should be evaluated for their impact on overall national security. Its members ask whether any agreement will have the necessary credibility or deterrence capability, or whether it can insure that one side will not try to gain a unilateral advantage. This group argues that any further integration of military commands for space is unnecessary.[17] To them, it appears that an unnecessary or prematurely unified organization could be counterproductive and might foster unneeded futuristic systems; they believe that recent government actions are sufficient to coordinate and integrate space operations. These actions have included:

the establishment of an Air Force Space Command at Colorado Springs as a four-star command under General James V. Hartinger;

the establishment of an Air Force Space Division (a major part of

the former Space and Missile Systems Organization—SAMSO)
and the naming of a deputy commander for Space Operations;
the establishment of a Manned Space Flight Support Group at
Johnson Spaceflight Center to provide support to NASA and
train Air Force personnel in shuttle operations;
the establishment of a Defense Space Operations Committee,
chaired by the secretary of the Air Force, to coordinate Department of Defense space operations;
the formation of a Directorate for Space Operations within the
Headquarters of the Air Force; the naming of Major General
James A. Abrahamson, U.S. Air Force, as the associate administrator for NASA responsible for the shuttle;
the formation of a course in space operations at the Air Force
Institute of Technology for training Air Force personnel;
the establishment of an Air Force Space Technology Center at
Kirtland Air Force Base;
the planned construction of an Air Force Consolidated space
Operations Center in Colorado Springs for control of Air Force
space and launch operations; and
the construction of Space Shuttle facilities at Vandenberg Air
Force Base.[18]

According to the high-ground group, further steps toward coordinating and integrating our space activities are not required. They
believe that the structure of Space Command should evolve through
need.

Space As a Military Theater

The school referred to here as the "theater" group argues that
more attention should be given to space as a military theater of
operations in its own right.[19] According to a noted commentator on
the military space program, Colonel Morgan W. Sanborn (USAF,
Ret.), just as air operations are uniquely different from land and
naval operations, so are space operations uniquely different from air
operations: "Space is a mission and not simply another medium only
to be used to augment existing military roles and responsibilities."[20]
Just after the launching of Sputnik, even General Thomas White,
who later originated the term "aerospace," prophesied that "whoever
has the capability to control space will likewise possess the capability
to exert control [over] the surface of the earth."[21] The theater group
argues that this concept—loosely defined as "space power"—is even
more compelling today. According to the Department of Defense
publication *Soviet Military Power*, "The Soviet Union is intensely
engaged in a program designed to achieve a dominant role in

space."[22] Representative Ken Kramer of Colorado, an advocate of a major military role in space, feels that the Soviet threat arises from the development of an ASAT system, the manned orbiting Salyut stations, and their satellite targeting of our naval forces.[23] The Department of Defense argues that the Soviet Union is working on a new booster that is similar in performance to the Apollo Saturn 5 booster, has from six to seven times the launch weight capability of the Shuttle, and will be able to launch a new series of Soviet projects.[24]

The theater group argues that the growing Soviet space threat illustrates the need for better American military space operations. In case of war, space could be the first battlefield.[25] They contend that lasers and particle beam weapon systems, if made survivable, could decrease the utility of long-range nuclear weapons, changing the present concepts of deterrence and arms-limitation agreements. Not only would lasers provide possible antisatellite weapons, but they would be an effective first-line ABM system, though this would raise questions concerning the need to abrogate the ABM treaty. The reported follow-on particle beam system could further improve space capabilities.[26] Lieutenant General Daniel O. Graham (USAF, Ret.), a former director of the Defense Intelligence Agency, recently proposed the development of a large number of "space cruisers" armed with antimissile projectiles and a military manned station in space for command and control.[27] A later version of these "space cruisers" would use a laser system. The theater advocates argue that more attention should be given to such systems and to the long-term problem of how to fight and win a war in space.

As for the shuttle, the theater group believes that the issue is people, not hardware. People will determine what can be done, how, and at what cost. According to Colonel Morgan Sanborn, "I predict that manned space systems will provide at least the same quantum jump in military capabilities as did the airplane."[28] Although it is difficult to quantify the benefit of having military people in space, their presence will demonstrate what military missions can be accomplished.

In the view of the theater group, greater attention should be given to the coordination and integration of space operations, especially Space Command.[29] According to Sanborn, "The first essential is a reorganization of Air Force command responsibilities to give proper recognition to the potentials of military space."[30] They also hold that a revolutionary change in military structure is required.

The General Accounting Office has recommended that the Department of Defense establish a focal point for space and the creation of a "Space Master Plan."[31] Other services, in particular the

Navy, are acutely aware of the military value of space and the need for protection from any Soviet threat from space.[32] For the shuttle and military space operations, full responsibility comes together only in the office of the president.[33] The office of the president, however, is too high in the organizational structure to deal with operational problems that might develop with the military use of the shuttle.

According to the theater group, the formation of the Space Command and the other changes are all steps in the right direction, but more should be done to integrate and coordinate our military space activities. Representative Kramer, who pushed the formation of the Space Command, advocates integrating the space activities of four other major Air Force commands and eleven other organizations and even advocates renaming the Air Force the "Aerospace Force."[34] Secretary of the Air Force Verne Orr rejected the name change but himself initiated the study that led to Space Command.[35] To the theater group these are welcome changes. In their opinion, if structures are not changed, the military potential of space may be underestimated.

SPACE STRATEGIES AND INITIATIVES FOR THE 1980s

It is difficult to argue either that space can be free of military considerations or that the United States need not provide for a military role in space. The superpowers have already made serious commitments in space. The Soviet Union has demonstrated its commitment to programs of historic firsts, and it continues to build a massive record of manned and unmanned launches. Although it has no separate military service for space, the Soviet Union does have a separate Strategic Rocket Force. The military use of space dominates the entire Soviet space program. A strong influence in Soviet military art extends their concept of combined forces and operations into space.

Both superpowers can use space for arms verification, warning, and command and control of terrestrial weapon systems. In general, space-based systems can enhance the effectiveness of conventional forces. Further, the superpowers can use space to decrease the usefulness of long-range nuclear weapons. Space systems may even constitute the first line of defense. It is difficult to argue that space is "just another place." Other services, in particular the Navy, are justifiably concerned about the space threat and the military use of space. Since the days of Sputnik, the integration of the roles and missions of the services has greatly increased. Further, there are differences between space and air operations and even between space and missile operations. Launch services, including shuttle operations, satellite operations, and command and control services, are all very specialized and distinct. Technology and the shuttle will not change astrodynamics and celestial mechanics—laws of nature that describe motion in space—any more than 1930's technology and the long-range bomber changed the laws of aerodynamics. Yet technology and the shuttle will inevitably change the use of space.

The long-term objective of the military role in space should be more than merely the enhancement of terrestrial forces. Although space is being used for that purpose now, and there is the new possibility of a Soviet threat of denial, other military space missions may emerge in the future. The role of the military is related to warfare, both its deterrence and its resolution. If space may be the first battleground, an enormous advantage may accrue to the side that is able to control space for its own benefit. Fundamental to the military role in space, therefore, is the concept of assured free passage and its use for national objectives. In the future, nations may first actually have to assure access and passage in space before using it to achieve their objectives. To control space and to deny it to the enemy may become major military objectives. The United States must develop the military capability to assure free passage in space.

The United States needs a balanced military space program, including a mix of the shuttle fleet and expendable launchers, manned and unmanned space systems, and survivable systems, as well as an operational ASAT capability and a vigorous technology program for space-based missile defenses. Highly survivable, autonomous satellite systems and unmanned launchers have many advantages, but military missions will require people and a shuttle. The enhanced capabilities of the shuttle will provide a revolutionary test of the best missions for people in space, but the shuttle must be balanced against the benefits of other programs. Training programs are needed for military specialists who are now being recruited for possible missions on the shuttle. Discussions of space-based radars and a permanent presence in space should continue. Clearly, better thinking is needed about space-based systems, their missions, and objectives for the military role in space.

A necessary condition for any arms-control negotiation for space must be a consensus on U.S. vital interests and our military role in space and a willingness to negotiate the nonvital interests. Warning and surveillance systems are vital, and other systems may be equally important. Any negotiations must avoid restrictions that might put these systems at risk. Perhaps the greatest uncertainty concerning the military role in space is the question of arms-reduction initiatives. In general, U.S. and Soviet military space programs are asymmetrical and do not lend themselves easily to common limitations.

The changing nature of the military role in space and shuttle operations will require better coordination and integration of military space activities. It may be necessary to form a unified organizational structure to utilize the shuttle's potential. The present structure for air operations of centralized command and control and decentralized execution may not be suitable for space systems. Although multimission space systems appear to be the design trend, each space system is a special and singular entity. In general, launch services, command and control telemetry, tracking, and satellite operations are interrelated functions, which should be integrated within a proper organizational structure. Further, any possible ASAT system should be included, as should advanced research and development.

A separate vertical structure of centralized command and control and centralized execution of those commands by the space system or on board the shuttle may be preferable to integrating space operations into the present terrestrial operational structure. A unified organization is needed to overcome the compartmentalization of military space projects that has developed over the last decades. This should help correct the layered misperceptions and interservice and intraservice rivalries concerning responsibility and authority for the military space programs.

The current organizational situation parallels the entrenched military organization in the 1930s. At that time, lack of proper organization led to the neglect of air power. To correct the situation, air power advocates concentrated on the unescorted bomber, with the result that the military further neglected other important elements of air power. With proper organizational support, they might have made better preparations for World War II. The United States cannot afford to repeat that error in developing space priorities and strategies.

If the Soviet threat is real, the United States must have an organization properly structured to plan and execute the space order of operations and the postattack reconstitution of space systems. If full responsibility for space operations comes together only in the office of the president, then this may be too high an organizational level to deal with the problems that might develop in military shuttle operations. Military space activities must be better integrated and coordinated.

By the mid-1980s the United States should have a major change in the military organization for space. The development by the middle of this decade of a unified (and some day separate) U.S. Space Organization would create the organizational means to address space objectives fully. It would provide a cadre of military space professionals, a center for long-range planning, and an advocate. These will be critical in the fight for the space share of the military budget and in the proper use of space for national security. The mid-1980s are appropriate for this change in our military organization for space. A unified U.S. Space Organization could be in existence for the first shuttle flight from Vandenberg Air Force Base, for the start of operations of the Consolidated Space Operations Center in Colorado Springs, and for the start of operations of the Defense Satellite Communication System III, the Global Positioning System, and possibly the ASAT system.

In summary, U.S. strategy for the military use of space during the 1980s should appreciate space as a major military consideration and not just as another place; therefore, the United States must provide for a military role in space. The long-term objective of the military role in space is more than enhancement of terrestrial forces. The United States needs a balanced military space program with a mix of the shuttle fleet and expendable launchers, manned and unmanned space systems, and survivable systems, as well as an antisatellite deployment capability and a program of research in space-based missile defense. Furthermore, the United States should have as a goal the negotiation of a meaningful arms-reduction agreement for space. A well-conceived domestic consensus on vital interests in space is of course a necessary precondition to space policy. Finally, major changes in the military organizations for space are needed by the mid-1980s. Shuttle operations will require a dedicated and efficient organization to utilize the shuttle's potential to its fullest.

NOTES

1. For a further discussion of these issues see Michael M. May, "War or Peace in Space," discussion paper no. 93, California Seminar on Arms Control and Foreign Policy, Santa Monica, March 1981.

2. The National Aeronautical and Space Act of 1958 is often quoted, although it does have provisions for the right of self-defense and a military

role in space. For further discussion see Richard D. Lyons, "Military Planners View the Shuttle as Way to Open Space for Warfare," *New York Times*, March 29, 1981, p. 1; Frank Asbeck, "The Militarisation of Space," *Armament and Disarmament Information Unit*, April–May 1980, pp. 1–3; Barry Scheider, "Preventing Star Wars," *Bulletin of the Atomic Scientists*, October 1981, pp. 13–15; David A. Andelman, "Space Wars," *Foreign Policy* no. 44, Fall 1981, pp. 94–106; Donald L. Hafner, "Averting a Brobdingnagian Skeet Shoot: Arms Control Measures for Anti-Satellite Weapons," *International Security*, vol. 5, no. 3, Winter 1980–81, pp. 41–60; and May, "War or Peace."

3. For an excellent discussion on space law see Major General Walter D. Reed, the Judge Advocate General, U.S. Air Force, address to the American Astronautical Society, "A Legal Regime for Space Activities," *Supplement to the Air Force Policy Letter for Commanders*, no. 1-1979, AFSINC/IIA, Kelly AFB, Tx., January 1979. See also Carl Q. Chrestrol, "Growth of Space Law," *Astronautics and Aeronautics*, December 1981, pp. 111–115; and Raymond L. Garthoff, "Banning the Bomb in Outer Space," *International Security*, vol. 5, no. 3, Winter 1980–81, pp. 25–40.

4. See Anthony Austin "Brezhnev Hints He Wants Talks on Space Arms Curbs," *New York Times*, April 18, 1981; and "Colby Calls Shuttle Spur to Arms Talks," *Washington Star*, April 22, 1981.

5. Andelman, "Space Wars," pp. 94–106.

6. Department of the Air Force, Air Force Manual 11-1, *Functions and Basic Doctrine of the U.S. Air Force*, Washington, D.C., February 1979, chap. 7.

7. Alton D. Slay, "Space: The Air Force's Future Initiative," *Astronautics and Aeronautics*, April 1979.

8. Dr. Frank Press, then director of the Office of Science and Technology, Executive Office of the President, statement before the Committee on Science and Technology, House of Representatives, Washington, D.C., February 14, 1979.

9. Hans M. Mark, then secretary of the Air Force and now deputy administrator of NASA, "The National Space Policy," statement to the Subcommittee on Science and Technology, House of Representatives, Washington, D.C., July 24, 1980; reprinted in *Supplement to the Air Force Policy Letter for Commanders*, AFSINC/IIA, Kelly AFB, Tx., September 1980, pp. 2–5.

10. "Our Role In Space," U.S. Air Force Fact Sheet, OIP No. 005.81, Air Force Systems Command, Andrews AFB, Md., February 1981.

11. Department of Defense, *Soviet Military Power*, Washington, D.C., 1981, p. 79.

12. Ibid., p. 68.

13. Ibid., pp. 75–76.

14. Alton G. Keel, Jr., Air Force Assistant Secretary, Research, Development, and Logistics, Letter to the Editor, *New York Times*, December 10, 1981.

15. Slay, "Space."

16. Caspar W. Weinberger, *Annual Secretary of Defense Report to the Congress, Fiscal Year 1983*, Washington, D.C., February 8, 1982, chap. 3, pp. 66–69.

17. Leonard Famigliette, "Orr Hopes for Separate Space Command by 85," *Air Force Times*, February 8, 1982, p. 6.

18. Edward C. Aldridge, Jr., Under Secretary of the Air Force, address to the National Space Club in Washington, D.C., November 1981, as reported by *Air Force Times*, "AF Already Promoting 'Space Command' Idea," December 14, 1981, p. 16; and *Air Force Policy Letter for Commanders from the Office of*

the Secretary of the Air Force, AFRP 190-1-12-82, AFSINC/IIA, Kelly AFB, Tx., January 15, 1982, p. 2.

19. For this point of view see Lyons, "Military Planners View...," in Donald W. Cox and Michael Stoiko, *Spacepower—What It Means to You* (Philadelphia: Winston, 1958); Dandridge Cole, "Response to 'Panama Hypothesis,'" *Astronautics and Aeronautics*, June 1961; Jacob E. Smart, "Strategic Implications of Space Activities," *Strategic Review*, Fall 1974; Richard E. Hansen, "Freedom of Passage on the High Seas of Space," *Strategic Review*, Fall 1977.

20. Morgan W. Sanborn, "National Military Space Doctrine," *Air University Review*, January–February 1977.

21. Thomas D. White, speech to the National Press Club, November 29, 1957, as reported by the *Wall Street Journal*, December 2, 1957, p. 2. It is ironic that the words of General White can be used by both the high-ground and the theater groups to argue their positions concerning the role of the military in space.

22. *Soviet Military Power*, p. 99.

23. Ken Kramer, "The United States Space Challenge: Can It Be Met?" *The Wichita Eagle-Beacon, September 27, 1981, p. 3B.*

24. Soviet Military Power, p. 79.

25. An interesting illustration of space as the first battlefield is noted in General Sir John Hackett et al., *The Third World War, August 1985* (New York: Berkley Books, 1980), p. 183.

26. Malcolm Wallop, "Opportunities and Imperatives of Ballistic Missile Defense," *Strategic Review*, Fall 1979, pp. 13–21; Lyons, "Military Planners View"; and "An Armada in Space," *St. Louis Post-Dispatch*, January 11, 1981.

27. Daniel O. Graham, "Toward a New U.S. Strategy: Bold Strokes Rather than Increments," *Strategic Review*, Spring 1981, p. 13; and John Ginovsky, "Plan Would Use Satellites to Fight Off Missile Attack," *Air Force Times*, March 15, 1982, p. 24.

28. Sanborn, "National Military Space Doctrine."

29. For further discussion of this issue see Major General Robert A. Rosenberg and Lieutenant Colonel Wayne L. O'Hern, Jr., "The Shuttle and the Second Great Era in Space," *Defense 80*, May 1980, p. 19; Edgar Ulsamer, "Dawn of a New Space Age," *Air Force Magazine*, February 15, 1982, p. 17; John Ginovsky, "Space Command: Not If But When: Gen. Abrahamson Interview," *Air Force Times*, February 15, 1982; and Sanborn, "National Military Space Doctrine."

30. Sanborn, "National Military Space Doctrine."

31. See "GAO Report Hits Space Center Plans," *Aviation Week & Space Technology*, February 15, 1981; and General Accounting Office, *Consolidated Space Operation Center Lacks Adequate DoD Planning*, No. 82-14, Washington, D.C., January 29, 1982.

32. See John F. Lehman, Jr., Secretary of the Navy, "Rebirth of a U.S. Naval Strategy," *Strategic Review*, Summer 1981, p. 12; and Eberhardt Rechtin, President of Aerospace Corp., address to the 1981 Navy Space Symposium at Monterey, Calif., October 1981, as reported in "Rechtin Sees Space Systems as Naval Opportunity, Threat," *Aerospace Daily*, January 29, 1982, p. 146.

33. Rosenberg and O'Hern, "The Shuttle and the Second Great Era in Space."

34. See Leonard Famiglietti, "More Jobs Seen in Space Command," *Air Force Times*, vol. 42, no. 22, December 21, 1981, p. 6.

35. Famiglietti, "Orr Hopes for Separate Space Command by 85." Secretary Orr reportedly rejected the idea proposed in a bill introduced by Representative Ken Kramer of Colorado to rename the Air Force the "Aerospace Force."

3

Technological and Operational Aspects of Superpower Space Systems

8

New Directions for the U.S. Military and Civilian Space Programs

PATRICK J. FRIEL

For the remainder of this century, the United States and the Western Alliance will rely heavily on a variety of space-based assets for strategic reconnaissance, communications, early warning of a ballistic missile attack, and command and control of the strategic nuclear forces. This chapter provides an overview of U.S. military space programs and their relationship to U.S. national security objectives; it examines also nonmilitary U.S. space programs with a view toward exploiting the space-based sensor technology involved for international arms control and verification of arms-limitation agreements.

THE TITAN FAMILY OF SPACE BOOSTERS

The deployment of U.S. military space assets is heavily dependent on the capability and reliability of U.S. space boosters. The two systems that will be available in the 1980s and beyond are the Titan III and the Space Transportation System (STS), frequently referred to as the Space Shuttle.

The Titan III family of space boosters has been the workhorse booster system for U.S. military programs for twenty years. The Titan IIIB, with the Agena upper stage, is the launch system that has placed in orbit the low-flying (100- to 200-mile orbit) photographic reconnaissance satellites. This system can place 8,400-pound payloads in low earth orbit (100 miles) and 2,700-pound payloads in geosynchronous equatorial orbit (23,300 miles). With the addition of solid rocket motors, the Titan IIIB becomes the IIIC, a versatile, reliable booster which can place 33,400 pounds in low earth orbit and 3,700 pounds in synchronous equatorial orbit from Cape Canaveral. The transtage space propulsion unit is used to place the payload into a wide variety of low earth orbits or on a deep space trajectory. A new Titan space launch vehicle—the 34D—is scheduled for flight test in 1982. The new launcher will be quite similar to the TITAN IIIC except that it will be fitted with the Inertial Upper Stage (IUS). The IUS was originally designed for the Space Shuttle only and would be used to transfer payloads from the Space Shuttle Orbiter in low-altitude orbit to high orbits, including synchronous orbits. The IUS will therefore be used both in the Titan 34D and the Space Shuttle. The Titan 34D will place a 4,000-pound payload in geostationary orbit and a 30,000-pound payload in low earth orbit.

THE SPACE TRANSPORTATION SYSTEM (STS)

The U.S. Air Force Space Division is presently planning to use the STS or Space Shuttle to launch all Department of Defense payloads in the mid- to late 1980s from a launch complex now being constructed at Vandenberg Air Force Base. The shuttle's successful flights have demonstrated its capability to carry large payloads into space, and continued tests may demonstrate that the STS can carry these at much lower costs than Titan III boosters. The STS can place a 65,000-pound payload at low equatorial orbits from Cape Canaveral, Florida, and a 30,000-pound payload in low polar orbits from Vandenberg. Later, the shuttle orbiter will carry the IUS, which will also be used on the Titan 34D. The IUS will occupy seventeen feet, about half of the payload section of the orbiter. When the shuttle orbiter is in low earth orbit the IUS will be deployed from the orbiter. The IUS is inertially guided and will place a 4,000-pound payload in geosynchronous orbit.

THE SPACE SHUTTLE: A RISK FOR THE U.S. MILITARY SPACE PROGRAM?

Air Force literature indicates that the U.S. military space program will rely on the Space Shuttle in the late 1980s to launch the Global Positioning System, the Defense Satellite Communications System, and the Defense Meteorological Satellites. These satellites will be placed in synchronous or subsynchronous orbits and will require the IUS to launch them from the shuttle. The existence of the Titan 34D program suggests that the decision to rely on the shuttle is not as firm as the public literature suggests.

Complete reliance on the shuttle poses many risks from the U.S. viewpoint. The number of vehicles available may not be adequate, and the cost advantage of the STS, compared with expendable systems, may not be as large as initially hoped. Aside from economic factors, military concerns suggest that total reliance on the shuttle may be unwise. For example, the shuttle may not be able to launch reconnaissance or communications, command, and control satellites in a crisis. A second vulnerability is that the two launch sites at Cape Canaveral and Vandenberg are vulnerable to low-level attacks or sabotage. Deploying reconnaissance or communications satellites from the shuttle orbiter by a vulnerable crew during a crisis may involve an unacceptable risk, and deploying the IUS from the shuttle to transfer a payload from low earth orbit to geosynchronous orbit would be particularly risky. It may be that the STS cannot reliably serve as the prime future launch system for the U.S. Department of Defense space systems. The highly reliable Titan III system probably will continue to be the prime military space launcher.

THE SPACE SHUTTLE AS AN ANTISATELLITE WEAPON OR BALLISTIC MISSILE DEFENSE SYSTEM

During the continuous negotiations with the Soviet Union to prohibit antisatellite (ASAT) systems, the Soviet Union has insisted that the STS will ultimately be an antisatellite weapon. Indeed it is not difficult to conceive of an ASAT system in which many infrared homing interceptors would be carried by the 60,000-pound STS payload into a low earth orbit. An infrared vidicon system would allow the pilot to acquire and track satellites in orbits as high as 1,000 miles, essentially challenging photographic reconnaissance satellites and low-orbit ocean surveillance and meteorological satellites. Because the principal communication satellites are in synchronous orbit, they probably cannot be challenged from a low-orbit shuttle. Even with the IUS, the number of interceptors that could be placed in geosynchronous orbit would be small. The principal satellites challenged would be the low-orbit reconnaissance satellites, which are probably the prime targets of the Soviet ASAT system. The orbiter's propulsion system could correct its orbit to engage any low-orbit satellite at a reasonable range.

It seems clear that the STS could have a technically credible ASAT capability. From a U.S. military viewpoint, however, the STS has virtually no credibility as an ASAT system. The STS cannot defend itself against the single-orbit Soviet ASAT with on-board interceptors because the STS propulsion system is small and could not engage the Soviet ASAT in its first orbit. Even ground-based lasers could be a serious threat to the 100-mile orbit STS. Certainly the infrared sensor would be susceptible to damage from a high-power laser at 100 miles. As a countermeasure, the STS's radar and optical characteristics would have to be reduced and a large number of decoys would have to be deployed in potential STS orbits. The pilots themselves would, of course, be highly vulnerable to the radiation from small nuclear devices. Adequate hardening against thermal radiation, penetrating X-rays, neutrons, and gamma rays would involve a prohibitive weight penalty for the STS. For these reasons, the STS does not appear to be a survivable, reliable ASAT system.

The shuttle could have some capability to engage warheads from ICBM launches. The impact of a nonnuclear warhead deployed from the shuttle would be comparable to that involved in the Homing Overlay Experiment (HOE) described below and would exceed the impact energy required to destroy either the booster, the "bus" used to deploy reentry vehicles, or the vehicles themselves. Assuming that a Soviet attack involved 500 ICBMs and that each space shuttle can carry as many as 40 kill vehicles (1,500 pounds each), then about 12 shuttles would have to be in battle-space at all times (if simply being in orbit were equivalent to appropriate battle formation—which is not the case). It can be shown that the number of satellites (N_S) required for single satellite coverage of the entire earth at space shuttle orbital altitudes (200–300 miles) actually is about 60. For every satellite in the proper geometry for battle, N_S are required in orbit. Thus, for this most optimistic case (40 kill vehicles per space shuttle), 720 (12×60) space shuttles with their crews would have to be in orbit at all times in order to have any ballistic missile defense (BMD) capability at all. In addition, the shuttles would be deployed in five or six different orbits. If the Soviet ICBM launches were not in these five or six planes, the interceptor would have to have a propulsion system capable of leaving the orbital plane of the shuttle. This capability would require a much larger interceptor and would sharply reduce the number of kill vehicles the shuttle could carry. Again, the space shuttle with a BMD capability would be vulnerable to direct attack by the Soviet first-orbit ASAT system or to any detonation of a nuclear weapon in space.

Thus the technical and military credibility of the STS for the ASAT or BMD mission is very low, although the Soviet Union has publicly attributed some ASAT capability to the shuttle. The STS would give the United States a significant capability to deploy reconnaissance or communications satellites in low earth orbit during a crisis. Thus the objective of the ASAT negotiations from the Soviet viewpoint may be to deny the United States this capability.

THE SPACE SHUTTLE AND THE POTENTIAL ANTI-SATELLITE TREATY

The Soviet position in the ASAT negotiations has been that all space-based systems that could destroy satellites should be banned, including the Space Shuttle. It is fairly clear that from the American viewpoint the shuttle is not a credible ASAT system and is certainly not a credible BMD system. The prime military mission of the STS will be to deploy in low orbits communication, reconnaissance, navigation, and meteorological satellites. While the primary advantage of the STS is its high payload, it is not clear that this capability gives it an overwhelming advantage over the Titan family of launch vehicles.

The Soviet ASAT system already poses a threat to low-orbit satellites. There have been reports that the Soviet Salyut low-orbit space station may have an ASAT capability, and the possibility exists for the Soviet Union to use the Salyut space station to challenge the U.S. early warning satellites. While the United States is attempting to reduce the vulnerability of military satellites, it is clear that Soviet ASAT systems represent a threat to world stability. The deployment of sophisticated sensors in satellites is part of the technological advantage the Atlantic Alliance has in monitoring Soviet conventional and strategic weapons development and deployment. U.S. space-based sensors and communications satellites would play a critical role in crisis management. Any arms-control initiative that would limit the Soviet ASAT capability would be a significant step toward a more stable world. The only real military capability that the Space Shuttle provides is the ability to place a large payload in low orbit. Therefore, an agreement to discontinue the military version of the STS and stop the development of the U.S. conventional ASAT system, in exchange for a ban on all Soviet ground or space-based ASAT systems, would be in the U.S. interest and a sound move toward world stability. The savings realized by the cancellation of the military version of the Space Shuttle may provide more than enough resources to correct the deficiencies in the military space program described later in this chapter. Verification of such a treaty could be accomplished through photographic observation of the dismantling of the present Soviet ASAT launch site and the absence of any ASAT tests.

SATELLITE COVERAGE REQUIREMENTS

In order to understand the size of the military satellite deployment, the number of satellites required to insure that every part of the earth is covered by at least one satellite from circular polar orbits must be known and this is shown in figure 8.1. The number of satellites required for single coverage of the globe is very high for low earth orbits. If low-altitude equatorial or inclined orbits are used, then the satellite requirement would be 50 percent higher. At low-orbit altitudes used by photo-reconnaissance satellites and the Space Shuttle, the number of satellites required for continuous earth

Figure 8.1

Single Satellite Coverage Requirements (Polar Orbit)

Number of Satellites		Altitude (Miles)
60		300
50		400
30		600
25		800
20		1,000
12		2,000
3	Geosynchronous	23,000

coverage is prohibitive. Consequently, U.S. reconnaissance satellites acquire only periodic data over the Soviet Union. As the orbital altitude increases, the number of satellites required for complete earth coverage decreases, particularly above altitudes of 1,000 miles. At orbit altitudes of 22,300 miles, each satellite views the same part of the world continuously, and only three satellites are required to cover the globe.

U.S. MILITARY COMMUNICATION SATELLITES

Defense Satellite Communication System (DSCS)

A description of the key U.S. military communications satellites is shown in figure 8.2 and is taken from *Aviation Week*'s annual survey of aerospace systems. The Defense Satellite Communication System (DSCS) is being deployed in geosynchronous orbit in three phases. The first phase involved twenty-six small satellites in near-synchronous orbit. Phase II (1,200-pound solar-powered satellites in synchronous orbit) involves more power and longer lifetimes for these satellites. The phase II satellites carry a propulsion system for orbit repositioning or emergency situations, two earth-coverage horn antennas, and two steerable antennas; they can use four communications channels. One phase I satellite still operates. Of the sixteen phase II satellites that have been procured, seven are operating in orbit and at least four failed to achieve orbit. The DSCS III is a much more advanced communication satellite which will provide high-power, multibeam, full-earth coverage, area coverage, or spot coverage. Apparently, the satellite uses a phased array with the ability to produce steerable nulls in the earth-coverage mode to negate jamming and interception. There are two transmit and two receive earth-coverage horn antennas, which provide additional communi-

Figure 8.2
U.S. Military Communications Satellites

System	Contractor/Gov. Agency	Weight	Launch Vehicle	Comments
DSCS II	TRW/Def. Comm. Agency	1,245	Titan IIIC or 34D/IUS	Synchronous orbit with earth-coverage and spot-beam antennas; provides up to 1,300 duplex voice channels 11-3-71
DSCS III	GE/Def. Comm. Agency	1,876	Titan 34D, Space Shuttle/IUS	Three-axis stabilized, next generation synchronous communications satellite 1981
FLTSATCOM	TRW/Navy/Air Force	2,100	Atlas/Centaur	UHF communications between ship-to-ship aircraft and SIOP forces 2-9-78; 5-4-79; 1-17-80; 8-6-81.
SDS	Hughes/Air Force		Titan IIIB/Agena	UHF communications for strategic forces; communications between Satellite Control Facility ground stations, strategic data relay

cations support. A high-gain, narrow-coverage, steerable dish antenna will provide a beam of increased radiated power for users with small receivers. DSCS III also includes a separate antenna set as part of the Air Force satellite link to the strategic alert forces. The receive/transmit frequencies are in the 7–8 GHz range and should minimize the vulnerability of DSCS III to electronic measures or signal interception. All of these satellites are powered by solar arrays. The DSCS satellites are hardened to nuclear radiation to prevent destruction by all but relatively close nuclear detonations.

Fleet Satellite Communication System (FLTSATCOM)

Five Fleet Satellite Communication Satellites (FLTSATCOM) are in geosynchronous equatorial orbit. Each satellite has twenty-three communication channels at the UHF and superhigh frequency bands. Ten channels are used by the Navy, twelve by the Air Force, and one by the National Command Authority.

The Satellite Data System (SDS) Air Force Satellite Communication System (AFSATCOM)

The Satellite Data System (SDS) provides UHF communication through a series of satellites in polar orbits. The AFSATCOM space segment consists of a series of communication transponders carried by various host satellites to several systems. FLTSATCOM is one host, and the SDS is another. Since FLTSATCOM satellites are in equatorial orbits and SDS satellites are in polar orbits, AFSATCOM transponders make up a worldwide communications network that relays data between airborne and ground teletype terminals.[1] The ground terminals are both fixed and mobile.

The NATO Communications System

The NATO Phase III Communications Satellite System consists of three satellites in geosynchronous orbit over the Atlantic Ocean. Two more are planned. The NATO III system provides rapid and secure communications among NATO member nations through a network of ground and shipborne stations. It is also interoperable with the U.S. Defense Satellite Communication System. The communication transponder is a three-channel frequency translating repeater operating in the 7–8 GHz range. Security is apparently provided by the transmit/receive pencil-beams and frequency shifting.

LASERCOM

The U.S. Air Force Space Division is developing a space-based laser communications system. The system will be capable of transmitting the entire text of the *Encyclopaedia Britannica* in slightly more than one second. Radio frequency satellite communication systems carry 24,000 voice channels or 8 color T.V. channels at a time. The "suitcase-size" LASERCOM can transmit 40,000 voice channels or 12 color T.V. channels. As a telephone relay it could carry over 250,000 conversations at a time. The LASERCOM is a modulated light beam with a wavelength much shorter than that of the microwave frequency satellite communications system (about 10^5 smaller for an 8 GHz system). The laser beam is extremely narrow (ten millionths of a degree) and probably cannot be jammed or intercepted. From a 22,000-mile orbit the beam on the earth's surface is much less than a mile wide; conventional satellites broadcast a signal that is three hundred miles wide. Test models of LASERCOM have been flown on aircraft transmitting to ground stations. The potential atmospheric attenuation of the laser beam suggests that the principal operational application of LASERCOM will be with the receiver on a high-flying aircraft.

U.S. NAVIGATION SATELLITES

The older U.S. navigation satellites in orbit now are in the Navy's Navigation Satellite System called TRANSIT. The TRANSIT system has been in polar orbit since 1960. In the TRANSIT system, a ship's position is determined by triangulation using the radar frequency signal transmitted by three satellites. The new NAVSTAR Global Positioning System (GPS) dramatically improves the military's ability to determine locations. When fully operational, the system will involve at least eighteen satellites in subsynchronous orbit with an orbit period of twelve hours. A user can determine his position within tens of feet, his velocity within a fraction of a mile an hour, and the time within a millionth of a second. The user equipment would automatically select four satellites most favorably located, observe them and their navigation signals, and compute the user's position, velocity, and time. User sets are being developed for integration into aircraft, land vehicles, ships, and even soldiers' backpacks. Data available from the Air Force indicates that a three-dimensional position accuracy of 52 feet and a velocity accuracy of 0.3 feet per second are possible. Six NAVSTAR satellites are now in orbit, and extensive testing of user equipment has taken place at Yuma Proving Grounds in Arizona.

One interesting application of GPS will increase the accuracy of American ICBMs. Presumably, after launch the Minuteman could update its position almost continuously, using GPS, before deploying the warheads, thus virtually eliminating guidance system errors. The total missile system error then would be that attributable to the flight of the reentry vehicle in the earth's atmosphere. The implication of the GPS capability for the accuracy of U.S. SLBMs—particularly Trident II—is obviously profound, since SLBMs could be as accurate as land-based missiles and attack hardened targets. This assumes, of course, that an adequate number of GPS satellites survive and that the communication link is available and secure. In any case, the GPS will have a significant impact on the accuracy of all long- and short-range U.S. military systems.

DEFENSE METEOROLOGICAL SATELLITE PROGRAM (DMSP)

The DMSP is a low earth orbit meteorological satellite system that provides continuous weather data for all U.S. military forces. The satellites carry an operational linescan system with a linescanning radiometer to take visual and infrared (day and night) imagery with a resolution of 0.3 miles or 1.5 miles. The combination of infrared and visible imagery can produce valuable meteorological data not observed by single-source satellites. The satellite also carries a precipitating electron spectrometer for auroral detection. This data forecasts the intensity and location of the aurora to aid radar and long-range communications operations in the northern hemisphere. There is also a microwave radiometer on board, which is used to measure temperature and moisture in the atmosphere. A microwave imaging system provides precipitation measurements, soil moisture estimates, sea state estimates, and ice formation measurements. There are three command readout stations for DMSP: Fairchild Air Force Base, Washington; Loring Air Force Base, Maine; and Offutt Air Force Base, Nebraska. Mobile ground terminals provide military commanders with photograph-like prints of cloud cover four times per day.

U.S. SURVEILLANCE, RECONNAISSANCE, AND EARLY WARNING SATELLITES

Ocean Surveillance Satellites

The table of military satellites listed in the annual aerospace system specifications by *Aviation Week* shows an ocean surveillance satellite that was first launched in 1976 and that involved three spacecraft per launch. Earlier press reports described Project White-Cloud as an ocean surveillance system involving three satellites that passively detect the electronic emissions from ocean-going vessels, including the communications and radar signals emitted by warships. The three satellites would then act as a long-baseline interferometer, and the direction and location of the ship would be accurately monitored by observing the interference fringes produced by the changes in distance from the satellites as the ship moves. This system, with the P-3C Orion antisubmarine warfare (ASW) aircraft and NATO ship surveillance vessels, is apparently considered adequate to monitor the deployment of the Soviet Navy. The Soviet Union has in orbit a nuclear-powered ocean surveillance radar satellite called RORSHAT, which is used to monitor the deployment of NATO ships. One of these satellites, and its nuclear power source, reentered the earth's atmosphere over Canada. Presumably RORSHAT could provide sufficiently accurate position data to launch long-range passive or active homing missiles. The United States apparently does not plan to develop a similar capabilitiy, although space-based radars could be powerful tools for continuous ocean surveillance since space-based passive visible or infrared sensors are limited by cloud cover. It may be very desirable to track the wakes of surface ships and, ultimately, the wakes of submarines. Space-based synthetic aperture radar technology could present an opportunity to monitor continuously the location, speed, size, and possibly the weight of all surface ships.

U.S. Reconnaissance and Space Surveillance Satellites

The 25,000-pound Big Bird satellite in low earth orbit apparently uses a visible photographic system that can radio photographs to earth or deorbit a recoverable film capsule. The C.I.A.'s KH-11 Strategic Reconnaissance Satellite also weighs 25,000 pounds and is in low earth orbit. The operations manual for this satellite was sold by a TRW employee to Soviet intelligence officers. There was little public knowledge of this important intelligence asset prior to the disclosure of this Soviet intelligence-gathering operation. The KH-11 is a broad-coverage, digital image transmission reconnaissance satellite in low earth orbit, presumably capable of providing a digital image of a Soviet scene every ninety minutes. A third reconnaissance satellite is the high-resolution film recon satellite in low earth orbit that the United States has used for over twenty years. This satellite uses the Discoverer film reentry capsule, which is deorbited with a retro-rocket and recovered. Three other surveillance satellites have been reported. The Teal Ruby experimental satellite, planned for the Space Shuttle, will attempt to track air-breathing aerospace systems. The Space Infrared Experiment (SIRE) would provide the United States with a space-based passive long-wavelength infrared surveillance capability, and a version is planned for a late 1980s shuttle launch.

Early Warning Satellite Systems

The U.S. early warning satellites are perhaps the only space-based U.S. early warning system for the detection of Soviet ICBM or SLBM launches. They are infrared tracking satellites in geo-synchronous orbit and were first launched in 1971. Their infrared sensors track the missile after launch by observing the infrared radiation emitted by the rocket plume. The booster plume emits an enormous amount of heat, and it can be easily tracked. The upper stages and the vernier engine emit less energy and are more difficult to track. The radiation emitted by the Multiple Independently Tar-geted Reentry Vehicle (MIRV) "bus" (from which the RVs are deployed) is very small, and the bus therefore is difficult to track, at least from geosynchronous orbit. By tracking the radiation from the booster plume, the infrared satellite can determine the missile's ballistic trajectory and its impact point. The missile impact point, however, may not be the reentry vehicle impact point, except in the case of a missile with only one reentry vehicle. The majority of U.S. and Soviet long-range missiles now carry MIRVs deployed from separate buses. Consequently, with a knowledge of the missile system impact point, the reentry vehicle impact point is known only within the envelope of possible impact points (called the "footprint") provided by the MIRV bus. For this reason, present early warning satellites are limited to measurements of the number of missiles launched, the direction of their trajectories, and a rough estimate of the points of impact. Since the present system uses mid-1960s infrared sensor technology, it is probably unable to track the upper stage and certainly cannot track the MIRV bus. A more capable satellite has not been placed in orbit during the past twelve years, owing to the Air Force belief that a determination of the launch time, size, and general direction of a Soviet attack is adequate for U.S. purposes. The warning provided by the present system (as much as thirty minutes) may be adequate to launch or disperse bombers or to launch American ICBMs.

An Advanced Early Warning Satellite System:
Detailed Boost-Phase Track

The technology associated with the present early warning sys-tems probably cannot provide an accurate prediction of each reentry vehicle impact point. The state of the art in passive infrared detection and tracking was advanced considerably during the 1970s. Detectors are more sensitive, and the amount of information that can be processed has increased enormously. Such progress in technology probably has made upper stage and even MIRV bus tracking possible, particularly at low-orbit altitudes. If the MIRV bus can be passively tracked and the deployment of an RV can be shown to be a unique event during the bus maneuvers, then the actual trajectory of each reentry vehicle can be determined. If the trajectory and impact point of each attacking reentry vehicle is known with sufficient accuracy, then the intent of any Soviet ballistic missile attack could be more readily determined. The U.S. response (including the extreme case of launch-on-warning) could be implemented in shorter time and with greater understanding not only of the number of launches and the launch time of a Soviet ballistic missile attack, but, more important, of the nature and military objective of the attack.

The ability of such a space-based MIRV bus tracking satellite would be greatly enhanced if the orbit of the passive sensor satellite were considerably lower than geosynchronous and if an active sensor were also deployed in low orbit. Two active sensors may be technically feasible in the foreseeable future, even very high frequency radars and lasers. Active tracking of any reentry vehicle after MIRV bus deployment would provide a very accurate prediction of its impact point. These low-altitude "pencil-beam" extremely high frequency sensors are probably the most promising active sensors, since it is not easy to take electronic countermeasures against super high frequency systems. A super high frequency space-based radar would have to be deployed in relatively low orbits because the radar power sources are limited. A dual passive and active sensor system of this type could possibly track several thousand MIRV buses and RVs.

Thus a satellite system in low or medium orbits that could passively and actively track Soviet MIRV buses or reentry vehicles would be a significant improvement in the U.S. ballistic missile early warning system. Such a system would also be invaluable in collecting intelligence data on any long-range Soviet missile and in the detailed verification of any nuclear-arms control treaty. Verifiable limitation on the number of missile warheads and the military mission of each missile system is one of the prime objectives of the new START process.

Boost-Phase Track Satellites and Ballistic Missile Defense

The space-based sensor system could provide the basis for a ballistic missile defense of the United States. For example, if the impact point of each reentry vehicle were predicted within a few miles by the dual sensor satellite system, interceptors could be launched long before the attack would break the visible horizon for a U.S.-based radar. The interceptor would carry homing infrared nonnuclear kill vehicles. The kill vehicle would locate the reentry vehicle and destroy the weapon. The predictions of the satellite would be subject to only a slight degree of error, and therefore the size of the propulsion system required for the kill vehicle would be relatively small. Such a system probably could not completely deny damage to the United States in a determined large-scale Soviet attack with sophisticated countermeasures. The system's principal advantage would be to permit the United States to absorb an attack of up to about a thousand reentry vehicles without immediately retaliating and implementing the assured destruction policy. Similarly, the United States would be able to absorb a limited ballistic missile nuclear attack from an "Nth" country without retaliating with the U.S. strategic nuclear forces. A space-based sensor system of this type would therefore make a major contribution to early warning and ballistic missile defense while vastly improving intelligence acquisition and strategic arms treaty verification capability. The ABM treaty modification that would permit such a system with clear interceptor limits would decrease the possibility of nuclear war by reducing reliance on reflexive retaliation. This change should be accompanied by parallel negotiations to ban short patrol range submarines, which can launch ballistic missiles on depressed trajectories and defeat the area defense system. The survivability of the space-based systems will always be an uncertain issue. Therefore, a treaty to ban ASATs would be the third element of the negotiations required to make such a system effective, and limiting the possibility of nuclear war.

THE SURVIVABLITIY OF U.S. MILITARY SPACE SYSTEMS

Hardening Satellites to
Nuclear Weapons and Lasers

Satellites in low earth orbits are vulnerable to a number of threats, including nuclear detonations, the deployed Soviet non-nuclear ASAT system, and possible high-power land-based lasers. The key communications and early warning satellites in geosynchronous orbits are vulnerable primarily to nuclear weapons. The capability of the Soviet ASAT system is probably restricted to satellites in lower orbits; it is possible that the Soviet Salyut space station may be developing a transorbit capability to threaten space assets in synchronous orbit. The new communications satellites are all being hardened against nuclear detonations. For example, DSCS III will be hardened to a set of Joint Chiefs of Staff (JCS) specifications of X-ray, neutron, and gamma levels, which are chosen to insure that only a close nuclear detonation will destroy the satellite.

The U.S. military space program is attempting to harden its early warning satellites whose focal planes and optical systems could be damaged by high-power ground-based lasers. Attempts are also being made to increase the survivability of the ground stations associated with communications and early warning satellites. In addition, DSCS II and III will be able to maintain communication links without constant ground-based monitoring.

Satellite Survival Aids

In addition to hardening, four techniques could improve the survivability of space-based assets: (1) satellite maneuvering; (2) decoys; (3) deep space-based "silent spares"; and (4) a reduction in the radar and infrared/optical signature of satellites. Satellite maneuverability is one of the prime survival techniques for American spacecraft. Radar and infrared signature reduction is an integral part of U.S. reentry system technology. The application of this technology to satellites would require design changes that are difficult to apply to satellites. The use of "pen-aids" technology to reduce satellite signature is difficult but not impossible. A silent spare with reduced signature and some maneuverability would increase the survival of the geosynchronous satellites. Reduced-signature satellites would also decrease the weight, size and complexity of replica satellite decoys. Thus, all four techniques could be applied to increase significantly the survivability of geosynchronous satellites.

Some of these survival techniques may not be applicable to reconnaissance satellites in low orbits. Signature reduction is ineffective because the range is short. Decoys may not be effective because they must be kept in low orbits with small rockets that may destroy the deception. The only attractive low-altitude satellite survival technique may be maneuvering; however, a sophisticated homing ASAT can probably negate the effectiveness of this capability.

The U.S. Antisatellite System

The United States has decided to deploy a low-orbit antisatellite system as a response to the Soviet system. The American ASAT system could also challenge the Soviet RORSHAT satellite and neutralize the Soviet ASAT in its first orbit. The American ASAT system involves the launch of a missile from an F-15 aircraft, which can be flown to a range of launch points and cover a variety of Soviet low earth orbit trajectories. The kill vehicle on the American ASAT missile is a Miniature Homing Vehicle (MHV), which would utilize long wavelength infrared homing combined with laser-gyro stabilization and lateral maneuvering capability to collide with and destroy the Soviet satellite. However, the MHV may be susceptible to simple countermeasures, such as replica satellite decoys near or even attached to the parent satellite. If several targets appear in the sensor's field of view, the sensor would have to be sophisticated enough to reject these false targets. The U.S. ASAT system, therefore, may not be effective. A complete ban on all ASAT systems, combined with survival aids, may be a more effective path to insure the survival of U.S. military space assets.

MILITARY SPACE PROGRAMS NECESSARY TO IMPROVE U.S.
SURVEILLANCE AND EARLY WARNING SYSTEMS

The proposed FY 1983 military space budget for the procurement of new space systems reveals the priorities that have been placed on important space assets (see figure 8.3).

The communication, navigation, and meteorological satellites are clearly the main emphasis of the Defense Department's space program. However, there is no plan or even a research and development program directed at a new ocean surveillance satellite or a new early warning satellite. The allocation for space surveillance is probably directed at ground-based optical and radar systems, and a small part may be allocated to passive infrared space surveillance. Almost a third of the military space procurement budget is directed at "special programs," which, presumably, are primarily reconnaissance satellites. The additional programs required to provide an improved surveillance, early warning, and reconnaissance capability are shown in figure 8.4.

There is a need for an ocean surveillance satellite, new passive and active boost-phase tracking satellites, and a passive infrared

Figure 8.3

**Proposed FY 1983 Department of Defense
Space Systems Procurement Program Budget**

AFSATCOM	$ 79 million
DSCS	243 million
FLTSATCOM	231 million
GPS	277 million
DSMSP	294 million
ASAT	213 million
Space Shuttle	582 million
Launch Support	257 million
Total	$2,194 million

Figure 8.4

**Space Programs Necessary to Improve U.S. Surveillance
and Early Warning Systems**

Requirement	Required Program
Ocean surveillance	High-resolution synthetic aperature radar; 1000–2000-km orbit; 10–20 satellites
Active and passive MIRV bus tracking	Passive infrared tracking of MIRV buses in low orbits; 5,000-km orbit; 6–10 satellites
	Active tracking at super high radar frequencies; 5,000-km orbit; 6–10 satellites
Space-based passive tracking of all U.S. and Soviet spacecraft	Long wavelength infrared tracking satellites; 5,000-km orbit; 6 satellites

space surveillance satellite. These applications would involve the deployment of from forty to sixty new satellites. The issue of survivability of the new satellites will always emphasize the need for an effective antisatellite weapon treaty and an aggressive survival aids program. The cancellations of the ASAT program and the military version of the Space Shuttle, as suggested in this chapter, should provide adequate funds to develop and deploy the three new space-based sensor systems.

THE U.S. NON-MILITARY SPACE TECHNOLOGY—AN
OPPORTUNITY FOR INTERNATIONAL ARMS CONTROL

The U.S. non-military space technology programs have demonstrated the remarkable power of near earth orbit space-based sensors to observe key features of the earth's surface, both land and sea. These sensors have already shown that significant aspects of the earth's resources can be systematically monitored, e.g., the location of new water sources, ocean fishing areas, crop development, geological surveys, ice formation, air and harbor pollution monitoring, and last, almost continuous meteorological observations. These sensors and the associated space technology could also present an opportunity to develop an internationally controlled space-based sensor system to monitor the development and deployment of strategic nuclear and conventional arms. The uniqueness of these sensor systems is that they were developed by U.S. civilian space programs so that the information obtained is available to the general public. These systems are the U.S. Landsat and Seasat satellites and more recently the space shuttle system. The sensors involved are primarily imaging sensors operating in the visible and infrared. Seasat and more recently the space shuttle have shown the spectacular images that can be obtained by the new synthetic aperture radars. These sensors can image the earth's surface day and night, in good and bad weather. The data obtained by the active and passive sensors on U.S. earth resources satellites show the dramatic, indeed revolutionary, impact of this space-based sensor technology for monitoring of the earth's surface. This tehnology could have equally dramatic impact if applied to an internationally controlled space-based sensor system to monitor the development and deployment of conventional and strategic arms. While such may seem a utopian suggestion, there is little question that the periodic publication of high resolution images of the world's trouble spots would act as some deterrent by galvanizing world opinion against countries deploying men and equipment for military action. The sensor technology, the space technology, and launch vehicle technology are well within the state of the industrial art. The unique aspect of this technology is that it is no longer constrained by our national security interests. In 1970 the technology associated with the synthetic aperture radar was declassified. During that decade visible and infrared imaging technology developed for national security interests were used in satellites to monitor the earth's environment and resources. There is now the possibility that the Landsat satellite itself may be transferred to the private sector. Even the space shuttle may be available for private use or even purchase.

The principal obstacle to an internationally controlled satellite monitoring system is obviously geopolitical—and this may prove to be an overwhelming obstacle. The United States and the Soviet Union have most of the world's satellite based sensors and technology. Since the U-2 incident, neither country has challenged the other's "right" to make satellite observations, which are clearly at the heart of the national security interest of both nations. Obviously neither country would be willing to provide its sophisticated intelligence gathering technology to an international body to monitor arms development and deployment. However, if the United States is apparently willing to transfer some of the Landsat and space shuttle technology to the U.S. private sector, then it may be possible that it could be made available to an international space agency. This transfer of technology to a space agency sponsored by a conglomorate of European countries and Japan may be politically feasible, particularly if there were guarantees that there would be adequate protection to prevent a subsequent transfer to a Soviet bloc country. A United Nations sponsored space agency would be an alternative but hardly a secure or even politically objective option. The international legal aspects of acquiring this data from space-based sensors would also have to be faced squarely. Acquiring an image from space of a country by a foreign entity could be considered by some to be an involuntary surrender of sovereign rights. Indeed, many countries have already involuntarily surrendered that right to the United States and the Soviet Union. The precedent has been established, therefore, and perhaps it could be universally established that an internationally controlled space agency may acquire such data, provided it were used only for international arms monitoring or earth resources management. Funding of such an agency would be through an assessment to the United States, Japan, NATO and Latin American countries and would amount to a few tens of millions each per year, hardly a heavy burden.

A similar proposal has been made by Adam Wasserman of the Office of Technology Assessment of the U.S. Congress. He points out that while there are risks for the United States and its allies in participating in such an organization, the gains far outweigh the losses. The United States should also recognize that an organization of this type may come into being with or without U.S. participation. France will deploy its SPOT system with 10-meter resolution in the mid-1980s. France also proposed a U.N.-controlled system in 1978. The chapter presented by Muyukio Honda at this conference clearly shows that Japan will have a significant, perhaps a dominating, capability in space-based sensor systems by the end of this century. In addition, an international space agency could provide detailed environmental and earth resources data on a routine basis to the entire world. This information from these space-based sensors would be an enormous asset in the development and monitoring of the resources for the third world.

Perhaps it is time that we see the exploration of space, or at least that space closest to the planet earth, from the viewpoint of its truly revolutionary potential in arms control and earth resources management and not to pursue ill-conceived space-based manufacturing plants or manned space colonies, or even worse, technically ill-conceived and potentially dangerous "star-wars" weapon systems.

NOTE

1. The description of the Titan III family of space boosters and the Space Transportation System (STS) developed by the U.S. Air Force to

deploy all U.S. military satellites in the late 1980s is contained in a series of fact sheets, which are available from the Office of Public Affairs, Space Division, Air Force Systems Command, Box 92960, Los Angeles, CA 90009. There is also a series of fact sheets available from the Air Force Space Division on various communications and navigation satellites. The descriptions of the Air Force managed satellites in this chapter are taken from these sheets and from *Aviation Week*, "*Aerospace Specification Tables 1982*," p. 22.

9

The Soviet View of U.S. and USSR Space-Based Intelligence-Collection Tactics

FREDERICK W. GIESSLER

The Soviet view of space-based intelligence collection focuses on the potential military use of space to support weapons and warfighting and emphasizes the integration of all sources of intelligence collection to create a comprehensive picture of the strategic and tactical posture of the enemy.[1] The fundamental differences between U.S. and Soviet conceptions of space-based intelligence operations have significant implications for U.S. security policy in the 1980s and beyond.

Basic to the Soviet view of space-based intelligence collection are the differences between the open society of the United States (and the free world) and the closed Soviet society. Because of the open nature of the United States, the Soviet leaders face a problem of source selection rather than a technical problem of intelligence collection. The kinds of tactical, strategic, and technical intelligence that the Soviet Union can obtain from American official, journalistic, and commercial sources is staggering. Although this abundance of information can lead to inaccurate conclusions or faulty analyses, it simplifies the Soviet intelligence-gathering effort. For example, the Soviet leaders do not need to rely heavily on satellite photography of the United States, nor do they have to collect fragmentary data to determine the readiness of U.S. forces. They can obtain construction drawings, official pictures, operational specifications, and mobilization capabilities from the United States and free world official and unofficial press. The task for the Soviet Union is not to collect more, so as to create speculations and substantiate hypotheses, but instead to decide what sources to believe.

Economics, entrepreneurial style, and management philosophy also present major asymmetries between U.S. and Soviet intelligence problems. In the West, private enterprise encourages the rapid deployment of available and maturing technology. Soviet centralized bureaucracy, however, focuses on its goals and objectives and develops accordingly the technology needed to meet military needs. In a sense, the United States mans its equipment while the Soviet Union equips its men.

Political forces drive the Soviet Union to incrementalism and prolonged adherence to initiatives. Contrary to the laborious annual rejustification of the U.S. space-related budgets, Soviet decisions appear to follow more consistently and closely their five-year plans.

Fundamental societal asymmetries make it relatively difficult for Moscow to compare its space-based intelligence-collection system with American methods. Our ability to comprehend the compartmentalized and narrowly circumscribed Soviet way of dealing with space intelligence collection may allow us to face fewer obstacles than Soviet officials do in their efforts to understand the voluminous discussions of the very broad spectrum of U.S. views.

COMPARING SPACE-BASED INTELLIGENCE COLLECTORS

Cybernetics, the science of information and control, is the foundation for the Soviet approach to intelligence collection, processing, and use. It is also fundamental to Moscow's approach to space exploration. At the highest levels, the Soviet Union evaluates the overall contribution of a system to the attainment of national goals. For simplicity this cybernetic system is divided into four subsystems: sensors; booster rockets; spacecraft; and ground support, processing and disseminating.

Sensors

The United States is compelled to rely upon satellites for intelligence collection to a much greater extent than the Soviet Union. In the Soviet view, space-based sensors are intended to collect or confirm information that is needed to improve the military "correlation of forces." Sensors are required to provide prompt discovery of enemy defensive nuclear weapons and continuous surveillance of these weapons. The Soviet objective in visual spectrum collection is to develop a highly sensitive analyzer with a large field of view for adequate spatial resolution and a capability to repeat and verify observations. Soviet technology is meeting these difficult requirements by using cosmonauts to speed up the information-collection process through selectivity, a reduction in the amount of information recorded, and its preliminary processing before transmission to earth. While man-machine sensors are preferred and emphasized, automated sensors are widely used and are being developed further. Some of these sensor systems have two modes, sensing from space and gathering from space. Eight nonvisual band sensors on board a scientific satellite launched in early 1981 were designed to produce better maps of shorelines and icefields, identify storms and hurricanes, locate schools of fish, and measure the thermodynamic temperature of the ocean's surface. In addition, the satellite had the capability to gather data over a unique earth-satellite-earth bridge from 256 buoys and platforms. This was necessary to collect information in areas that are difficult to reach or cover by human observation.

Published Soviet evaluations of U.S. satellite-borne sensors focus on unmanned radar, photographic (scanning and detailed), radio/telecommunication, infrared, television, and electronic detectors that are used to locate military forces. The Soviet leaders believe that America concentrates on military "targets" and other intelligence of use in preparing for war. In the Soviet view, the United States is determining the location of military targets. Moscow also believes that the United States is determining the location of air defense systems, gathering technical information on Soviet radar installations, locating trucks, tanks, and radio communication centers, providing accurate target coordinates for nuclear weapons, and tracking planes and ships.

The Soviet leaders assume that the United States has a variety of radio reconnaissance sensors that complement photoreconnaissance systems and are sometimes carried on the same spacecraft. Soviet experts in the early 1970s described the sizeable number of U.S. programs and defined the objective of the sensors. From SAMOS through the plans of the mid-1970s for three stationary geosynchronous satellites, details of sensors and associated spacecraft were analyzed for their contribution to U.S. warfighting abilities. The Soviet Union also believes that the United States has ocean surveillance sensors. Soviet analysts considered that deployed satellite sensors would be able to determine the location of all ships, intercept radio communications, and have all-weather, day and night capability through the use of sophisticated radar. Finally, the Soviet Union believes that the United States supports its strategic submarines with a global system of reconnaissance and surveillance.

Boosters, Rockets, Transportation Systems, and Cosmodrome Sites

Baykonour Launch Complex, the launch site of the first artificial earth satellites, is described in Soviet literature as a new town fulfilling a political mission of enormous significance. Soviet publications indicate that Kaputin Yar and Plesetsk also are involved in launching satellites used for collection of data vital to the attainment of the long-term goals of the Soviet Union. These three launch complexes service the needs of the hardware that is produced and sponsored by the

Ministry of Aviation Industry and the Ministry of Defense. In conjunction with the launch complex, the flight control center at Kalingrad is in charge of satellites from preparation through operation. The center is reported to participate in the design of the space vehicle and to develop the new means and principles of control that are required.

As far as Soviet views of American booster technology are concerned, Moscow has paid attention to the Titan IIID agenda booster and has placed an eleven-ton payload into low polar orbit.

Spacecraft and Military Space Equipment

The Soviet Union emphasizes manned spacecraft for data collection because they expand the opportunities for research and lead to accomplishment of the tasks laid down in the eleventh five-year plan. Many special mechanisms and subsystems are required to support the cosmonauts; thus, there is an increase in the probability of malfunction in the spacecraft. This is more than offset, however, by the ability of the crew to restore important elements that may fail in flight. For unmanned missions the Soviet Union focuses on single-purpose spacecraft. One way of categorizing these spacecraft is by titled space programs. Thus, starting with the 1957 Sputnik flight, the Soviet space program grew to include Vostok, Voskhod, Soyuz, Salyut, Kosmos, Polyot, Elektron, Proton, Prognoz, Interkosmos, Molniya, Luna Venera, Mars, and Zond. Of these programs, Kosmos is reported to include the military intelligence collection satellites. The Kosmos series has had more than 1,200 launches, of which more than 50 percent were military related.

The published Soviet views of U.S. spacecraft design and use for intelligence collection emphasize the belief that U.S. spacecraft would have direct impact on terrestrial and eventual space warfighting. Soviet literature maintains that, beginning in 1958, spacecraft such as the "Dyna-Soar" project were developed to be armed with bombs having atomic warheads, nuclear rocketing, and equipment for conducting espionage from space. The Soviet Union reportedly views American intelligence collecting spacecraft as being of significant help to the United States on the tactical battlefield. Soviet literature states that American satellites gather intelligence on radar and radio stations, use infrared to detect ICBM launches, obtain radar maps of terrain, detect tanks and trucks by thermal radiation collection, and combine electronic and photoreconnaissance gear on spacecraft that record both signals and images, which are later transmitted to earth. Soviet publications assert that most U.S. reconnaissance collection satellites have multiple purposes: photo, signal intelligence, weather, launch detection, and nuclear detection.

Processing and Production of Intelligence

The Soviet Union indicates that three general categories of military space applications characterize the Soviet collection-through-dissemination subsystem: intelligence collection, communications, and antisatellite operations. Soviet open-source literature indicates that several types of intelligence collection are conducted on a daily basis and include photographic, ocean surveillance, and electronic missions. Significant progress is being made in analyzing, interpreting, and evaluating information collected from space.

Image recognition of Soviet space-collected information by computer is still limited. Current and developing technology is reported to focus on interpretation of space-collected image data by specialists, storage in computer data banks, and interpretation by researchers. This man-computer system imposes high requirements on the volume of computer memory but contributes to overcoming the unsolved image recognition problem. While the availability of information concerning Soviet military intelligence collection is very sparse in the open Soviet literature, significant insights are revealed in the description and analyses of data collection concerning non-military subjects, including Soviet diagrams that compare the manned and unmanned space systems. These factors provide a basis for understanding the intelligence collection, processing, and dissemination system.

For many years the Soviet Union has been describing what it believes to be the television, photographic film capsule recovery, and direct impact on the battlefield of the information from U.S. intelligence satellites. Open Soviet source descriptions of the direct military use of intelligence data from space imply a capability for near-time collection, processing, and dissemination.

AN OVERVIEW

With the last flight of Gary Powers, America's need to rely upon intelligence collection methods other than aircraft became obvious. From that point on, the United States began a series of highly productive programs to meet this requirement.

In comparing the U.S. and the Soviet space collection efforts, it is necessary to comprehend that their approaches are inherently asymmetrical. Several different issues are crucial to understanding and integrating the Soviet view of USSR and U.S. approaches and assets. Societal asymmetries in the two countries produce different concepts and actions concerning space-based intelligence collection. Basic asymmetries exist between the economies, societies, educational philosophies, political systems, and cultural heritages of the two states.

For instance, the Soviet approach to micro and macro resource allocation starts with an articulated objective, develops alternate effective strategies to accomplish that objective, determines what resources and organizations are necessary and optimal to implement the strategy chosen, develops tactics to mix resources in the face of problems, procures the resources and hardware necessary to fulfill strategies, and proceeds toward the objective set, while conducting analysis to insure that operations and capabilites continue to be adequate for the attainment of those goals. Shortfalls are identified from time to time, and goals are altered accordingly. The United States tends to make changes on the margins to meet near-term goals. While its practices may avert great pitfalls, the United States rarely focuses on strategic long-term goals. The Apollo and other space-related programs are some of the few exceptions where the United States has focused on major goals with classic strategic planning. However, even in the case of the moon landing, it is not clear that the United States had a strategic plan to proceed and exploit the achievement.

The result of such asymmetry is that the United States and the Soviet Union approach problems from different paradigms, and therefore have different views of technology, whether in manned space, unmanned space, intelligence collection, or communications.

One approach to understanding Moscow's view of U.S. and Soviet space-based intelligence collection technologies is to subdivide the latter into four different categories: sensors; boosters; spacecraft; and communication, processing, and dissemination systems.

Cybernetics, the science of information and control, seems to be the foundation for the Soviet approach to space-based intelligence collection, processing, and use. The Soviet leaders appear to be interested in adapting critical variables in the system for eventual manned control. Although man in space requires much more technology than an unmanned space system, the Soviet Union believes that there are more than offsetting advantages. The United States recognized this and acted accordingly during earlier stages, when the manned orbiting laboratory was developed, but that effort was abandoned when costs rose and goals were questioned. The Soviet Union, on the other hand, understood the need for adaptation and continues to comprehend the vital role that crews could play in accomplishing goals in space.

The Soviet Union thus designs its space-based capabilities to accomplish strategic goals. If these technological capabilities fail to meet the goals set, Moscow insures that the man in space or the design bureaus will make the incremental improvements to accomplish the objective.

In the sensor area Soviet literature acknowledges U.S. space-based collection sensors in a very interesting manner. Soviet publications view U.S. space sensors as being highly supportive of war, of warmaking, of conflict in general, and of actions that would make a significant difference in the outcome of fighting. The Soviet Union describes U.S. imaging sensors, like infrared sensors, as being good enough to tell the difference between a tank and a truck. The Soviet Union evaluates U.S. ocean surveillance as capable of locating all the ships in the world, whether they are friendly or not, and of determining direction of travel and speed.

Soviet publications tend to denigrate their own space-based intelligence collection capability. They maintain that the United States is far ahead in this area. They assert that they are simply trying to make some technological progress, while the United States is using all its space collection capability for military purposes. It is unclear whether such material is intended, at least in part, to serve "disinformation" purposes.

The Soviet Union subdivides U.S. sensors into photographic "elint," "comit," and "sigint." Furthermore, it describes these sensors according to functions they supposedly serve in meeting the military needs of the United States. Very little is written about Soviet space-based military sensors. Nonmilitary Soviet sensors are discussed and described, although many of the facets addressed are obviously applicable no less to sensors designed for military requirements.

In discussing boosters, the transportation system, and the cosmodrome sites, Soviet literature describes new towns inhabited by talented, intelligent individuals, living in pleasant surroundings and having access to high-grade facilities. U.S. launch sites are described in Soviet publications as places where weapons are launched into space and where sinister experiments are carried out which will have disastrous results in the future. These publications compare Vandenberg Air Force Base with the Kosmos launch facility and their other launch facilities with Kennedy and Wallop's Island.

The Soviet Union has continued to focus on single-purpose, single-sensor spacecraft, often of limited life. Soviet publications speak of U.S. large, multipurpose, multisensor spacecraft that can operate for a lengthy period of time. They recognize some of the advantages and disadvantages, respectively, of each approach. Soviet literature states that, with shorter-lived systems and a large number of launches, the Soviet Union has more flexibility and can be more adaptive; it recognizes, at the same time, that U.S. spacecraft are much more automated, sophisticated, integrated, and technologically advanced.

When considering the processing, production, interpretation, correlation, documentation, and utilization of the intelligence gathered from space, the Soviet Union focuses on integrating intelligence supplied by a variety of sensors. The Soviet Union integrates photographic, elint, sigint, and comint right from the start, while also integrating space-collected intelligence with other kinds of information (including material obtained from the U.S. open society). Soviet publications also speak about use of such information by military commanders on the battlefield or in planning military operations. They focus on the actual conversion of this highly technical intelligence into information usable for military purposes.

Soviet literature appears to view U.S. intelligence collection from space differently than it regards its own. The Soviet Union proceeds from a different paradigm, related to its whole concept of strategic long-range planning, of knowing its goals, doctrine, and objectives and wedding these to technology so as to accomplish strategies over the long term.

NOTE

1. Serious research on this topic is difficult to conduct without infringing on classified sources. Intelligence gathering from U.S. space-based vehicles to support treaty verification, particularly over the Soviet Union, became a necessity after Gary Powers's last U-2 flight over the Soviet Union. Other intelligence collection technologies continued to evolve and ground- or aircraft-based sensor devices have been used where proximity allowed. Unclassified Soviet literature indicates that the Soviet leaders realized this and have tried to minimize this U.S. ground- and air-based collection. Alleged facts about this subject have been printed in periodicals, newspapers, scientific publications, and "exposés" of intelligence organizatons, but it is neither legally nor ethically possible for a government employee or a defense intelligence analyst to confirm or deny such speculation. Therefore this chapter looks at the Soviet view of U.S. intelligence gathering technologies. Speculations and studies can be gathered about Soviet technologies involved in their collection of intelligence from space. However, here, too, security limitations exist. This chapter avoids such problems by attempting to focus primarily upon openly published Soviet authorities concerning Soviet space programs. Where Soviet sources are not available, international sources are used.

10

Crew Roles in Military Space Operations

DAVID LEINWEBER

There is a wide-ranging debate on the role of the armed forces in space. This issue has begun to attract substantial attention not only in the defense community, but from Congress, the executive branch, and the public.

In simple terms, the debate centers on the question of the degree of involvement of space systems in our future military operations. The military uses of space to date have been largely in support of terrestrial military functions, such as communications, navigation, reconnaissance, and surveillance. The systems have been passive and without capability of initiating hostile actions. Many civilian and military analysts believe that no further expansion in the military use of space beyond the current support missions is necessary. Some take this position because of general opposition to the "militarization" of space, while others feel that space systems are far too vulnerable to be relied on for important military purposes.

Another group would contend that it is necessary and prudent to expand the military capacity for operations in space by taking on new missions and expanding existing roles. Such an increase in capacity might include space defense systems to protect U.S. space assets and counter hostile actions. In this view, space systems would still be a supporting, rather than a central, element in the nation's military posture. It has become apparent from Soviet activities that the Soviet Union has incorporated these notions in its policy for military space activity.

Such activities would be limited to earth orbit only in the early stages of a determined effort to expand the strategic role of space. As is cited often in plans for civilian space colonization and industrialization, the earth-moon system contains two points of stable equilibrium (known as L_4 and L_5), which are natural locations for the economical conduct of large-scale military and civilian space activities. These points will be of critical importance if the United States and the Soviet Union develop the capability to conduct space operations beyond the confines of low and geostationary earth orbits.

A concerted effort to establish military superiority by control of the "high ground" in space would require substantial revision of the treaties now governing space activities. The national security consequences of today's decisions on the military role of space will affect international relations for years to come. They should be made in a reasoned and deliberate fashion, rather than by default or by haphazard attempts to apply both manned and unmanned space techniques in an uncoordinated way.

THE ROLE OF SPACE CREWS IN MILITARY OPERATIONS

Regardless of the outcome of the military space debate, questions of appropriate roles for crews in the development, support, and operation of military space systems will remain. These issues arise whether the systems are unarmed observation and support platforms or powerful weapons.

Soviet attitudes on these matters are in some ways clearer than our own. The extended six-month Salyut missions would have been impossible without the repairs, both scheduled and unscheduled, made by the crews. During the life of the Salyut spacecraft, major modifications were made to the life-support systems, communication systems, and other components, including the manual release of a large dish antenna that had not deployed successfully on its own.

Arguments can be made that the Soviet Union's more backward technology, particularly in areas of information processing, forces it to use crews in space, while American systems can rely on superior computing. In fact, the Soviet experiences, as reported, confirm the American conclusion that the most illuminating episodes of crew utility in space have not been of the "the computer could have done it" variety. The rapid advance in American electronic technology will not eliminate useful roles for military crews in space.

The tasks best suited for crews are, first, those that can be conducted in relatively safe environments. They should be non-repetitive and relatively complex, requiring degrees of physical dexterity, perceptual acuity, learning ability, intuitive decision making, attention to detail, and an ability to deal with a wide range of contingency applications requiring the use of mechanical or electrical procedures. Some duties are best left for machines, including tasks that are repetitive or rigidly defined, such as beam fabrication, and those in acutely hostile environments or very remote locations, such as translunar space.

Figure 10.1

Limits of Movement for an EVA Suited Crew Member

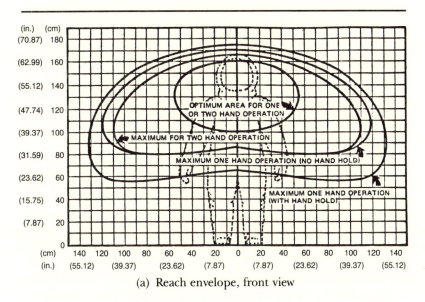

(a) Reach envelope, front view

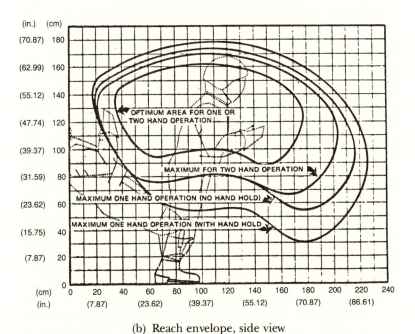

(b) Reach envelope, side view

SOURCE: Marshall Space Flight Center

We do know that in some ways astronauts are at a disadvantage. Many assembly tasks, such as bolting together components, are far more tiring in space because of the lack of gravity and the limited mobility of suited crew members. While on earth many physical forces are provided by the friction between our feet and the ground; in space much greater muscular effort must be expended, for instance, just to stand still and turn a screw driver. As seen in figure 10.1, mobility limits are restrictive but not prohibitive, and many designs for individual work modules intended to attach directly to a spacecraft and hold the crew member in place have been proposed. These would allow mechanical work to be performed with far greater efficiency.

For some tasks, any mechanical disadvantage is outweighed by the perceptual and cognitive abilities of human crew members to notice unexpected and subtle phenomena.

A dramatic illustration of this important aspect of manned space activity occurred when astronauts on board Skylab noticed unexpected eddy current phenomena in the sea currents below. Their findings are important both for the military application of minimization of submarine observables and for the interpretation of sonar returns. The potential value of oceanographic data gathered by trained observers in developing an understanding of these eddy currents is sufficiently high for the Office of Naval Research to have planned a seven-shuttle flight program to study the effects.

TYPES OF CREW INVOLVEMENT

Space systems can be "manned" to different degrees. While manned systems are commonly thought to be those in which the crew plays a central and continuing role, there are different degrees of crew involvement in such systems. Experimental research and development activities to develop new space systems; service, support, and maintenance of spacecraft by means of periodic crew visits of varying durations; and the active operation and participation by crews in ongoing manned space activity on continuously populated space platforms are three levels of human involvement possible for "manned" space systems.

The Marshall Space Flight Center has characterized the interactions between crews and space systems that apply in all three contexts. They cover a wide range of activities, from simple experimental setup to manned satellite and subsatellite operations (see figure 10.2).

Figure 10.2

Man/System Interaction Definitions

Man/System Interaction	Definition
Experiment setup, direction	Crewman physically moves equipment/ experiment from stowage to operation location, configures support systems (pre and post), and returns equipment to stowage after experiment completion.
Experiment start/stop	Crewman initiates and terminates experiment operations.
Monitoring at C&D panel	Monitoring experiment/payload status at display panel in orbiter (PSS) or Spacelab module; minimal crew activity.
Experiment control, direct	Crewman mechanically or electronically controls experiments directly (adjust, select modes, identify/acquire targets, react to data, etc.); crewman and experiment are in the same physical location.
Experiment control, remote	Crewman electronically controls experiments indirectly; crewman and experiment are physically separated.
Experiment observation, direct	In situ observation of experiment progress; crewman and experiment are in the same physical location.
Experiment observation, remote	Observation of an experiment physically located away from crewman (i.e., crewman in orbiter, experiment on pallet); observation either through viewing port/ window or T.V. system.
Housekeeping	Crewman performs activities such as film or tape changing, store/dispose of throwaway items, general cleanup, etc.
Maintenance	Unscheduled or scheduled repair or service activities performed directly (shirtsleeve), remotely (shirtsleeve with manipulator or free-flying teleoperator), or EVA.

SOURCE: Marshall Space Flight Center Manned System Specifications.

Figure 10.2 (continued)

Man/System Interaction	Definition
Calibrate instrumentation	Crewman performs procedures (direct or remote) to calibrate or recalibrate instrument prior to or after experiment data taken.
Data reduction/analysis	Crewman reviews experiment data and determines next experiment functions based on that data; redirects emphasis of experiment as necessary.
Remote pallet operations	Display/align/retract booms or antennas on pallet-mounted equipment; activities controlled from orbiter or Spacelab module.
Free-flying teleoperator (FFTO) operations	Checkout, deploy, track, operate (precise on-orbit control from FFTO panel), and retrieve; T.V. system observation utilized to perform remote tasks.
Subsatellite operations	Checkout, deploy, track, operate (majority of control from ground; on-orbit, control from PSS), and retrieve; observation through window or T.V. system.

ROLES OF CREWS IN SPACE EXPERIMENTATION

Development of a new space system can be a long and frustrating process. Thirteen test launches were required to bring the early Discoverer reconnaissance spacecraft to even a shaky operational status. A multitude of tiny oversights and minor failures, such as circuit-breaker trips, blown fuses, or neglect of a "remove before flight" tag, which could be remedied with five minutes of an astronaut's time, have cost hundreds of millions of dollars in lost spacecraft and space experiments.

The coming generation of space experiments, which will be carried on a shuttle mission and returned to earth following a test, tries to avoid many of these problems by having crew members (payload specialists) available for contingency actions as well as normal operations. In addition, substantial cost reductions may be realized. Equipment can be refurbished and refined for use in subsequent experiments, and much common equipment, such as power supplies and communications, data handling, cooling, and pointing devices, could be used in several different experiments. Other savings arise since the availability of an intelligent crew to deal with contingencies places less-demanding requirements on the experimental designers.

There may be some initial cost increases for payloads not designed for the shuttle, since reengineering may be required. Common support equipment for space research must be designed, procured, rated, and installed on the shuttle. The personnel to operate the experiments must be selected and trained. These initial costs may be seen by some experimenters as introducing unacceptable delays in programs already delayed by the extended shuttle development program, but when amortized over a large number of experiments conducted over the lifetime of the shuttle fleet some of these costs may be offset by a greater degree of technical productivity.

Other factors would also tend to lower costs of manned experiments. The intelligence of the human operator who can reconfigure the experiment or make use of spare parts reduces the need for redundant hardware and complex computer programs. A payload specialist can direct the experiment and data collection. The results would therefore be subject to real-time examination, and postflight data reduction costs could be diminished and the probability of making all of the desired observations would be increased. These factors could occasionally make the difference between a fully successful experiment and one that must be reflown in order to acquire data that were missed.

Experimentation and system development on space shuttle missions have limitations as well as advantages. The most significant is the limit on the duration of any test to the maximum twenty- to thirty-day shuttle mission. Other difficulties include the effects of both chemical and electromagnetic contamination from the shuttle environment, and the power and communications constraints imposed by the shuttle's payload provisions.

These limits have been the motivation for the design of autonomous space experimental platforms, such as the Science and Applications Support Platform (SASP), discussed in a subsequent section of this chapter.

CREW MAINTENANCE AND SUPPORT OF THE SPACECRAFT

For many missions it is possible to envisage a spacecraft that would operate autonomously, without a crew, for long periods. Service and maintenance would be performed during manned visits scheduled on a regular basis, or as required by indications of failing or failed components on the spacecraft. If the satellite were in a shuttle-accessible orbit or could be brought into one for service, the crew would have the option of repair in orbit or recovering the satellite and returning it to earth for more extensive reworking.

The absence of a crew on a permanent basis from a spacecraft has certain benefits. Spacecraft sensors can be made larger, and the vibration induced by crew motion will not degrade the quality of the observations. More power will be available for primary mission functions. A fully manned design was considered for the NASA Large Space Telescope but was deemed inappropriate, in part because movement of the crew members would substantially degrade the pointing accuracy of the apparatus.

The designs of hypothetical manned and unmanned space systems to perform the same mission can be compared. Program lifetime is assumed to be fifteen years, and the estimated mean time between failures on the satellite is estimated at three years. The manned support option would be to launch a single satellite with manned repair or recovery scheduled nominally every three years, though conducted on an as-needed basis in order to realize the benefits of extended satellite lifetime. The unmanned option would be to procure five satellites in a block and launch them as required on expendable launch vehicles. For purposes of this comparison, assume a cost of $40 million per ELV launch, $180 million per manned recovery/refurbishment mission, and $240 million per satellite. The nominal fifteen-year program cost, based on fixed three-year satellite lifetimes, would then be $1 billion for the manned program and $1.4 billion for the unmanned. Both program costs will vary with the mean satellite lifetime if recovery and refurbishment missions or new launches are deferred when the satellite in place continues to operate satisfactorily.

The detailed cost comparison of the two programs is strongly sensitive to the assumptions regarding the cost of the individual components. However, an illustrative calculation using these assumed figures is presented here. The program cost now depends on the satellite lifetime L as shown below, where the square brackets indicate the greatest integer function.

$$\text{Manned program cost} = \$280M + [(15/L) - 1]*\$180M$$

$$\text{Unmanned program cost} \begin{cases} = \$1400M + [(15 - 5L)/L]*\$280M \text{ for } L <= 3 \\ = \$1240M + [(15/L) - 1]*\$40M \text{ for } L > 3 \end{cases}$$

These equations are graphed in figure 10.3, which shows the dependency of the total program cost on mean satellite lifetime. If the fifteen-year program lifetime assumption is rigidly observed, the

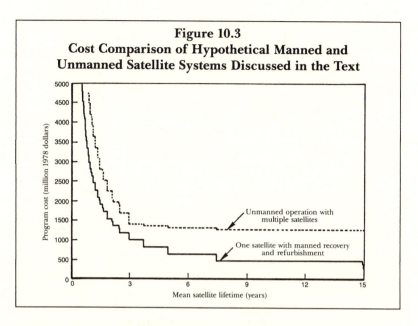

Figure 10.3
Cost Comparison of Hypothetical Manned and Unmanned Satellite Systems Discussed in the Text

Program cost (million 1978 dollars) vs. Mean satellite lifetime (years)

Unmanned operation with multiple satellites

One satellite with manned recovery and refurbishment

manned program dominates the unmanned program over all satellite lifetimes, since recovery operations are less costly than new satellites and only relatively small savings are realized by eliminating ELV launches. In fact, it is unlikely that the unmanned program would continue in the way shown in this chart for lifetimes of less than three years. In the face of multiple early failures the satellites would be extensively evaluated and redesigned rather than replicated and relaunched. There are many other difficulties with this sort of cost comparison; reasonable alternative programs are not included, and the results are sensitive to initial assumptions.

The manned and unmanned systems can be compared in terms other than cost, such as versatility. A single satellite system with manned servicing would require recovery, refitting, and replacement to modify the satellite substantially. The cost of this kind of activity would be much higher than that incurred in modifying a satellite already in production. The other side of this issue is that long satellite lifetimes with adequate performance result in substantial savings ($180 million per cancelled manned service mission, compared with only a $40 million savings per cancelled ELV launch, in the previous example). In the case of short satellite lifetimes, the schedule of manned service missions can be accelerated. If short lifetimes persist despite efforts to improve reliability, the conventional program would continue but with increased costs for valuable payloads, such as the one discussed here.

In the manned program, the possibility of accidents in which the crew inadvertently damages the satellite will always exist. This will not occur in a conventional program. A major advantage offsetting this risk is the far simpler recovery from certain electromechanical accidents in a manned program.

A single catastrophic event destroying the satellite will require termination of the single satellite manned program, while an accelerated launch schedule can allow the conventional program to proceed as long as satellites remain in inventory or production.

The collateral opportunities in the manned program include the experimental test of the utility of crews in space but exclude the possibility of multiple satellite observations. The conventional program does nothing to resolve further the questions of human space capabilities, but if satellite lifetimes are extended and multiple platforms are placed in space at the same time, additional observation opportunities can arise.

Another risk in the manned program is that the satellite may become unserviceable, or fail catastrophically during a service visit, in the worst case causing the loss of the crew and shuttle, as well as the satellite. In the conventional satellite program only the loss of equipment, satellites, and ELVs can occur.

Irrespective of the particular numbers involved, it is clear that certain very expensive satellites using fuel, film, and other consumables, both for today's passive or tomorrow's active military functions, could benefit from manned servicing. This would be even more valuable for orbiting space weapons systems requiring a large number of platforms arranged in orbits allowing multiple visits in a single shuttle mission.

MANNED SPACE RESEARCH AND DEVELOPMENT PLATFORMS

The discussion of experimentation on shuttle missions noted the limitations and the advantages of sortie research and development activities, particularly the twenty- to thirty-day limit on mission duration, imposed by use of the shuttle as the experimental platform.

To circumvent these limits, NASA has undertaken detailed studies of systems to support manned space research, development, testing, and evaluation (RDT&E). One system, called the Science and Applications Space Platform (SASP), consists of a proposed shuttle cargo to be placed in orbit as a long-term base for large payloads. Crew involvement could include setup and maintenance or extended operation from a habitat module. The SASP would be similar to the

Long Duration Exposure Facility (LDEF) in that it would stay in low orbit and be serviced by shuttle flights over a period of years. Unlike the LDEF, it would provide support functions to experiments in a manner compatible with the sortie. Electric power, computer support, data services stabilization, and heat radiation could all be handled by centralized systems. The central computer would operate the platform, and individual experiments could operate under the control of smaller computers.

NASA's study concluded that major improvements in low earth orbit payload accommodations could be provided over the sortie mode with minimal payload conversion. Experiments would benefit from longer flight duration, an environment without chemical and electromagnetic contamination from the shuttle, greater heat dissipation and power, greater viewing freedom, and lower cost per day of flight.

There would also be reductions in the load on NASA support systems, such as the TDRSS and the shuttle itself. The SASP package of resources available for payloads would free the experimenters from having to provide their own solar arrays, antennas, radios, recorders, and other equipment, and thus would be an economical alternative to a series of smaller free-flying spacecraft.

The current designs do not include a long-term crew habitation module, which would be required for a resumption of manned space activity similar to the American Skylab and Soviet Salyut programs. Crew involvement on an unmanned SASP would be limited to initialization, maintenance, and equipment change-outs during brief visits.

ACTIVE CREW OPERATION OF CONTINUOUSLY MANNED FACILITIES

An orbiting space station, long envisioned by writers of science fiction, is now viewed as a potentially valuable asset in the development, deployment, operation, maintenance, and recovery both of military and commercial spacecraft, as well as the conduct of space operations. Space station concepts range form the modest, such as the manned habitation module attached to an SASP as described earlier, through a full-blown multiport structure capable of accommodating large crews involved in the construction and service of large space systems.

The only currently funded manned experimental program to provide a Skylab-like environment is the European Space Agency's Spacelab, which is designed as a shuttle mission payload. It has the duration, power,and heat limitations imposed on other payloads.

Spacelab is a modular system consisting of various manned and unmanned equipment pallets installed in the shuttle bay.

The Spacelab accommodations are short-term facilities, limited to a few weeks of continuous use at a time. In a recent study, the Aerospace Corporation examined the possibility of an independent Spacelab, modified to support a crew of three for ninety days. Their design proposal is based on the use of current or planned hardware elements: the 25-kilowatt solar power module is under development by NASA for extended STS and SASP operation, the Remote Manipulator System arm has been flown on shuttle missions, and the reboost module and other support equipment are based on Skylab designs.

The shirtsleeve satellite service area is composed of Spacelab pallets enclosed in a new pressurized fiberglass fabric enclosure. The original Spacelab long habitation module is extended by an additional segment to accommodate the crew and equipment that otherwise would be carried on the orbiter (see figure 10.4).

A major new component is the Teleoperator Maneuvering System (TMS), a remotely controlled vehicle designed to extend the range of manned satellite serviceability. This is one of a number of proposals for such reusable transfer vehicles; others are discussed in a subsequent section of this chapter.

Development cost for an Independent Spacelab is estimated at $2 billion, though such preliminary estimates must be regarded with some caution. The facility would make good use of existing components and thus allow a relatively modest investment to expand substantially the planned U.S. crew presence in space. Evaluation of the

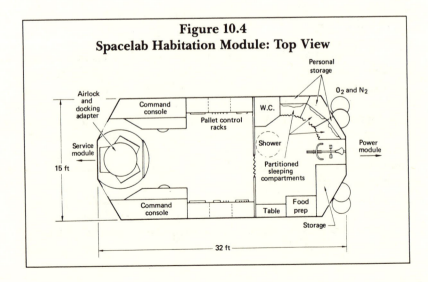

Figure 10.4
Spacelab Habitation Module: Top View

services provided and experimental results of a small facility such as this could form the basis for a decision on more elaborate platforms, such as the Space Operations Center (SOC), a less modest undertaking of potential military importance. This is a NASA concept that could evolve from a small initial configuration to a full-blown, high-volume satellite construction and service facility, serving a wide range of military and civilian missions.

Much more must be known about the relative economies and abilities of crews performing construction and heavy maintenance tasks in space before informed decisions can be made on whether to initiate such a program and which design should be pursued.

ADVANCED DEPLOYMENT CONCEPTS

The space operations that have been proposed for the remainder of this century are principally in low earth orbit (LEO) or at geostationary (GEO) altitudes. Looking further into the future it is reasonable to ask whether we will confine our activities to LEO and GEO. The answer given by many futurists is that the domain of space activities will expand to encompass the earth-moon system.

In addition to the earth and moon there are five points of interest in the earth-moon system, called the Lagrange points (known as L_1 through L_5), where the gravitational forces exerted by the two bodies are such that an object at one of these points will remain at that point. Of the five points, only two (L_4 and L_5) are stable; that is, slight perturbations in the position of an object result in restorative forces that tend to maintain the equilibrium. The others are of less interest, since a space platform trying just to maintain position at L_1, L_2, or L_3 would require substantial energy expenditures to do so.

The military importance of L_4 and L_5 stems from their position at the top of a pair of gravitational "wells," one going down toward the earth and the other toward the moon. A platform placed at L_4 or L_5 has considerable strategic importance in the earth-moon system since gravity assists the transfer of mass to the earth or moon and resists any effort to transfer mass to the equilibrium point from the earth or moon. This is a case where the "high-ground" analogies of some military space planners are quite appropriate.

It should be noted, however, that occupation of the L_4 and L_5 "high ground" offers no additional protection from directed energy devices.

The use of these points for any purpose, military or civilian, is many years away. Decisions regarding them will be made in political and technological contexts that differ greatly from today's circumstances.

MANNED MILITARY SPACE VEHICLES

While illustrations of space stations often show one or two space shuttles parked nearby, actual operations will require the development of a different kind of vehicle, designed for use only in space and not intended to cross the atmospheric barrier. Such a vehicle would be lighter, smaller, and far less expensive than the shuttle, which must operate in space and in air, two very different environments.

The primary reason to develop a space-only vehicle is that the shuttle will be needed for its space launch missions and will not be available to any great extent for ongoing orbital operations. The need for the vehicle arises as well from the orbital limitations of the shuttle, which can reach only as high as 600 miles, whereas many military payloads orbit at altitudes far beyond, and almost all commercial payloads (desirable as cost sharers for any manned space operation) are in geosynchronous orbit. The Teleoperator Maneuvering System (TMS) is one such vehicle, envisaged as an unmanned robot.

Orbital transfer vehicles are essential for a mature operation in space. Support and additional propulsion modules could be added to the exterior of the vehicle, since it would never be required to fly through the atmosphere and no streamlining would be necessary. It could be operated in a manned or autonomous mode as deemed appropriate for the mission. A known minor component replacement for a satellite in geosynchronous orbit would certainly not call for bringing a large and potentially delicate satellite down into low earth orbit. A crew member would be sent to do the job as a "housecall." An undiagnosed failure on a nearby satellite would justify a recovery mission.

The transfer vehicle would need some means of dealing with satellites spinning out of control. This is an area of considerable uncertainty, but it is clear that direct personal action by crew members would be unwise. Grappling systems or nets operated by remote teleoperators would be more appropriate.

ANOTHER APPROACH

Much of the preceding discussion has been based on the implicit assumption that it is useful and economical to place crews in space to perform complex functions. This may well be the case in peacetime, but during a period of hostilities the use of a Space Operations Center or similar base may well be denied even though the nation's military need for space operations would be substantially increased. There are proposals for hardened silo launchers to place small payloads in space, but this does not allow for the flexibility and adaptability of manned operations. Thus another approach to the military use of space is that of quick turnaround, single-stage to orbit, Reusable Aerodynamic Space Vehicles (RASV). One concept for a RASV uses space shuttle main engines in a wet wing airframe holding the cryogenic fuels. With slight upgrading, such a vehicle could place payloads of over 30,000 pounds in 28.5 orbits and over 15,000 pounds in polar orbits of 50 by 100 miles with takeoff turn-around times measured in hours. This design is actually reminiscent of the original proposals for the shuttle, which were based on similar advanced materials technology. The metal exterior of the craft would eliminate the turnaround delays associated with the tile maintenance that must be performed on the shuttle, and other systems would also benefit from shuttle experience.

CONCLUSIONS

An examination of the future military roles of crews in space reveals that military space programs have neither clear goals nor well-defined limits. Organizations to carry out required training and development activities have not yet fully emerged. What is needed today above all else is a commitment to explore the possibilities, to experiment, and to acquire a sound base of knowledge on which to make an informed judgment on the future military role of men in space.

4

Organizational Dimensions of Space: Unilateral and Multilateral

11

U.S. Organizational Infrastructure for Space Programs: Strengths and Weaknesses

JOHN M. LOGSDON

INTRODUCTION

It is now over twenty years since the initial debate over the goals of the U.S. space program was resolved by John F. Kennedy's commitment to across-the-board preeminence, with a series of manned expeditions to the moon as the centerpiece of a national enterprise. This commitment energized the development of an impressive institutional and organizational capability for carrying out the U.S. civilian space program which, at its peak, involved hundreds of thousands of skilled individuals in an integrated government-industry-university undertaking. In recent years, as the priority assigned to government's civilian space efforts has diminished, there has been a corresponding decline in the vitality of the institutional base for that program. The future of the civilian component of government space efforts is currently under intensive review, with the appropriate role, mission, and character of the National Aeronautics and Space Administration (NASA) a central concern.

The evolution of the national security component of the country's space program has followed a different path. Certainly the Apollo commitment was driven by concerns of national security, broadly defined, and considerations of national power and prestige continue to underpin, however implicitly, decisions on civilian space programs. In contrast to the NASA program, which by the mid-1960s had become a highly mobilized and highly visible national undertaking and which has existed since then on residual momentum, national security efforts in space have steadily and quietly grown over the past two decades. They now command a budget larger than the civilian space program, and there is a distinct possibility within the next few years that space technology will play a more central and visible role in the nation's defense.

The continuing growth in national security space efforts has not been accompanied by the creation of an integrated institutional and organizational base. The current fragmentation reflects the fact that various elements of the armed forces and the intelligence community have found space technology a useful means for carrying out their responsibilities. The mission requirements of a variety of agencies have provided the main impetus to the growth of national security space programs. No single powerful organization acting as an advocate of the benefits of space has emerged in the national security community. In general, however, it can be said that civilian officials within the Defense Department, particularly at the level of the Office of Secretary of Defense, have been more enthusiastic about exploring the defense potentials of space technology than have the leaders of the uniformed services.

Whether this fragmented approach to both space research and space operations for security purposes is now dysfunctional is an important issue and is being debated extensively within the defense community. This chapter does not address that issue directly. Rather, the focus will be on evaluating the widely discussed suggestion that formal separation between government's civilian and military space efforts is no longer in the national interest. In particular, the chapter will address the question of whether the institutional, facility, and human resources that together comprise NASA could, and should, be brought into a closer relationship to national security space efforts.

Such a suggestion arises from a recognition that the relationship between civilian and national security efforts in space is defined much more by policy than by differences in technology. The technological reality is that almost any space capability—earth observation, environmental monitoring, communications, transportation, in-orbit construction, and so forth—can be used for either civilian or national security purposes.

How best to develop these capabilities to serve a full range of national objectives, from fundamental science to strategic surveillance, is a policy problem that has persisted since the origins of the U.S. space program almost a quarter of a century ago. The world is a much different place in the mid-1980s than it was in the late 1950s, when the current policy and institutional framework for the national space program were developed. The political and economic context within which the U.S. space program exists, and thus the national priorities and objectives to which that program should be responsive, have shifted from a Cold War focus to that of a much more complex environment of global economic and political interdependence. The United States and other leading countries have had almost twenty-five years to assess the ways in which space achievement might, as President Kennedy suggested in 1961, "hold the key to our future on earth."

In the civil sector the United States has achieved a position of space leadership, and the Space Shuttle program is a central element in maintaining that leadership. By any reasonable criteria, NASA has been successful in carrying out the primary mission assigned to it: developing and demonstrating advanced space technology. NASA grew into an extremely capable organization and became larger than anyone had anticipated in 1958. In just over two decades of experience, NASA has also developed into a particular kind of institution in the eyes of the world, of the U.S. public, and of its own staff. Any consideration of changes in the overall structure of the U.S. space program cannot ignore the results of the past twenty-five years of activity.

The U.S. national security space program is larger and more vital than all but a few expected in 1958. As the Department of Defense and the intelligence community use existing space capabilities and explore the potentials of future space systems, there is a growing realization of the central role space technology might play in U.S. security planning. The national security space program has evolved with particular institutional characteristics, and two decades have demonstrated that there are substantial differences in organizational style and methods between the civilian and military space programs. These differences include the relationship between users and developers, and the closed style of the military program when contrasted with NASA's openness.

There have been repeated interactions since 1958 between the separate space programs, and those interactions reflect a mixed record of cooperation and conflict. Previous assessments of this record and of the reasons for maintaining separate program structures have all concluded that the existing relationships are fundamentally sound. The following discussion identifies issues that should be considered in determining whether this conclusion remains valid in the 1980s.

THE ORIGINAL RATIONALE REVISITED

Controversy surrounded the 1958 decision to set up a pluralistic institutional structure for the U.S. space program. Intense debate among executive and legislative branches, the military services, the scientific community, and the nascent aerospace industry led to the conclusion that national security and civilian space efforts should be managed in separate institutional structures. One reason for this decision was a belief that defense and intelligence applications of space technology were best carried out under the management of national security agencies, rather than by a single space agency for both civilian and military purposes. There were also scientific, economic, and political justifications for space activities that were not tied to national security applications, which added up to a nonmilitary space program large enough to require a sizeable organization to carry them out. Separate programs seemed best to serve the national interest, because civilian space projects were not relevant to the Defense Department mission and could interfere with security-oriented space projects by competing for resources and technical talent and by complicating the security process required for military projects.

The existence of a separate civilian space program meant that the United States could exploit that program as a tool of domestic and foreign policy, could openly engage in both cooperative and competitive international space efforts of a nonmilitary character, and could more easily transfer the results of the government's space research efforts into the civilian economy.

The validity of the rationale for the 1980s could be questioned in two different ways. One approach would examine whether there is continuing justification for committing significant financial, technical, and institutional resources to a civilian space effort when there are competing national security requirements for their use. The other would ask whether the perceived political, diplomatic, and economic benefits of separate civilian and military space programs continue, or whether the benefit calculus has shifted to support a more integrated national space program driven primarily by explicit national security concerns. This chapter assesses the implications of a closer relationship between civilian and national security space programs and evaluates institutional alternatives for creating that closer relationship.

ADVANTAGES OF CLOSER NASA-MILITARY RELATIONSHIPS

Several advantages might result from unifying the government's civilian and national security space programs into a closer relationship. The military program would benefit from bringing the capabilities possessed by NASA into a role of more direct support for the top-priority space objectives of the country. NASA would gain a more secure political base, since the agency would be carrying out both civilian and security-related research and development programs. Both programs would be improved as a result of the greater flow of technology between civilian and security programs and the new opportunities for sharing the costs of research, technology development, and operational activities. Cooperative activity could range from basic work in space propulsion to jointly managed development and operational programs in such areas as meteorology, ocean observation, navigation, and space transportation. Finally, although the government's space programs are organized in separate federal agencies, they draw upon the same aerospace industry. Closer program relationships might lead to more efficient utilization of this industrial and technical base.

DISADVANTAGES OF CLOSER NASA-DOD RELATIONSHIPS

The potential consequences of a closer NASA-DoD relationship include impacts that may not be desirable from a national point of view. First, the United States has invested a lot of time, money, and effort in a civilian space program with an open, peaceful image. This image has proven useful both as a rallying point for creating national pride and a sense of common accomplishment and as a propaganda tool for creating a positive attitude toward the United States among the other countries and peoples of the world. Closer ties with military missions might undermine NASA's peaceful image. In more concrete diplomatic terms, the civilian space program is party to a wide variety of agreements for international cooperation and joint activities with space programs of other countries. These cooperative activities are valuable in scientific, economic, and political terms. Other countries might be less willing to cooperate with a U.S. space program closely linked to defense and security missions, and the U.S. managers of such a program might be less willing to open elements of it to non-U.S. participation. The less open nature of a military program might also cause highly motivated and qualified technical personnel to seek careers elsewhere. At a minimum, bringing the civilian and national security space programs into closer contact could limit the potential for mutual learning between two separate research and development efforts aimed at differing but complementary objectives. Planners and managers of the national security space program are likely to give lower priority to research and development opportunities without clear security applications; the results of a program driven largely by such security requirements could include a lack of balance in research and development investments and development programs and the subsequent loss of U.S. leadership in space technologies. This danger seems acute in view of the determined efforts by Europe and Japan in pursuing space development for civilian payoffs.

Another problem is raised by the lack of a single Department of Defense space program and the conflicting institutional relationships among the space efforts of the Army, Air Force, Navy, defense intelligence agencies, and other strategic intelligence programs. Another major actor, NASA, outside the defense framework but with major research and development responsibilities related to military programs, could simply add to the current conflict. Within DoD, various agencies perceive themselves as competing for scarce resources, for which space efforts are only one claimant. It is not clear that DoD would support any NASA-managed space research and development except efforts closely tied to military needs.

CHARACTERISTICS OF CIVILIAN AND NATIONAL
SECURITY SPACE EFFORTS

Even if it were desirable to bring civilian and national security efforts in space into a more integrated framework, the question of feasibility would remain. The NASA and national security space efforts have evolved rather differently, and each has different institutional and programmatic characteristics.

Mission

NASA is a research and development agency chartered to develop space technology, demonstrate space systems, and use those systems for scientific research. Although in theory NASA's research and development efforts are linked to the requirements of various users, in practice NASA is largely dominated by its scientists and engineers.

Space research and development activities within the Defense Department framework are primarily responsive to the requirements of military operations and supporting structures. The military users of space technology are within the Defense Department, and the problems of transfer from developer to user are less than if the two were in different organizations.

NASA has a mixed record in its efforts to conduct research and development responsive to the requirements of users outside the agency. Programs in support of the needs of the National Oceanic and Atmosphere Agency and various users of communications satellites have been successful, but those in the remote sensing area have been less productive. Applications efforts have not been a large part of NASA's experience, and to make NASA's mission the support of other users, rather than space technology development, will require substantial reorientation.

Openness

NASA is somewhat conservative in operating style, but it carrries out its missions in the full glare of public scrutiny and also actively seeks such publicity and attention as a means of gathering support and gaining political advantages for the country. Full disclosure of NASA's activities (with a few recent exceptions) has no potential for compromising national security issues.

The Department of Defense operates through a closed and compartmentalized system; extensive precautions are taken to avoid disclosure of any information potentially useful to an adversary. Space activities other than routine operational support are among the most highly classified DoD programs. NASA could not become intimately associated with national security space activities without major modifications in its policy of open access and full disclosure.

Involvement of Other Countries

International cooperation was one of the objectives set for NASA in 1958, and the United States has pursued an extensive cooperative program with technical, economic, and political benefits. While there is foreign participation in some DoD space activities, this participation is based on joint defense objectives and is of a quite different character than NASA's international activities.

There would undoubtedly be tension between security requirements and any extensive interaction between the United States and other countries in civilian space efforts. Some of these tensions are already evident in planning for the use of the shuttle by military and foreign users. Scientists in foreign countries may be less willing to deal with a U.S. space program closely linked to national security activities.

Institutional Base

NASA has developed an extensive set of field centers and facilities to carry out its programs, despite its substantial use of outside contractors. The Department of Defense has a smaller base for its activities and makes extensive use of government-owned, contractor-operated support organizations to perform tasks similar to those carried out by NASA field centers. It is not clear that DoD would be comfortable with or effective in assuming managerial control over some or most of NASA's laboratories, or that efficient means could be found for civilian-run government laboratories to work on national security programs.

NASA and DoD draw on substantially the same base of aerospace industry contractors, and this common base may facilitate closer cooperation between civilian and military management structures.

Program Emphasis

NASA has extensive experience, trained personnel, and appropriate facilities in two space technology areas in which the Department of Defense has limited capabilities: manned space flight and space propulsion. DoD's emphasis has been on unmanned spacecraft development. This complementarity may make it easier to mobilize civilian capabilities for new national security missions than if both programs had been emphasizing the same kinds of technologies.

Mutual Distrust

The various differences in the Department of Defense and NASA discussed above have resulted in a working relationship between the two organizations better characterized by distance and mutual lack of understanding than by close collaboration. Neither NASA nor the Department of Defense has been eager to share control of any of its programs with the other agency. The organizations have different internal and external priorities, and attempts at initiating jointly funded and/or jointly managed programs have not been successful. Recent attempts to define an operating framework for the Space Transportation System, including the shuttle and an orbital transfer vehicle, have demonstrated the complexities of NASA-DoD relationships.

The emphasis in the discussion above on the differences between NASA and DoD activities in space is meant to suggest the barriers to bringing those agencies into a more intimate relationship. It is important to note, however, that there are significant commonalities in what both organizations do and need. Both are working on advancing the state of the art in space science and space technology; both require similar kinds of infrastructure, such as reliable and inexpensive space transportation services, tracking and control systems, data acquisition and processing capabilities, and in the future, in-orbit facilities for power, construction, and servicing. The space activities of the civilian and national security programs are together a national asset; the policy issue is how best to employ that asset in service of the national interest.

CONCLUSION

A general conclusion on the issues discussed in this chapter requires decisions on the goals and character of future national security and civilian space efforts. Organizational frameworks and institutional capabilities are means, not ends, and should be adapted to the ends they serve. In space, those purposes may change dramatically in coming years.

Substantial institutional barriers resist bringing NASA's capabilities to bear in direct support of national security requirements. Perhaps a less complex approach would be to develop the necessary institutional resources and technical capabilities within the Department of Defense, rather than depend on NASA for security-related research and development efforts. Specific elements of NASA, or technical capabilities now operated under NASA auspices, might be part of the DoD space structure. Clearly, there must be continued close cooperation between NASA and national security space programs. From the perspective of national security interests, however, the provisions of the 1958 Space Act, which assigned military space efforts to the Department of Defense, remain valid today. The debate over future national security applications of space technology should include an institutional component that asks what organizational resources are required within the Defense Department to carry out the space programs that are selected and to explore future space technology.

NASA's future should not depend on closer links to national security efforts in space. A separate and vigorous civilian government space program should continue, with its own goals and with a revitalized NASA at its core. It appears that the U.S. national interest has been well served by a commitment to leadership in space technology; that commitment should be renewed for the decade to come.

12

The Other Space Powers: Europe and Japan

JOHN H. HOAGLAND

EUROPE AS A SPACE POWER

Following the confusion and indecision that marked the early years of the European space effort, in the era when the first collaborative organizations were emerging from a welter of competing national projects, the European effort has become purposeful, successful, and, to a remarkable degree, integrated.

Europe's main purpose is to reduce or eliminate its dependence on the United States for launching and operating satellites, especially those with a direct economic or commercial benefit, such as communications and earth resources satellites. Of less importance in European space activities are purely scientific or exploratory missions; and military space programs, with a few exceptions, are not given a very high priority. (Admittedly, many Europeans would argue with this judgment.) Commercial and political independence has been the primary consideration, and the result is a well-directed effort with early benefits.

It is useful to recall that, just fifteen years ago, as the first decade of the space age was ending, Western Europe's policy makers and institutions were still in the throes of an effort to close the "technology gap." They watched on the sidelines, with growing concern, as the United States and the Soviet Union made spectacular advances in orbital, lunar, and planetary exploration programs. As one eminent British engineer observed at the time:

> Western Europe enters the second decade of space flight still with no clear idea of her eventual destination in space or even of the initial route that must be followed. The simple purpose of the United States and the Soviet Union to explore the moon and planets both with manned and

unmanned spacecraft (which is the most powerful reason for a space program) is missing. It is too expensive for Europe to contemplate, at least in the next 10 years, and important subsidiary objectives must therefore be found.[1]

Britain, France, Germany, Italy, and others possessed important technological resources, but there was no national mandate in any of these countries or, even more important, any real progress in the formation of a European space consortium that would permit the collaborative pursuit of agreed-upon objectives, under the direction of a single authority. In particular, the Convention Establishing a European Organization for the Development and Construction of Space Vehicle Launchers, signed by seven European countries in 1962, had encountered frustrating and costly delays caused by lack of agreement on objectives and work sharing. This organization, known as ELDO (European Launcher Development Organization), of which Britain was the technological and financial leader, was finally dissolved; but ELDO and its companion organization ESRO (European Space Research Organization) became effective precursors of later collaboration.

By 1975, ESRO and ELDO had been supplanted by a truly effective collaborative organization, the European Space Agency (ESA), which is the most successful example to date of an organizational form in which European governments and industries have become preeminent: an international agency that defines goals and contracts to multinational industrial consortia made up of chosen national firms, which share the work in proportion to national financial contributions.

Eugene Skolnikoff and this author observed in 1967 that

Even in the unlikely event that some of the other industrial powers, such as Britain, France, West Germany, and Japan, were to increase their space expenditures drastically—for example, to about one-half of one percent of GNP per year—the United States and the Soviet Union would still remain the predominant space powers by any standard of measurement. But this kind of assertion, although factual, may also be somewhat misleading. It is important to keep in mind that the two superpowers have made an extremely large investment in both manned and unmanned space exploration, . . . [including] a manned lunar landing. . . . If the cost of a manned lunar program or other highly ambitious programs of manned space exploration were omitted, then smaller budgets of other countries would appear more competitive, especially in the practical application of artificial earth satellites.[2]

This is, in fact, the course that the Europeans have chosen; and if, in the 1980s, the United States shifts its space effort even moderately from civil to military applications, Western Europe could assume a leading role in commercial uses of the space environment. In the intervening fifteen years, the European nations have managed, against many obstacles, to organize a consortium of interests in support of practical and achievable objectives. In the process, Western Europe has indeed become a space power in spite of the fact that its total budget is still far less than that of the United States. There are two reasons for this development. First, in launch vehicles, Western Europe acquiesced in French leadership. Second, the Europeans concentrated their interests primarily on developing sophisticated satellites for communication, navigation, meteorology, and resources capable of offering Europe itself or Europe's customers a direct economic or commercial payback. In the discussion that follows, these are recurrent themes.

Although Western Europe has indeed become a power in space, it is a power according to its own definition. The exploration of space, manned orbital missions, and major military applications lie beyond Europe's priorities and independent capabilities, which are tailored to the criteria of possibility and profitability.

SOME BUDGETARY COMPARISONS

Europe's combined expenditures on space projects typically amount to less than 20 percent of the NASA budget.[3] It is instructive to match this fact against Europe's growing competitive challenge to American predominance in the launching of commercial payloads. In recent years, the French national space budget has often represented over 40 percent of total European space expenditures; the Federal Republic of Germany on the order of 30 percent; Britain about 15 percent or more; and all other European countries from 10 to 15 percent.

Within each country's space budget, expenditures are divided between purely national programs and contributions to the European Space Agency (ESA), the international agency responsible for harmonizing and coordinating the major European programs. The ESA budget has typically accounted for 65 percent or more of European space outlays as a whole. Generally, therefore, contributions to ESA have been somewhat larger than purely national portions of each national budget; but there is some speculation that, with the completion of major ESA development projects, such as the Ariane booster and Spacelab, many national programs—especially satellites—will become more important in the 1980s.

Even within the various national contributions to ESA, each of the principal countries has carefully earmarked its own contribution to fulfill particular national interests. For example, French contributions have been devoted largely to Ariane booster development; British contributions to communications, weather, and navigation satellites in which British industry played a leading developmental role; and German contributions to Spacelab, the manned scientific laboratory which will be launched by the American Space Shuttle beginning in 1983 and in which the German government and industry have special interests. In fact, the contributions of each ESA member country take two forms: first, the mandatory contribution to meet the rather modest fixed costs of the ESA organization and facilities; and second, the optional contributions to particular programs.

THE EUROPEAN SPACE AGENCY

Currently, eleven European countries are members of ESA: Belgium, Denmark, France, Germany, Ireland, Italy, the Netherlands, Spain, Sweden, Switzerland, and the United Kingdom. Austria, Canada, and Norway also participate in some of the agency's programs. ESA's purpose is to provide for and promote cooperation among European states in space research and technology leading to nonmilitary space applications. ESA fulfills this mission by:

defining and implementing a long-term European space policy, recommending space objectives to the member states, and harmonizing the policies of the member states;
implementing collaborative activities and programs in the space field;
coordinating the total European space program with separate national programs, and integrating the latter as completely as possible in the European space program, particularly with respect to the development of applications satellites; and
defining and carrying out a coherent industrial policy appropriate to its programs and serving as a contracting agency.

The basic policy of ESA is to create European autonomy in space activities by developing its own independent technological and industrial capabilities. Autonomy in the domain of boosters was considered absolutely critical, and for this reason the Ariane launcher became ESA's highest priority. France has been both the largest single contributor and the largest industrial work-sharing beneficiary of the Ariane project.

ESA has a modest staff of approximately 1,500 people drawn from the member states, located at the headquarters in Paris and in other establishments. ESA maintains the European Space Research and Technology Center at Noordwijk, in the Netherlands, which is responsible for applied research in space technology. The European Space Operations Center located at Darmstadt, Germany, is responsible for satellite orbital operations and tracking, as well as data acquisition and processing. This center controls a network of four ground stations located in Belgium, Germany, Italy, and Spain. It is responsible for operation of the most powerful automated documentation system in Europe, containing more than 12 million bibliographic references.

Since 1975, when ESA was created, a major policy has been to make the maximum use of industry in all aspects of the space program. Under this policy, all activities that do not absolutely require reliance on ESA personnel are delegated to industrial contractors. This includes maintenance and operating contracts for the operations center, ground stations, and computer facilities; technical assistance in the maintenance and operation of environmental test installations and check-out equipment; technical assistance in software development; management of laboratories; and, most important, development and production of boosters, spacecraft and their support systems. Given the need for complicated national work-sharing arrangements and the use of chosen national instruments, competitive bidding has often been set aside in favor of negotiated contracts.

To the greatest possible degree, a "Buy European" policy is followed. Another major policy is that of "indirect intervention," favoring the formation of multinational industrial structures adapted specifically to the implementation of particular ESA programs. These include the formation of multinational industrial consortia for important development and procurement contracts, the consequent reduction of the number of prime contractors, and increased competition at the subcontractor level for major development programs. Typical examples in recent years have been the MESH (Matra, ERNO, Saab, and British Aerospace) and STAR (British Aerospace, Dornier, AEG Telefunken, VFW, and others) consortia formed to carry out specific types of projects.

ESA is, of course, anxious to improve the competitiveness and marketing presence of the European space industry in world markets. To achieve this, ESA's priorities include the active promotion of

ESA systems and technologies in the Third World and in other industrial countries, and support in the creation of powerful commercial ventures such as Arianespace.

Only when it has been necessary to fill obvious gaps in the technological or financial resources—as in the area of manned orbital projects—have the Europeans established governmental and industrial collaboration with the United States . The most notable U.S.-European program is Spacelab. There are also, however, a number of collaborative efforts at the industrial level, in which U.S. corporations participate, through membership in European consortia, in ESA programs in order to contribute technologies, especially in electronics, that are currently lacking in Europe. Finally, it is worth noting that France has engaged in bilateral projects with the Soviet Union, including the joint Soviet-French manned space mission that took place in 1982. These, however, do not directly involve ESA; and whatever importance it may have is more political or psychological than technical or industrial.

BRITISH SPACE ACTIVITIES

In the first decade or so after World War II, Britain established an early lead in the development of large boosters, but it failed to capitalize on this leadership and, during the 1970s, fell behind France and the Federal Republic of Germany in its commitment to space activities. Now, after a period of comparative apathy on the subject, the British government is showing new vitality concerning space projects for the 1980s and 1990s, especially in developing and manufacturing satellites with commercial applications.

Britain has given particular attention to communications satellites, both for commercial and for military use. In the military area, the Skynet military communications satellites have provided a basis for intensive collaboration between British and U.S. industries since the late 1960s. The next satellite in this series, Skynet IV, will provide communications with ships and submarines and mobile as well as fixed land terminals. It will probably be launched by late 1984. British Aerospace Dynamics Group and Marconi Space and Defense Systems are the leading British contractors for satellite systems.

The most important new satellite project for British industry during the 1980s will be L-SAT (Large Communications Satellite), which will measure more than 55 feet in length. British Aerospace will be the prime contractor for this program, and British industry will dominate the program as a whole. L-SAT, with seven kilowatts of on-board power, will provide direct-broadcast television to rooftop antennae as well as a high volume of telephone and data communications traffic. Although L-SAT is an ESA project, Britain will contribute about one-third of the total cost. France and Germany will not participate in the project because of their own concentration on a directly competitive joint project for direct television broadcasting and communications.

British Aerospace Dynamics Group (BADG) will lead the consortium of companies building L-SAT. Britain's contribution of 34 percent of the estimated $430 million project cost will be nearly matched by Italy. Canada, the third largest partner, has a 10 percent share. L-SAT will probably be launched by Ariane III in 1986. Britain is clearly placing a great deal of importance on this strong entry into the direct-broadcast satellite market; British estimates have indicated a market for between 50 and 100 direct broadcasting (DBS) units in the foreseeable future. In keeping with this goal, BADG has teamed with the Rothschild Merchant Bank to create Satellite Broadcasting Company to launch and operate direct-broadcast satellites for British and other customers.

L-SAT is only one of many communications satellite projects in which Britain is involved, but it is the largest in terms of capacity and commercial promise, and it represents an evolving competition within Europe. Other important programs include the INTELSAT series, in which BADG has received an important share of the work; MARECS (Maritime European Communications Satellite); and ECS (European Communications Satellite), which will provide telephone services within the Eutelsat group of countries. In keeping with these programs, BADG has created a joint venture with Matra of France, known as SATCOM International, for overseas marketing of communications satellites based on ECS and MARECS.

FRENCH SPACE ACTIVITIES

In 1965, France became the third nation, after the Soviet Union and the United States, to orbit a satellite independently. In the late 1960s there were several launches by the Diamant booster from Hammaguir in North Africa, and by 1970 Diamant B was putting satellites in orbit from the launch site in Kourou, French Guiana (now Guyana). While Britain, which had invested heavily and early in large ballistic systems, vacillated in its commitment, France maintained a steady and determined program to develop its own independent capability in both large ballistic missiles and space boosters. Immediately after World War II, the French government established the Laboratoire de Recherches Balistiques et Aérodynamiques (LRBA) at Vernon to begin laying the groundwork for a ballistic missile program. In addition to French personnel, LRBA was also staffed by experienced German engineers who began, by 1949, to develop the Veronique rocket. The LRBA complex at Vernon laid an effective foundation for all subsequent work on rocket engines and boosters, including the land- and sea-based strategic deterrent and the Ariane booster.

Currently, there are three major and highly competent industrial contractors that work closely with CNES (Centre Nationale d'Etudes Spatiales), the French equivalent of NASA. These are Société Européenne de Propulsion (SEP), specializing in rocket motors; Matra, specializing in satellites; and Aerospatiale, the general contractor for RDT&E of entire space systems. It is an impressive team.

In 1981, the total budget, all of it allocated through CNES, was on the order of $500 million, of which roughly 40 percent was allocated to ESA, primarily for Ariane. Aside from ESA, the budget can be divided into three broad headings: supplemental contributions to the Ariane program; bilateral programs; and national programs, coordinated with the European effort.

About 20 percent of the 1981 budget went to supplementary contributions to the Ariane project, over and above the basic ESA operating budget. European bilateral projects also represented roughly 20 percent. Here, the major current program is the Franco-German five-channel direct television broadcast and telecommunications system, which will result in two very similar spacecraft, developed in a common project, for national use by each country: the TDF-1 for France, and the TV-SAT for Germany.

In the category of national programs, which amounted to something less than 15 percent of the 1981 budget, the two major current activities are a domestic and Francophone telecommunications satellite, TELECOM I, and the earth resources satellite, SPOT. Matra is the prime contractor in both cases. A great deal of attention is being given by CNES to the SPOT remote sensing satellite (Système Probatoire d'Observation de lat Terre), which will be launched by Ariane into a sun-synchronous polar orbit in 1984. SPOT itself is being marketed actively to customers worldwide for earth observation, with direct readout to foreign ground stations or by data access through France.

The SPOT satellite is designed to provide 1:100,000 scale stereoscopic pictures in visual and IR wavelengths to allow land-use and geological investigations by ground stations. The basic SPOT vehicle will also serve as the platform for two ESA-developed earth resources satellites, ERS-1 and ERS-2. ERS-1, a land application satellite system, may be launched by 1986. ERS-2, a coastal and ocean monitoring system, is to be launched about one to two years later. ERS-1 will use a synthetic aperture radar as well as optics, and ERS-2 a new microwave radiometer.

The first SPOT satellites will have a ground resolution of about ten meters in black and white and twenty meters in color and will observe in three spectral bands, including visible and IR portions of the spectrum. Although the SPOT "bus" will be a standard multipurpose platform, the payload can be varied for different types of earth observation. Services will be marketed to users worldwide through the licensing of foreign receiving stations. In addition, data received through French stations can be marketed and distributed to foreign users on a commercial basis. SPOT will also provide the basis for Matra's development of a military reconnaissance satellite, SAMRO, which will have better ground resolution and improved capability to transmit military reconnaissance imagery by radio and video links. It will be launched by Ariane.

Soviet-French cooperation is not significant in a budgetary or technological sense, but it has some political significance. In 1981, CNES allocated only about 1 percent of the budget to this program, the most spectacular element of which was the presence of a French astronaut, along with two Soviet astronauts, aboard a Soviet craft in 1982. There are also various other scientific and experimental projects being carried out in cooperation with the Soviet Union. The Mitterrand government, which inherited the project, has probably been somewhat uncomfortable with it politically, especially after the Polish crisis.

GERMAN SPACE ACTIVITIES

Spacelab is a versatile, multipurpose manned laboratory for scientific activities in near earth orbit, using palletized loads. It will be launched by, and remain attached to, the Space Shuttle throughout its mission. Germany, the European leader in the collaborative U.S.-European Spacelab program, has contributed roughly 55–60 percent of the total Spacelab development costs, currently amounting to about $1 billion. The next largest contributor is Italy, whose contributions now amount to about 18 percent. In addition, Germany has been an important minority partner in the Ariane program. German industry has captured about 20 percent of the development work (especially for the second-stage structure and integration), matching Germany's 20 percent contribution to Ariane's development cost.

Spacelab represents a major German and European investment that is heavily dependent on the quality and commitment of American partnership. Given the political and technological importance of this collaboration, it is essential that the United States be as supportive as possible of the European effort and avoid unnecessary complications, such as those that arose in the International Solar Polar Mission.

Several delays and cost overruns have already occurred in the Spacelab project, which is not surprising in view of the project's complexity and its close dependence on the Space Shuttle. The fundamental purpose of Spacelab is to provide, under joint American and European control, a reusable orbiting manned laboratory where space technology experiments can be conducted by scientists rather than astronauts. Spacelab will be highly flexible in its applications and adaptable to a wide variety of experiments.

The program began in 1973, when an agreement was signed between NASA and the ESA member states. At that time, a cost to completion of about $400 million was specified. The current program calls for three Spacelab launchings: in mid-1983, mid-1984, and early 1985. The second Spacelab is an all-German project. The two others are ESA-NASA projects. The combination of inflation and changes has now brought the completion cost to more than twice the original amount. German spokesmen have indicated that about a third of the total increase is attributable to system and interface changes requested by NASA in the course of the project.[4] Although these are regarded as unavoidable because the shuttle was being developed simultaneously with Spacelab, it has certainly added to European difficulties in bringing Spacelab to completion.

The German government has encountered increasing difficulties in gaining support from other European countries, and even from the U.S. government and industry, in extending the future of the experimental capacities of Spacelab. NASA and the Reagan administration need to remain alert to the commitment that the Germans have made to this program. The German project manager recently noted that some device must be invented for encouraging potential industrial customers to rent space on Spacelab. He suggested, for example, the possibility of governmental loans to companies or tax allowances to stimulate such activity.

The Germans have correctly pointed out that Spacelab is the only manned facility for actually carrying out work in space, while the shuttle orbiter is merely a transportation vehicle. On this basis, ERNO has argued that spacelab should be an integral part of any future U.S. or European manned space scientific activities. However, the American view of the future Spacelab role appears to be divided.

ESA, for its part, foresees several possibilities for the evolution of Spacelab, including three phases: first, to develop an improved vehicle capable of extending mission endurance from one week to about three weeks; second, to develop a "free flier," which could be detached from the shuttle orbiter and spend up to six months in space between launch and retrieval; and third, to identify alternative future evolutions, including an unmanned Spacelab that could be launched by Ariane rather than the Space Shuttle.

ARIANE: THE EUROPEAN SATELLITE LAUNCHER

Some two hundred geostationary satellites are expected to be launched in the 1980s to support the growing world market for telecommunications and other commercial applications. Europe is well positioned to share in the extensive launcher market. In 1973, it was decided to develop Ariane as a launcher suitable for the requirements of the next ten or fifteen years. The European Space Agency assigned the primary responsibility of managing this development program to CNES, the French national space agency, under whose direction more than fifty European manufacturing companies have participated. Ariane is a three-stage launcher weighing 213,000 kilograms at liftoff. It is optimized to place unmanned satellites in geostationary or polar heliosynchronous orbit.

The Ariane booster's capabilities will continue to grow. Ariane I will place a 1,800-kilogram payload, consisting of one or two satellites, in geostationary transfer orbit. The comparable values for Ariane II and III will be 2,000 and 2,400 kilograms, respectively, and will be available by 1983. It is typical of European and especially of French programs that modest incremental improvements are made in aerospace systems in order to reduce risk and cost. Thus ESA has indicated that the total cost of developing both Ariane II and III is an incremental increase of about $115 million over Ariane I, development of which has been estimated at about $1 billion. ESA's latest budget, for 1982, includes about $285 million for the initial development of Ariane IV, which will be capable of placing a payload of more than 4,000 kilograms in geostationary transfer orbit. This will, in fact, be a highly modular vehicle, with various capabilities ranging from 2,700 to 4,300 kilograms injected into geostationary transfer orbit. Ariane IV will be available in 1985.

Although Ariane is certainly a serious competitor in the satellite launcher market, there is a lingering European concern that the Space Shuttle, with its reusable vehicle and massive thrust, will in the foreseeable future reach a stage of development in which its comparable launch cost per pound will drop below that of expendable boosters. To keep pace technologically and economically, ESA planners believe that they will be forced to develop a more advanced version of Ariane with some degree of reusability.

Thus the relatively massive development funding that has already gone into Ariane I is not likely to put an end to European expenditures for advanced boosters. Already, ESA is considering a winged version of the Ariane booster, of which the first of two stages would be recoverable. Although it seems likely that Ariane will remain cost competitive for some time to come, especially for launching payloads into high geosynchronous orbits, Europe may hedge its bets by laying the groundwork for a Future European Launcher (FEL), in which France would inevitably play a leading role. The consequent next step would probably be Ariane V, which would be operational in 1995 if initial project approval were given by 1985. Such a vehicle would be capable of placing about 5,000 kilograms in geostationary orbit. In 1981, a plan was being considered in which the first stage of such a booster could descend by parachute about 340 kilometers downrange from the launch site. This would be a complicated procedure because the first stage uses a liquid propellant, requiring pumps and valves that would be susceptible to salt water damage.

By 1981, the Ariane production rate had been fixed at one every 2.5 months or five per year. Until 1982 CNES acted as prime contractor to ESA; Aerospatiale as system integrator and manufacturer of major structural parts of the first stage; SEP as engine manufacturer; Dornier as second-stage tank structure fabricator; ERNO as responsible second-stage contractor; and other firms in a variety of subcontractor roles.

Recently, a new and unique organization, Arianespace, has succeeded CNES as prime contractor and program manager.

ARIANESPACE

This new commercial organization was created in 1980 to market the launch capability of Ariane. There are many shareholders in Arianespace, including 37 aerospace and electronics firms in the eleven European member countries of ESA, 13 European banks, and CNES itself. French interests hold, in combination, 59 percent of the shares, West German members hold about 29 percent, and the rest is divided among nine other European countries. (This is also the approximate division of work sharing.) In addition to marketing, Arianespace is gradually becoming responsible for production management of the boosters themselves (currently being built at about five per year), financing and management of production, and other aspects of the program. According to current plans, Arianespace will also take over full launching reponsibility in early 1983.

Arianespace has vigorously marketed the Ariane booster,

especially for geostationary satellites, targeting such major customers as AT&T, RCA, Western Union, and INTELSAT. This effort, combined with perceived uncertainties in the Space Shuttle program, has resulted in a growing order book. In December 1980, Arianespace signed an agreement with Grumman Aerospace to act as its North American representative for sales, marketing, and technical liaison with customers to ensure compatibility between the booster and spacecraft. Grumman will receive a percentage commission on sales and services.

By the end of 1981, Arianespace had an order backlog worth about $500 million. This provides a minimum base of about $125 million a year from 1983 through 1986, rising to about $300 million a year (in constant 1980 dollars) when the second launch site becomes available some time in 1986.

It is a mark of the competitive spirit of Arianespace that it will charge a higher launch price to ESA members than to other customers in order to be as competitive as possible with the three U.S. boosters: Thor Delta, Atlas Centaur, and Space Shuttle. Generally, the cost of a launch will be discounted by 15–20 percent for non-ESA members. Currently, quotations are probably running at about $36 million for ESA members and $30 million for outside customers.

The stated goal of Arianespace is to capture at least 30 percent of the projected two hundred launches of applications satellites— especially communications satellites—through the 1980s. This may prove, in fact, to be a modest goal, since it would involve only sixty launches, or from six to eight a year, from now until the end of the decade. By the mid-1980s, the capacity of the launch facility at Kourou, Guyana, will increase rapidly, as noted above, when a second pad becomes operational. Currently, the complex is capable of about six launches per year, but the second pad, now under construction, will provide at least double that number starting in 1985. This fact, combined with the prospect of accelerating the schedule through extra workshifts, gives Arianespace a chance to exceed its stated goal.

To reserve a launch position, the customer pays a nonreturnable deposit of $100,000, which is applied toward launch cost. This is merely a reservation, which can be preempted if another customer should purchase an option or a firm order for the same slot. In that case, the reserving customer has thirty days to match or better its competitor. The option, which has a higher priority (and price) than a reservation, involves paying 1 percent of the launch price each month from months 36 to 27 prior to the flight. From months 27 to 24, the payment increases to 1.5 percent. If a competitor decides to place a firm order for the same slot, the option holder has thirty days to match this offer. For this reason, the advance launch schedule issued monthly by Arianespace changes constantly.

As a nonrecoverable booster, Ariane is directly in competition with two U.S. expendable launch vehicles: Delta and Atlas Centaur. These vehicles are launched, for the most part, from Cape Kennedy. (A few are also launched from Vandenberg Air Force Base.) Recently, a spokesman for the Delta program said that, as soon as a second launch pad is available at Cape Kennedy, the McDonnell Douglas launch team will be able to launch at a sustained rate of one every five weeks. Thus the launch capabilities of the Delta team and Arianespace are—or will be—generally comparable.

Ariane is also, however, in competition with Space Shuttle for civil launches. Any delays or cutbacks in the Space Shuttle program or heavier commitments to Defense Department payloads could result in many more bookings for Ariane. Already, bookings for launches at Kourou are being made by such companies as AT&T, Western Union, GTE, RCA, and others which have reserved launch positions aboard Ariane as a hedge against such eventualities. By February 1982, with a launch reservation placed by the Swedish Space Corporation for a direct broadcast satellite for the Nordic countries, Arianespace had firm orders in hand for thirty-two launches, including launches made prior to 1982.

Europeans were especially impressed when, in late 1981, INTELSAT reserved two Ariane launches and only one Atlas Centaur launch for three INTELSAT 5A payloads. INTELSAT planners were obviously concerned about the uncertainty of launches on the Space Shuttle due to NASA budgetary constraints. INTELSAT, the multinational communications satellite organization, has ordered a number of INTELSAT satellites from the prime contractor Ford Aerospace, which in turn subcontracts to aerospace and electronics firms in France, Germany, Italy, and Japan. The INTELSAT 5A, three of which were ordered in early 1981, has a capacity of about 1,500 telephone calls and two television channels. The first INTELSAT 5A will be launched in 1984. Prior to the orders placed in 1981, there had been nine previous INTELSAT 5 orders, the first of which was launched in December 1980. From 1981 to 1988, there will be about nine INTELSAT 5 launches, at least three of which will probably now be orbited by Ariane.

JAPAN AS A SPACE POWER

With important help from the United States, implanted in already-fertile technological ground, Japan has developed a space

program that is growing rapidly and becoming increasingly independent. Like the Western Europeans, the Japanese are emphasizing applications programs such as broadcast, communications and
weather satellites, which are likely to yield the greatest financial
advantage. Such programs are developed mainly under the National
Space Development Agency (NASDA). However, scientific satellites—such as the earth observation and maritime observation
series—are steadily gaining in importance. Much of the scientific
work is done at the Institute of Space and Astronautical Science
(ISAS), which was formerly part of the University of Tokyo. In a
major reorganization in 1981, ISAS was separated from the university
and became an independent entity under the Japanese Ministry of
Education. Another important space-related organizaton is the
national Aerospace Laboratory, which supervises the production of
rockets and missiles.

Among future programs planned by the Japanese are remote
sensing satellites and space materials processing, as well as a manned
spacecraft. The latter is still on the drawing boards and resembles the
U.S. Space Shuttle, although its dimensions are much smaller. Thus
Japan's space programs, although still relativley small compared with
those of the United States, embrace the whole gamut of applicatons.
Clearly, Japan is leaving its options open in the field of space.

The Japanese space budget has increased rapidly throughout
the 1970s and early 1980s, from about $100 million in 1972, to about
$234 million in 1975, to $480.1 million in 1982. (This last figure
reaches almost $800 million, if later-year appropriations are
included.) Of this total, NASDA is currently receiving 80 percent,
ISAS is awarded 10 percent, and the rest is allocated to a number of
smaller agencies.

In keeping with these budgetary increases, Japan's space industry has also grown. Total turnover in 1978 was estimated at $527
million, about half of which was from sales of rockets and satellites
and half from ground equipment and stations. Exports constituted
20 percent of this total. Japanese industry spokesmen currently
forecast sales of as much as $5 billion per year by 1990.

Several of the largest Japanese manufacturers are involved in the
space program. They include the following companies:

> Mitsubishi Heavy Industries, which developed the N-1 and N-2
> launch vehicles, engines, and ground-support equipment.
> Mitsubishi is currently working on a more powerful launcher,
> the H-1A, which will be able to launch a 1,2000-pound
> payload into geostationary orbit.
> Mitsubishi Electric Corporation, a subsidiary of Mitsubishi

Heavy Industries, which built (with Ford Aerospace Communications) the CS communications satellite, launched in
1977, and the ISS-A and ISS-B scientific satellites for
ionospheric sounding.

Nippon Electric Company, which has built scientific satellites,
such as the EXOS series, to study the earth's magnetosphere
and ionosphere, and the CORSA series, to study X-rays and
gamma rays; the GMS meteorological satellite (built with the
aid of Hughes in the United States); and support equipment.
The same team of Nippon and Hughes is developing MOS-1,
Japan's maritime observation satellite, scheduled for launching in 1986.

Nissan Motor Company, Ltd., the only Japanese manufacturer
of solid-propellant rocket motors, has built the Mu rocket
series for scientific launches. One of the latest in the series, the
Mu-3S, launched the ASTRO-A scientific satellite in February
1981.

Toshiba, which built the BS-1 TV broadcast satellite, in conjunction with General Electric Company.

Hitachi, which is reportedly joining with Nissan to develop
rocket engines. It is possible that another major industrial
conglomerate, Fuji Heavy Industries,will also join this team.

Space activities in Japan began in the 1950s, with the designing
and building of rocket launchers for nonmilitary satellites. The early
programs, sponsored by Tokyo University, produced single-stage
rockets that flew at altitudes of less than one hundred miles. Later in
the 1960s, larger, multistage rockets were launched, reaching altitudes of several hundred miles and often carrying scientific payloads.

In 1969, the National Space Development Agency of Japan was
established, and a well-planned and well-directed national effort
began for the production of satellites, launch vehicles, tracking systems, and equipment. Although the Japanese, like the Western
Europeans, have as their ultimate goal the establishment of an independent and indigenous space program, since the 1970s they have
made use of American technology and equipment. Thus, in the
mid-1970s, Japan signed contracts with NASA and U.S. manufacturers (including Hughes, McDonnell Douglas, Ford Aerospace,
and General Electric) for the development and launching of two
types of communications satellites (the CS and BSE series) and one
type of geostationary meteorological satellite (the GMS series).

The first satellites in each of these series were launched by NASA
in 1977 and 1978, using a McDonnell Douglas Delta launcher. The
Japanese received a license to build this launcher, which is now called

the N launch vehicle. An improved version, the N-2, with a payload of 800 pounds, has been developed, and Mitsubishi is now working on an even more powerful launcher in the series, designated H-1A, which will be able to lift a 1,200-pound payload into orbit by 1985. The H-1A will use Japan's first liquid hydrogen/liquid oxygen rocket motor, produced by Mitsubishi.

Japan has two satellite launch centers, both in the southern part of the country. The Tanegashima Island site, covering an area of 3.3 square miles, has employed the N-1 launch vehicle to launch applications satellites, such as the ECS communications satellite, into geostationary orbit. The University of Tokyo operates the other launch center, at Kagoshima, which was established in 1962. This site is mainly involved with scientific launches. By the end of 1979, 250 rockets had been launched from here. The facilities are scheduled to be expanded in the 1980s to accommodate the M-3S launch vehicle, which will send up the Venus and Halley's Comet probes.

Another important space facility is the Tsukuba Space Center, fifty miles north of Tokyo, which is the country's chief tracking and control station. Tsukuba is also a test center for spacecraft and equipment.

The Japanese launching capacity is limited to at most three launches per year, owing to an agreement with the fishermen's union prohibiting such activity in January, February, August, and September, and also because of the limited launch facilities. By the end of 1981, however, the Japanese had launched eleven applications satellites and twelve scientific payloads. The applications satellites included the ETS (engineering test) series, developed by Mitsubishi and Ford Aerospace, which have flight-tested, three-axis stabilization; the GMS meteorological satellites (Nippon Electric/Hughes) for photographing clouds; the CS-1 communications satellite, for experiments in the quasi-millimetric wave band; and the BS-1 broadcast satellite (Toshiba/General Electric).

Applications satellites scheduled for future launch include ETS-3 (August 1982), GMS-3 (1984), CS-2A and CS-2B (1983), CS-3 (1988), BS-2A and BS-2B (1984–1985), and MOS-1 (maritime observation, 1986).

A number of scientific missions are planned for the future. These include:

Planetary probes (Planet A, B, and C, to survey Halley's Comet and Venus; a lunar probe, not yet funded; and a Saturn probe, SOP-2, also not funded);
ASTRO-B, to be launched in 1982–83, with ASTRO-C to follow in 1986–87;

Additional launches in the EXOS series, with EXOS-C scheduled for 1983 launch and EXOS-D and E in the study stage;

OPEN-J, to study the origin of plasma in the earth's neighbor-
hood, planned for the late 1980s;

ERS-1, an earth resources satellite, which will be Japan's largest
spacecraft, to be launched into a sunsynchronous orbit in
1988 by the H-1A rocket;

GS-1, a geodetic survey satellite, to be launched in 1985; and

UvSat, for ultraviolet investigations, now under study.

Another funded program is FMPT, or first material processing
test, in which a Japanese scientist/astronaut would perform materials
processing and life science experiments on a U.S. Space Shuttle
flight in 1985. Japan is also reportedly interested in flying experiments on the European Spacelab. In addition, as already stated, the
Japanese have plans for a space shuttle of their own, although this is a
project for the distant future.

Early in 1982, a Tokyo newspaper, *Sankei Shimbun*, reported that
Japan was studying the possibility of developing a reconnaissance
satellite to monitor Soviet operations in the Far East and that it is
seeking U.S. assistance in the program. At present, the United States
furnishes Japan with information from its reconnaissance satellites,
but Japan wants to develop its own capability. Such a program would
make Japan the third country to launch a military security satellite. It
would also be another step in establishing Japan as an independent
space power. U.S. technology, however, would continue to play an
important part since the N-2 rocket, which might be used to power
such a spacecraft, contains about 56 percent of domestically produced parts, with the remainder made in the United States or
produced under license in Japan.

To sum up, it is clear that the Japanese are involved in a varied,
although relatively small-scale space program, that they are determined to develop self-sufficiency in both launch vehicles and satellites, and that they are equally interested in scientific and applications
projects. In the near future, their communications and broadcasting
satellites will continue to earn them some profit, especially among
less-developed countries. Nippon Electric, for example, has already
provided ground stations for communications satellites in Malawi,
Libya, Colombia, Malaysia, Mexico, Peru, the Philippines, Green-
land, and Greece.

CONCLUSIONS

To the United States and its allies and partners of Western
Europe and Japan, the coordination of outer space policies will

continue to present challenges of the first magnitude from now to the end of the century. At least three issues emerge from the preceding discussion: the prospect of further divergence of strategic concepts as the United States expands its strategic military use of space; the effective balancing of healthy competition with needed forms of collaboration and cooperation in commercial space applications; and the potential for technological sharing and collaborative risk-taking in the further evolution of space technology.

Concerning the first issue, there appears to be a growing and fairly broad-based support in the United States for greater investment in a strategic space force whose primary mission would be strategic defense. Obviously, neither the Europeans nor the Japanese would be able, nor would they attempt, to match this kind of effort. They would view it, for the most part, as the latest instance of a U.S.-Soviet vertical proliferation in which they could have no role. Even in the unlikely event that America's allies were interested in contributing, financially or otherwise, to such an effort, there would have to be an acceptable form of participation, probably involving commensurate work sharing, which in turn would require the export of critical technologies associated with such systems—and that is difficult to imagine.

If an American strategic defense force in space were gradually to become credible in the late 1980s and 1990s, the clearest and most intelligent communication between the United States and its allies would be required concerning the geographic scope and operating conditions of the defensive coverage. In an alliance already experiencing severe strains, with a prospect of deeper challenges ahead, the first signs of progress toward a really viable defensive shield over the American continent would give critics of the alliance an open field, especially in Western Europe, and might change some American perceptions as well. Obviously, it would also, at the very least, place some further distance between the leadership and military high command of the two continents in their strategic planning and coordination.

On the questions of commercial competition and technological sharing, it is useful to note that in space activities Western Europe has harmonized its programs. This provides an unusual opportunity for effective U.S.-European collaboration, because there is a single European terminus in the form of ESA. Collaboration, wherever possible, can provide a useful counterweight to the vigorous European-American commercial competition in launching satellites. NASA and ESA have engaged from time to time in some very significant joint planning, as in the Spacelab project; but the prevalent European view is that America lacks any genuine commitment to trans-Atlantic collaboration. Unfortunately, there are some specific instances that appear to confirm this to European observers. One particular grievance was caused by the decision to withdraw from full participation in the International Solar Polar Mission (ISPM), a joint venture of ESA and NASA which was to send two spacecraft over the sun's poles. This decision resulted in a formal protest by all the ESA member states, and it probably did permanent damage to the NASA-ESA relationship, especially in view of the fact that ESA had already expended about half of the estimated cost to completion of its share of the program. Although the program is continuing on a curtailed basis, American vacillation has certainly damaged prospects for future joint activities in space exploration and technology acquisition.

The ISPM cancellation also aroused European, and especially German, fears about the future of Spacelab. The Federal Republic has made a major commitment to Spacelab. The U.S. commitment is probably irrevocable, but a perceived lack of full commitment tends to diminish the value of the program and recent delays that have resulted from changing U.S. civil or military requirements have added to European unease. The presence of joint European-American scientific teams in space may prove, in the 1980s, to have a great deal of symbolic importance, especially after the Franco-Soviet manned mission. Spacelab can prepare the way for further collaboration in meeting the common strategic, technological, and cultural goals of the Western countries.

The question of commercial competition has already been discussed in detail. In this concluding section, it is probably worth pointing out that, if the Space Shuttle launch schedule appears to commercial operators to be susceptible to a great deal of reduction or change, or if there is a significant military preemption of its use, then these customers will naturally tend to book rides in Ariane or a more reliable alternative. Although, at least in theory, Ariane launches will become more expensive as operating experience with the Space Shuttle accumulates, customers may be willing to pay a premium to the vendor who offers on-time performance and a strong commercial orientation. If, as press reports suggest, the American expendable launchers, Atlas and Centaur, are phased out in the next few years, Ariane and Space Shuttle will be the two main choices. At the moment, the civil and commercial marketing skills of NASA compare poorly with those of Arianespace. Thus it seems likely that Europe will become the champion of the civil use of outer space.

Although Europe's effort will be primarily commercial, there will be some military programs. There is likely to be a French strategic reconnaissance satellite that would give French leaders the oppor-

tunity to play an important political role in conflict situations. There
is a similar prospect in Japan. There will also continue to be a
number of European military communications and navigation satellites for joint NATO and national use, some launched by the United
States. The NATO III series, for example, handles telex, facsimile,
and data communications. The first was launched into orbit over the
Atlantic in 1976, and at least two more will be launched by Thor-Delta
boosters in 1983 and later. In general, however, this type of activity
represents the limit of European commitment to military space
appiictions. If, in the U.S. view, there are or can be benefits to
European and Asian security in the forthcoming generations of U.S.
strategic systems in space, then consideration must be given very
soon to the twin issues of burden sharing and work sharing. In this
regard, Spacelab cooperation seems to be an important precursor.

No grand designs for space cooperation are presented here. The
growing commercial competition is probably a healthy one and
should not be suppressed. On the other hand, American policy
makers should review and probably increase the visibility of their
commitment to major collaborative programs. The ISPM cancellation was probably a mistake. Any additional hesitation in or hin-
drance to Spacelab would be especially serious, especially when
placed in juxtaposition with Soviet-French cooperation. If, in audit-
ing America's techology acquisition needs, NASA or even the
Department of Defense should find opportunities to propose collab-
orations with ESA and NASDA, where genuine work sharing is
possible, the alliances would benefit in a number of ways. In the
meantime, the real U.S.-European collaboration is likely to be that
which exists, not between governments, but between U.S. corporate
satellite users and the Ariane launcher organization; and U.S.-Jap-
anese arrangements will be embodied in the developmental contracts already described.

NOTES

1. L. R. Shepherd, "The First Decade of Space Flight on the European
Scene," *Aeronautics and Astronautics*, October 1967, pp. 62–68.

2. See John H. Hoagland and Eugene B. Skolnikoff, "The World-Wide
Spread of Space Technology," in *Outer Space: Prospects for Man and Society*, ed.
Lincoln P. Bloomfield (New York: Praeger, 1968).

3. For a recent tabulation of European space budgets, see *New Scientist*,
February 25, 1982, p. 483. For example, NASA's budget plan in 1981 was on

the order of $5.54 billion, compared with a little over $1 billion in Europe during the same year.

4. See, for example, comments of Ants Kutzer, Project Manager at ERNO, in *Interavia*, November 1981, p. 168.

13

U.S. Government-Industry Relations and Space-Based Technologies: The COMSAT Example

JOHN B. GANTT

INTRODUCTION

There are essentially four major types of government-industry relationships for the purpose of development and use of space-based technologies in the United States. In the first and most common type, industry provides hardware or services to the government under contract for use in government military and civilian space programs.[1] These contracts often involve a major prime contractor, with numerous subcontractors and suppliers working as a team to meet a common procurement objective. The second type of relationship is one in which the government is the contractor in providing services to industry in association with space activities. A prime example is the furnishing by NASA on a cost reimbursement basis of launch services to private commercial entities.[2] The first of these was the American Telephone & Telegraph Company experimental TELSTAR satellite launched by NASA for AT&T in 1962. Since then, NASA has launched over fifty spacecraft for U.S. commercial companies and INTELSAT using expendable launch vehicles. These contracts which with certain exceptions have changed little over the years, provide for the customer to pay for the launching on a full cost reimbursement basis regardless of whether the launch is successful or not. The government does not guarantee the success of a launch but instead leaves this risk to the commercial entity, which can obtain insurance in the commercial market to cover these risks. With the advent of the shuttle, use of expendable launch vehicles will be phased out.

The third type of relationship is the government-industry joint

---

The opinions expressed in this chapter are solely those of the author.

venture, a recent example being the joint endeavor between NASA and several U.S. companies for experiments in connection with the manufacture of certain pharmaceuticals in space. The introduction of the shuttle will encourage such activities, since now, for the first time, the experiment packages can be launched economically and readily returned from orbit to earth for examination of the results. NASA has issued guidelines for certain joint endeavors with U.S. companies for materials processing in space.[3]

The fourth type of government-industry relationship is exemplified by the Communications Satellite Corporation (COMSAT), a privately owned company incorporated in 1963 in the District of Columbia pursuant to provisions of the Communications Satellite Act of 1962 (the Satellite Act) for the purpose of establishing in conjunction with other countries a global communications satellite system.[4]

BACKGROUND

The launching of the Soviet Sputnik in October 1957 provided a direct challenge to U.S. leadership in the development of space technologies and research. The response of the United States was not long in coming. On 2 April 1958, President Eisenhower called for the establishment of a strong civilian agency to direct a national program for the peaceful use of outer space.[5] Under the guiding efforts of Senate Majority Leader Lyndon Johnson, the National Aeronautics and Space Act of 1958, P.L. 85–586, was enacted just five months later, on 15 July 1958.[6] This act created the framework for subsequent government-industry relationships in the peaceful exploration and use of outer space. Pursuant to contracts that have amounted to many billions of dollars over the years, this government-industry effort spearheaded by NASA has contributed immeasurably to the present U.S. leadership in space. The act stresses several basic intentions: that activities in space should be peaceful and for the benefit of all mankind,[7] that control of U.S. space developments should be lodged in the civilian sector,[8] and that international cooperation in peaceful space activities should be promoted.[9]

These themes of peaceful use and international cooperation in space activities were underscored internationally when on 20 December 1961, the U.N. General Assembly adopted Resolution 1721 (XVI). This resolution stated "that communications by means of satellite should be available to all nations of the world as soon as practicable on a global and nondiscriminatory basis" and recognized "the need to prepare the way for the establishment of effective operational satellite communications."[10]

At the same time, rapidly advancing technological developments were demonstrating the technical feasibility of a global communications satellite network that could meet the demands for higher quality and more reliable international communications than afforded by the existing modes of cables and HF radio.

A major milestone on the road to the development of such a network occurred on 24 July 1961, when President Kennedy announced a national policy looking toward the formation of a global communications satellite system; the United States' portion would be privately owned and operated, provided that such ownership and operation met certain policy requirements.[11] This policy recognized that communications satellite efforts were still being developed and that making them operational required a government-industry arrangement committed to that end. There followed a year of intense national debate on the question of U.S. ownership and operation of such a system, which culminated in the enactment of the Communications Satellite Act of 1962.[12]

By August 1964 the U.S. government and COMSAT had succeeded in developing multilateral arrangements with a number of other nations, which led to the formation of INTELSAT, at first under interim arrangements.[13] In 1973, under new definitive arrangements, INTELSAT became an intergovernmental organization; it now numbers 106 members.[14] It is this organization that has successfully established a system of global satellites carrying more than two-thirds of all intercontinental telephone and telex traffic and all intercontinental television. Each of the newest INTELSAT 5 satellites is capable of carrying, simultaneously, 12,000 telephone calls and two television programs.

A further development of importance was the coming into force in 1967 of the Outer Space Treaty.[15] This treaty, signed by all the major space powers, is the fundamental international charter for the peaceful exploration and use of outer space, including the moon and other celestial bodies. Of particular importance is Article VI, which clearly recognizes that national activities in outer space can be conducted by nongovernmental entities, but provides that such nongovernmental activities "shall require authorization and continuing supervision by the appropriate State Party to the Treaty." This provision imposes a legal requirement on the signatory state to regulate activities in space by private companies under their jurisdiction. This requirement of authority and supervision already existed in the Satellite Act enacted five years earlier.

The Satellite Act provides that COMSAT shall be a communications common carrier fully subject to regulation by the Federal

Communications Commission.[16] Aside from being the U.S. investor in the global system of satellites, COMSAT also operates and is a 50-percent owner of the U.S. earth stations that communicate with these satellites.[17] In simplest terms, COMSAT utilizes the communications capacity acquired by virtue of its ownership in INTELSAT to establish, through U.S. earth stations, channels of communications (such as voice circuits) with INTELSAT satellites in the Atlantic and Pacific regions. COMSAT then sells these channels, pursuant to tariff, to such U.S. international communications carriers as AT&T. Thus COMSAT is a "wholesaler" of these channels; or, in industry parlance it is a "carriers' carrier."

Other INTELSAT investors (such as British TELECOM) likewise establish channels from the satellite through their respective earth stations. This permits the creation of a satellite communications path between the United States and Britain. AT&T and British TELECOM use these channels, appropriately extended through their domestic networks, in providing international telephone service (for example, between New York and London) on a per minute (message toll) basis to their respective customers.[18]

COMSAT is also a retailer in a limited sense, since it is authorized to sell television capacity directly to U.S. broadcasters.[19] COMSAT can also sell communications capacity directly to the U.S. government in limited authorized-use situations.[20] The primary example of this is the communications service that COMSAT furnished directly to the government for the NASA Apollo program, and which made financially possible the early replacement of the first INTELSAT satellite "Early Bird" by the technically improved INTELSAT II series of satellites.[21]

On 5 August 1982, the Federal Communications Commission adopted a report and order modifying its authorized user policy; under the new order, COMSAT must provide satellite communications capacity at the U.S. INTELSAT earth stations to private and public entities, as well as to the U.S. international communications carriers. Furthermore, the commission, subject to certain conditions being fulfilled, authorized COMSAT, through a separate subsidiary, to enter the retail international communications service business, should it desire to do so. This order has been appealed to the courts by one of the international communications carriers.

GOVERNMENT-INDUSTRY RELATIONS PROVISIONS OF
THE COMMUNICATIONS SATELLITE ACT OF 1962

As one of the major policies and purposes of the Satellite Act, Congress provided that:

> In order to facilitate ... [the establishment of the global
> system] and to provide for the widest possible participation
> of private enterprise, United States participation in the
> global system shall be in the form of a private corporation,
> subject to appropriate governmental regulation.[22]

This provision reflects the culmination of a long debate in the
Congress as to whether the government should proceed to establish
the global system through a government corporation or a private
corporation and, if the latter, whether it should be owned entirely by
the U.S. international communications common carriers such as
AT&T, or in some proportion by both the carriers and the investing
public.[23] The result was the latter; namely, a private for-profit corporation whose ownership was split into two classes of stock. One class
was held by communications common carriers authorized by the
Federal Communications Commission to hold stock in the corporation, and the other class by individual public stockholders.[24] Consistent with this initial division of the ownership between carriers and
the investing public, the board of directors of the company was
likewise split, six directors being elected by the carriers and six
directors being elected by the public shareholders.[25] The common
carriers have drastically reduced their ownership in the corporation
over the years to a point where it now constitutes less than 8 percent;
therefore, under an amendment to the act, all twelve elected directors are now chosen by both the public shareholders and the common carriers.[26]

In addition, the Satellite Act provided that the president of the
United States should appoint three directors to be confirmed by the
Senate, bringing the total number of directors to fifteen.[27] The
appointment of three directors gives the president the opportunity
to ensure a broad spectrum of representation on the board from
various fields involved in the work of the corporation. The presidentially appointed directors have the same responsibilities to the shareholders as do the elected directors.[28]

Other important structural controls of the government-industry relationship provided for in the Satellite Act include the limitation
on the ownership of stock by any one stockholder (other than a
common carrier) or any affiliated group to 10 percent of the stock of
the corporation.[29] This limitation is further reduced to 5 percent,
pursuant to the articles of incorporation, which were approved by
the president.[30] As a result, no one person or group can gain
significant control of the corporation, an important element given
the nature of the quasi-governmental functions that were bestowed
upon the corporation. Likewise, under the provisions of Section 310

of the Communications Act of 1934, as amended, which also applies to the corporation and other licensed common carriers, the total alien ownership of shares of stock of the corporation may not exceed 20 percent.[31] In other major respects, the corporation's structure resembles that of a normal stock corporation, and COMSAT was organized under the District of Columbia Business Corporation Act with the usual powers conferred by that act on a stock corporation.[32] The Satellite Act expressly provides that COMSAT is not an agency or establishment of the U.S. government.[33]

The major relationships of the government to the corporation are essentially set forth in Title II of the Satellite Act and divided among the president, the National Aeronautics and Space Administration (NASA), and the Federal Communications Commission (FCC). The responsibilities of the president can be grouped into three categories.[34] The first calls upon the president to aid in the planning and development and to foster the execution of a national program for the early establishment and operation of the communications satellite system and to ensure that timely arrangements are made under which there can be foreign participation in the establishment and use of this communications satellite system. Second, the president is given certain coordination responsibilities, including the coordination of the activities of the governmental agencies with responsibility in the field of telecommunications so as to ensure effective compliance with the policy set forth in the Satellite Act. In discharging this responsibility, the president is to provide for a continuous review of the development of the system and to exercise his authority in a manner that will help achieve a coordinated and efficient use of the electromagnetic spectrum and encourage the development of a system that is compatible with both existing U.S. and foreign facilities.

The third area of presidential responsibility is to:

> exercise such supervision over relationships of the Corporation with foreign governments or entities or with international bodies as may be appropriate to assure that such relationships shall be consistent with the national interest and foreign policy of the United States.[35]

This requirement for supervision combines with the responsibility to coordinate the activities of the government in the field of telecommunications to form the basis for the process under which COMSAT receives guidance from the government as to the national and foreign policy interests of the United States on those issues for which the government wishes to provide guidance.[36] The process is not static, and it remains fluid often up to and during a particular meeting of INTELSAT. Following the meeting, the government is formally debriefed as to the outcome of the meeting. Although some maintain that the process is not perfect, it appears to accomplish the desired balance that the legislation intended.

In addition, the Satellite Act also requires the corporation to give advance notice to the Department of State of foreign business negotiations with respect to the facilities, operations, or services authorized by the Act, in order to permit the department to advise the corporation of relevant foreign policy considerations.[37] This process has proved beneficial to the corporation in its foreign negotiations. No other private corporation is required to coordinate with the government, although many companies do seek and obtain information from the government as to the environment for foreign negotiations and commerce.

On the other side of the equation, the president is required to take necessary steps to ensure not only the availability of the satellite system for general governmental communications purposes but also the appropriate utilization of the system by the government for these purposes, except where a separate system is required to meet unique governmental needs or otherwise is required in the national interest.[38] The exceptions were intended to permit, for example, separate military systems.[39] Although this mandate to assure appropriate utilization of the system for general governmental purposes would appear to ensure a large and lucrative customer base, direct government utilization has become embroiled in the "authorized user" issue, and direct governmental use through COMSAT of the system has therefore been limited.[40] This is not, however, to deny that there is considerable indirect government usage of the system through the services of the international carriers who purchase capacity at "wholesale" from COMSAT.

The major responsibility given to NASA under the Satellite Act is to furnish the corporation on request and on a reimbursable basis satellite launching and associated services required for the establishment, operation, and maintenance of the communications satellite system.[41] NASA has furnished more than thirty launches to COMSAT since the initial launch of the Early Bird Satellite in June 1965. In addition NASA has certain advisory roles to the FCC concerning the technical characteristics of the system, as well as responsibility to cooperate with the corporation with respect to the technical characteristics of the system.[42] The relationship with NASA has been a productive and harmonious one which has had mutual benefits for both parties.

The responsibilities set forth for the Federal Communications Commission pertain both to its administration of the provisions of the Communications Act of 1934, as amended, and the provisions of the Satellite Act, as they supplement the Communications Act. Among the major additional responsibilities given to the FCC under the Satellite Act is the responsibility for ensuring effective competition, essentially through the use of competitive bidding, in the procurement by the corporation of the necessary hardware and services required for the establishment and operation of the system.[43] This power is not conferred on the commission under the Communications Act of 1934; it was added in the Satellite Act in view of the fact that COMSAT was being granted a lawful monopoly as the U.S. participant in the single global system. Thus it was essential to ensure that fair and competitive procurement procedures apply in the procurement by the corporation of the necessary services and hardware, since there would be no competing systems. The commission subsequently issued regulations with respect to the procurement activities of the corporation[44] and also made special provisions that accommodate the regulations adopted by INTELSAT in the case of the international procurements by INTELSAT of the satellites.[45]

In general, the requirement under the commission's regulations is for COMSAT to conduct procurements on a competitive basis and notify the commission upon its selection of the contractor. The commission then has ten days to determine if its rules were properly followed. After that, COMSAT may award the contract unless the commission issues a request for comments upon the proposed award and within thirty days notifies COMSAT that it is unable to find that there has been compliance with the regulations. The commission's role is not to participate in the selection of a contractor or in the contract negotiations, but rather to ensure that all interested entities, including small businesses, are afforded an equitable opportunity to compete for the award of the contract. The commission neither acts as a contracting officer nor approves the contracts awarded.[46]

The operational communications satellite system in its totality consists of satellites; their associated ground tracking, telemetry, and command (TT&C) facilities; and communications earth stations. While the international arrangements setting up INTELSAT provided for the establishment, ownership, and operation of the satellites and their respective TT&C facilities,[47] these arrangements did not provide for the establishment, ownership, and operation of the communications earth stations. Instead, the establishment and ownership of the communications stations was left to national determination. This is consistent with the generally prevailing international practice of regarding the operation of national communications functions as either a sovereign activity or one that is carried out by the private sector under some form of close supervision or regulation by the government.

The authorization of the establishment and operation of the U.S. earth stations is another major responsibility given to the commission under the Satellite Act. While the commission clearly had broad authority under Title III of the Communications Act to authorize the construction and operation of radio facilities, the Satellite Act establishes the policy that the earth stations can be owned by the corporation or by one or more authorized common carriers or jointly by the corporation and one or more carriers.[48] Furthermore, the Satellite Act is explicit in instructing that the commission is not to give preference, as between the carriers and the corporation, in determining where the public interest lies in granting such authorizations. As a result there have been extensive proceedings in the commission over the years dealing with the question of earth-station ownership.[49] Presently, the stations are owned 50 percent by the corporation and 50 percent by various U.S. international communications carriers.

As for the satellites themselves, the commission is given responsibility to approve the technical characteristics of the system and to ensure the technical compatibility and operational interconnectivity of the system, the earth stations, and the existing communications infrastructure.[50]

The commission exercises these regulatory responsibilities with respect to the satellites and earth stations through its regular adjudicatory process. For example, when COMSAT wishes to construct an earth station, it makes application to the commission, and the application is then placed on public notice.[51] Other interested persons may comment on or oppose the application, after which the commission makes its decision as to whether it is in the public interest, convenience, and necessity to grant a construction permit. The permit specifies the technical parameters (such as location and frequencies) of the station. Once constructed and tested, COMSAT then applies for a license to operate the station[52] and an authorization to establish channels of communications, as a common carrier, between specified geographical points.[53] In the case of satellites to be established and owned by INTELSAT, the process is different in that COMSAT applies for authority from the commission to participate in a decision by the governing body of INTELSAT to construct and launch the satellites. This procedural difference is owing to the fact that the action is taken by an international organization, which cannot be required to submit its activities to the jurisdiction of a national regulatory body.

Another provision for which there is no parallel in the Communications Act of 1934 is the authority of the commission regarding the capitalization of COMSAT (other than the initial issuance of stock) and borrowings by COMSAT.[54] Under this provision, COMSAT must obtain the commission's approval to issue any new shares of stock, to borrow money, or to assume any obligation (such as a guarantee) with respect to the securities of another person. The commission may grant such approval after finding that it would be compatible with the public interest, convenience, and necessity—the standard criteria for commission action under the 1934 act—and furthermore is "necessary, appropriate for, or consistent with" COMSAT carrying out the purposes and objectives of the Satellite Act. The purpose of this provision, which is unique to COMSAT, was further to ensure its ability to provide efficient and economical service by avoiding excessive capitalization and disproportionate amounts of debt or equity, which could have adverse effects on COMSAT's revenue requirements and thus on its tariff rates.[55] Although this provision is unique to COMSAT as among communications common carriers, similar provisions appear in the Federal Power Act,[56] with respect to electric utilities and once appeared in the Interstate Commerce Act.[57] Though the commission has proposed rules under which to exercise its power pursuant to this section, it has never adopted those rules as final regulations.[58]

Another responsibility of the commission is outlined in a provision under which the Secretary of State, upon receipt of the necessary technical advice from NASA, can institute proceedings in the commission to require the corporation to extend communications by satellite to a particular foreign point in the national interest.[59] This provision has never been utilized, and given the extensive global network of communications earth stations now operating through the INTELSAT system (315 earth stations operating in 136 nations and territories), it seems doubtful that this provision will be invoked in the future.

EXPORT CONTROL MATTERS

Another form of government regulation that applies to COMSAT's activities, but because of its general applicability to the U.S. export industry is not specifically described within the Satellite Act, is the export of technical data and equipment relating to communications satellites. To the extent that they constitute "defense articles" or "defense services" such data and equipment are regulated by the Office Of Munitions Control (OMC), Department of State, under Section 38 of the Arms Export Control Act, as implemented through OMC regulations.[60] An item constitutes a "defense article" or "defense service" if it appears on the U.S. Munitions List, as do certain components associated with spacecraft and technical data related thereto. Likewise, the export regulations of the Department of Commerce generally apply to communications earth station equipment and technical data.[61]

COMSAT's major involvement with the OMC regulations has been in connection with the technical and management services it has performed under various arrangements for INTELSAT; under those arrangements it has been necessary to disclose to INTELSAT certain technical data. Similar problems arise for U.S. companies that wish to sell satellites and related hardware to INTELSAT. Since INTELSAT is an international organizaton, the delivery of data to the organization constitutes an export. Furthermore, INTELSAT, under the terms of the Operating Agreement, is required to acquire license rights to inventions and technical information generated by work performed on behalf of INTELSAT involving a significant element of study, research, or development.[62] These rights include the right to disclose and license to others, within the jurisdiction of any member of INTELSAT, the subject inventions and technical information. As the membership of INTELSAT has expanded beyond the original eleven countries in 1964, so has the geographical scope of distribution of inventions and technical information. This has necessitated the requirement for a close working relationship between those elements of the U.S. government concerned with export control matters and the satellite-related industry.

In the early days of INTELSAT, when COMSAT was manager, industry submitted proposals to COMSAT, and it was COMSAT's responsibility to obtain appropriate licenses required under the OMC regulations before submitting technical data contained in the proposal to the governing body of INTELSAT. COMSAT discharged this responsibility in close coordination with OMC under agreed procedures that were designed to alleviate concerns expressed by foreign members of INTELSAT. This was achieved in a manner fully compliant with U.S. regulations and serves as another example of the government-industry cooperation—a declared national policy objective—that fostered INTELSAT.

CONCLUSION

The COMSAT example serves as an excellent demonstration of a government-industry relationship that advances national space policies and goals. The example is unique in that the industry member, as the U.S. participant, performs certain roles that have been referred to as "quasi-governmental." The legitimate requirements and responsibilities of government and a private company with over 70,000 public shareholders were successfully balanced in the Satellite Act, which has as its goal the establishment of an operational global communications satellite system.

NOTES

1. The government-industry relationship in this category is governed by contract based on procurement regulations, such as the Defense Acquisition Regulations (DARs) promulgated pursuant to 10 U.S.C.A. 2301 et seq. (Cum. Supp. 1982) and found in 32 CFR Parts 1 to 39 (1981), and the Federal Acquisition Regulations (FARs) promulgated pursuant to Title 41 USC and found in 41 CFR (1981).

2. See 14 CFR Part 1214 (1981), Regulations governing the provision of launch services on the Space Transportation System (Shuttle).

3. See 44 Fed. Reg. 47650 (1979).

4. Communications Satellite Act of 1962, 76 Stat. 419, 47 U.S.C.A. 701 et seq. (1962) (hereinafter cited as "Satellite Act"). The major reports accompanying the Satellite Act were Report of the Senate Comm. on Aeronautical and Space Sciences, S. Rep. No. 1319, 87th Cong., 2d Sess. (1962); Report of the Senate Comm. on Foreign Relations, S. Rep. No. 1873, 87th Cong., 2d Sess. (1962); Report of the Senate Comm. on Commerce, S. Rep. No. 1584, 87th Cong., 2d Sess. (1962); Report of the House Comm. on Interstate and Foreign Commerce, H.R. Rep. No. 1636, 87th Cong., 2d Sess. (1962). Senate Reports 1584 and 1873 are reprinted in *1962 Code Cong. and Adm. News* at 2269–2329.

5. Message to Congress, 2 April 1958, reproduced in *1958 Code Cong. and Adm. News* at 5429–31.

6. National Aeronautics and Space Act of 1958, 72 Stat. 426, 42 U.S.C.A. 2451 et seq. (1973).

7. 42 U.S.C.A. 2451(a), 2471, 2473 (Cum. Supp. 1982).

8. 42 U.S.C.A. 2451(b) (1973).

9. 42 U.S.C.A. 2451(c)(7), 2475 (1973).

10. *United Nations General Assembly Official Record*, 16th Sess., Supp. No. 17(A/5100), pp. 6, 7.

11. Reprinted in Senate Report No. 1584, pp. 25–26.

12. See Throop, "Some Legal Facets of Satellite Communications," 17 *American University Law Review* 12 (1967). Also see Note, "The Communications Satellite Act of 1962," 76 *Harvard Law Review* 388 (1962); Levin, "Organization and Control of Communications Satellites," 113 *University of Pennsylvania Law Review* 315 (1965).

13. Agreement Establishing Interim Arrangements for a Global Commercial Communications Satellite System, with special agreement, 20 August 1964, TIAS No. 5646. For discussion on the establishment of INTELSAT, see Throop, supra, pp. 17–20; Colino, "INTELSAT: Doing Business in Outer Space," 6 *Col. Journal Transn. Law* 17 (1967); Simsarian, "Interim Agreement for a Global Commercial Communications Satellite System," 59 *American Journal of International Law* 344 (1965). See, for discus-

sion as to the renegotiation of the interim arrangements in the form of permanent (definitive) arrangements, Trooboff, "INTELSAT: Approaches to the Renegotiation," 9 *Harvard Journal of International Law* 1 (1968).

14. Agreement Relating to the International Telecommunications Satellite Organization "INTELSAT" and Operating Agreement, 20 August 1971 (entered into force 12 February 1973), TIAS No. 7532. For discussions of the definitive arrangements negotiations, see Colino, *The INTELSAT Definitive Arrangements: Ushering in a New Era in Satellite Telecommunications*, European Broadcasting Union Legal and Administrative Series, Monograph no. 9., 1973; Mizrach, "The INTELSAT Definitive Arrangements," *Journal of Space Law* 129 (1973); Washburn, "The International Telecommunications Satellite Organization," International Cooperation in Outer Space: A Symposium, Senate Doc. No. 92–57, 92nd Cong., 1st Sess. (1971), p. 437.

15. Treaty on Principles Governing the Activities of States in the Exploration and Use of Outer Space, Including the Moon and Other Celestial Bodies, 27 January 1967 (entered into force 10 October 1967), 18(3) U.S.T. 2410, TIAS No. 6347.

16. Section 401, 47 U.S.C.A. 741 (1962).

17. The FCC decisions that resulted in COMSAT obtaining its present 50 percent share were Report and Order, Amendment of Part 25 of the Commission's Rules and Regulations with Respect to Ownership and Operation of Initial Earth Stations in the United States, 38 FCC 1104 (1965), *modified*, Second Report and Order, 5 FCC 2d 812 (1966). In 1969 the commission reopened the matter but never issued a decision. Notice of Inquiry FCC 69-1330 (3 December 1969). On 5 August 1982, the Federal Communications Commission adopted a notice of inquiry concerning the modification of its policy on the ownership and operation of U.S. earth stations that operate within the INTELSAT system. *Notice of Inquiry*, C. C. Docket 82-540 (released 17 August 1982). See also Throop, supra, pp. 24–28.

18. See Johnson, "The International Activities of the Communications Satellite Corporation," International Cooperation in Outer Space: A Symposium, Senate Doc. No. 92–57, 92nd Cong., 1st Sess. (1971), p. 195.

19. Spanish International Network, 70 FCC 2d 2127 (1978).

20. Memorandum Opinion and Statement of Policy: Authorized Entities and Authorized Users Under the Communications Satellite Act of 1962, 4 FCC 2d 421 (1966), *modified in part*, 6 FCC 2d 593 (1967). See Throop, supra, pp. 28–32. The commission modified its policy further to permit COMSAT to provide satellite capacity directly to international television braodcasters. Spanish International Network, supra. The commission's Authorized User Policy was substantially revised by a recent decision of the commission. *Report and Order*, C. C. Docket 80–170 (released 19 August 1982).

21. Order and Authorization: Application of Communications Satellite Corporation, 1 FCC 2d 1216 (1965).

22. Satellite Act, Section 102(c), 47 U.S.C.A. 701(c) (1962).

23. See Throop, supra, pp. 14–15.

24. Satellite Act, Section 304, 47 U.S.C.A. 734 (1962).

25. Satellite Act, Section 303(a), 47 U.S.C.A. 734 (1962).

26. Satellite Act, Section 303(a), *as amended*. 47 U.S.C.A. 733 (Cum. Supp. 1982).

27. Ibid. However, legislation recently introduced by Senator Gold-

water, if adopted, would do away with the presidentially appointed directors. S. 2469, 97th Cong., 2d Sess. 304(a) (1982).

28. See letter dated 25 October 1962, from the attorney general to the president, reprinted in Hearings on Communications Satellite Incorporators Before Senate Commerce Committee, 88th Cong., 1st Sess., at 87 (1963).

29. Satellite Act, Section 304(b)(3), 47 U.S.C.A. 734(b)(3) (1962).

30. The purpose behind authorizing the board of directors to further reduce this percentage limitation below 10 percent was to "encourag[e] the widest distribution of shares of Common Stock to the American public." Articles of Incorporation of Communications Satellite Corporation, Art. 502(c) (1 February 1963). Reproduced in Hearings on Communications Satellite Incorporators Before Senate Commerce Committee, 88th Cong., 1st Sess., at 43 (1963).

31. 47 U.S.C.A. 310 (Cum. Supp. 1982).

32. Satellite Act, Sections 301, 305(c), 47 U.S.C.A. 731, 735(c) (1962).

33. Satellite Act, Section 301, 47 U.S.C.A. 731 (1962).

34. Satellite Act, Section 201(a), 47 U.S.C.A. 721(a) (1962).

35. Satellite Act, Section 201(a)(4), 47 U.S.C.A. 721(a)(4) (1962).

36. For a fairly recent discussion of the government guidance process, see "In the Matter of Implementation of Section 505 of the International Maritime Satellite Telecommunications Act, COMSAT Study, Final Report," C. C. Docket 79–266, 77 FCC 2d 564, 723 (1980); and the comments of Communications Satellite Corporation, dated 30 November 1979, pp. 56–60.

37. Satellite Act, Section 402, 47 U.S.C.A. 742 (1962).

38. Satellite Act, Section 201(a)(6), 47 U.S.C.A. 721(a)(6) (1962).

39. See testimony of John H. Rubel, Assistant Secretary of Defense (Deputy Director of Defense Research and Engineering) in Hearings on Communication Satellite Legislation Before Senate Aeronautical and Space Sciences Committee, 87th Cong., 2d Sess., at 261–62 (5 March 1962).

40. Supra, note 20. The latest action by the FCC on this matter is its *Report and Order*, C. C. Docket 80-170 (released 19 August 1982).

41. Satellite Act, Section 201(b)(5), 47 U.S.C.A. 721(b)(5) (1962).

42. Satellite Act, Section 201(b), 47 U.S.C.A. 721(b) (1962).

43. Satellite Act, Section 201(c)(1), 47 U.S.C.A. 721(c)(1) (1962).

44. 47 CFR 25.151 et seq. (1981).

45. Memorandum Opinion and Order: "Amendment of Part 25 of the Commission's Rules and Regulations," 11 FCC 2d 779 (1968).

46. "Report and Order: Amendment of Part 25 of the Commission's Rules and Regulations with Respect to the Procurement Apparatus, Equipment and Services Required for the Establishment and Operation of the Communications Satellite System or Satellite Terminal Stations," Docket No. 15123, 1 Radio Regulations 2d 1611 (9 January 1964), reproduced in 29 Fed. Reg. 345 (1964).

47. Agreement Relating to the International Telecommunications Satellite Organization "INTELSAT," Arts. II(a), III(a) and V(a).

48. Satellite Act, Section 201(c)(7), 47 U.S.C.A. 721(c)(7) (1962). The pending Senate Bill, S. 2469, would expand the right of ownership to include persons other than COMSAT and authorized international carriers "as will best serve the public interest, convenience, and necessity." Section 304(i).

49. See FCC decisions cited in note 17.

50. Satellite Act, Section 201(c)(6), 47 U.S.C.A. 721(c)(6) (1962).

51. 47 U.S.C.A. 308, 319 (1962).

52. 47 U.S.C.A. 308 (1962).

53. 47 U.S.C.A. 214 (Cum. Supp. 1982).

54. Satellite Act, Section 201(c)(8), 47 U.S.C.A. 72(c)(8) (1962). The pending Senate Bill, S. 2469, would repeal this provision. Section 304(b).

55. See Senate Rep. No. 1584, at *1962 Code Cong. and Admin. News*, 2280.

56. Federal Power Act, 49 Stat. 850, 16 U.S.C.A. 824 (1974).

57. 41 Stat. 494, *repealed*, P. L. 89–86, 24 July 1965, 79 Stat. 263.

58. Proposed Financial Rules, 38 Fed. Reg. 16245 (21 June 1973), *terminated by order*, 46 Fed. Reg. 18720 (26 March 1981). See, however, the commission's *Memorandum Opinion and Order, Changes in the Corporate Structure and Operation of Communications Satellite Corporation*, C. C. Docket 80-634 at paragraphs 105–109 (released 13 August 1982).

59. Satellite Act, Section 201(c)(3), 47 U.S.C.A. 721(c)(3) (1962).

60. Section 38 of the International Security Assistance and Arms Export Control Act of 1976, *as amended*, 22 U.S.C.A. 2778 (Cum. Supp. 1982); 22 CFR Part 121–130 (1981).

61. Export Administration Act of 1979, P. L. 96–72, 50 U.S.C.A. App. 2403 et seq. (Cum. Supp. 1982); 15 CFR Part 368–399 (1981).

62. Supra, note 14. See Operating Agreement Article 17 (Inventions and Technical Information).

5

National Interests and the Legal Regime in Space

14
Present and Prospective Military Technologies and Space Law: Implications of the 1967 Outer Space Treaty

S. NEIL HOSENBALL

Before discussing in detail the 1967 Treaty on Principles Governing the Activities of States in the Exploration and Use of Outer Space including the Moon and Other Celestial Bodies,[1] which will hereafter be referred to as the 1967 Outer Space Treaty, it should be noted that two other treaties bear upon military activities in space. The 1963 Treaty Banning Nuclear Weapons Tests in the Atmosphere in Outer Space and Under Water[2] provides in Article 1 that "each of the parties to this Treaty undertakes to prohibit, to prevent, and not to carry out any nuclear weapon test explosion or any other nuclear explosion, at any place under its jurisdiction or control: in the atmosphere; beyond its limits, including outer space; or under water, including territorial waters or high seas." Over one hundred countries are parties to the Nuclear Test Ban Treaty.

In addition to the Nuclear Test Ban Treaty the treaty between the United States and the Soviet Union on the limitation of antiballistic missile systems, the ABM Treaty of 1972,[3] provides in Article V, paragraph 1, that "each party undertakes not to develop, test, or deploy ABM systems or components which are sea based, air based, space based or mobile land based." Article II of the ABM Treaty provides that for the purposes of the treaty an ABM system is a system to counter strategic ballistic missiles or their elements in flight trajectory, consisting of: (1) ABM intercept missiles, which are interceptive missiles constructed and deployed for an ABM role or of a type tested in an ABM mode; (2) ABM launchers, which are launchers constructed and deployed for launching ABM interceptor missiles; and (3) ABM radars, which are radars constructed and deployed for an ABM role, or of a type tested in an ABM mode. With these descriptions of the Test Ban Treaty and the ABM Treaty, disarmament experts are more fully able to discuss their implications for the military uses of space.

There are four space treaties presently in force for the United States. These treaties were negotiated under the auspices of the United Nations Committee on the Peaceful Uses of Outer Space, which was established as a standing committee of the United Nations in 1959. They are the Treaty on Principles Governing the Activities of States in the Exploration and Use of Outer Space including the Moon and Other Celestial Bodies, which entered into force on 10 October 1967;[4] the Agreement on the Rescue of Astronauts, the Return of Astronauts, and the Return of Objects Launched into Outer Space; which entered into force on 3 December 1968;[5] the Convention on the International Liability for Damage Caused by Space Objects, which entered into force on 9 October 1973;[6] and the Convention on the Registration of Objects Launched into Outer Space, which entered into force on 15 September 1976.[7] A fifth treaty, the Agreement Governing the Activities of States on the Moon and Other Celestial Bodies, was opened for signature and ratification on 5 December 1979.[8] This treaty has not been signed by the United States, and by my last count it has been signed by only eleven countries. The treaty will enter into force when five signatory states have deposited their instruments of ratification. As of my latest information, only three states have deposited instruments of ratification.

Of the four U.N. treaties in force, only the 1967 treaty has implications for present prospective military technology. Article I provides that "outer space including the moon and other celestial bodies shall be free for exploration and use by all states without discrimination of any kind, on a basis of equality and in accordance with international law, and there shall be free access to all areas of celestial bodies." Article III of the treaty repeats that the exploration and use of outer space shall be in accordance with international law but adds the phrase "including the charter of the United Nations" and further provides that "activities in the exploration and use of outer space shall be carried out in the interest of maintaining international peace and security and promoting international cooperation and understanding."

Article IV specifically and expressly places limitations on certain potential military uses of space and on activities conducted on celestial bodies. Under Article IV "States Parties to the treaty undertake not to place in orbit around the earth any objects carrying nuclear weapons or any other kinds of weapons of mass destruction, install such weapons on celestial bodies, or to station such weapons in outer space in any other manner." In addition to banning nuclear weapons and weapons of mass destruction from space and from celestial bodies, Article IV in its second paragraph goes on to state that:

the moon and other celestial bodies shall be used by all states parties to the treaty exclusively for peaceful purposes. The establishment of military bases, installations and fortifications, the testing of any type of weapons and the conduct of military maneuvers on celestial bodies shall be forbidden. The use of military personnel for scientific research or for any other peaceful purposes shall not be prohibited. The use of any equipment or facility necessary for peaceful exploration of the moon and other celestial bodies shall also not be prohibited.

Note that the first sentence of paragraph 2 of Article IV requires only that the moon and other celestial bodies shall be used exclusively for peaceful purposes and that the prohibition against testing of any type of weapon is also limited to celestial bodies. Neither use of military personnel for peaceful purposes nor use of any equipment or facility necessary for peaceful exploration of the moon and other celestial bodies is prohibited. Article IV therefore expressly prohibits in paragraph 1 the placing of nuclear weapons or any other kinds of weapons of mass destruction in orbit around the earth in space or on celestial bodies, while paragraph 2 covers only prohibited and permitted activities conducted on the moon and other celestial bodies.

It is therefore clear from a reading of paragraph 1 of Article IV of the treaty that the only limitations on military activities in outer space are on placing in orbit around the earth or otherwise stationing in outer space nuclear or other weapons of mass destruction. The prohibitions contained in the second paragraph of the article apply to celestial bodies only. This view is fully supported by the negotiating history, since several delegations—the Indian, the Iranian, the Austrian, the Japanese, the Brazilian, and the Mexican—all questioned the propriety of excluding outer space from the coverage of the second paragraph.[9] These delegations, in effect, expressed concerns that by excluding outer space from the coverage of the second paragraph there was an implication that outer space may be used for nonpeaceful purposes. In his response to these concerns the Soviet delegate stated that "a number of questions would of course remain to be dealt with after the elaboration of the Treaty, particularly the use of outer space for exclusively peaceful purposes."[10]

Article IV, paragraph 1, however, still leaves several questions unanswered. What are other weapons of mass destruction? Are there other international legal norms or treaties that restrain in any way the military uses of space?

No references to discussions that took place during the negotiation of the 1967 Outer Space Treaty indicate the intent of the negotiators when they used the words "other weapons of mass destruction." However, in the hearings before the Senate Foreign Relations Committee on the ratification of the 1967 Outer Space Treaty[11] Senator Carlson asked, "What is a weapon of mass destruction?" To this Ambassador Goldberg responded, "This is a weapon of comparable capability of annihilation to a nuclear weapon bacteriologically. It does not relate to a conventional weapon." Pursuing the matter further, Senator Carlson stated, "This sounds ridiculous and wild but I think I am correct in stating there was some thought of placing a satellite over Vietnam to keep that country lighted all night. Mr. Goldberg responded, "This would have no application."[12] This question was pursued further by Senator Cooper, who asked if "the treaty refers to weapons of mass destruction as well as nuclear weapons. Can you give us some statement about that?" To this request Deputy Secretary of Defense Cyrus R. Vance responded, "Yes, I believe it would include such other weapon systems as chemical and biological weapons, sir, or any weapon which might be developed in the future which would have the capability of mass destruction such as that which would be wreaked by nuclear weapons."[13] Mr. Goldberg was testifying in his capacity as U.S. ambassador to the United Nations and was one of the principal negotiators of the 1967 Outer Space Treaty.

The Senate hearings also provide some insight into the views of the United States as to what military activities were clearly permissible in outer space under the 1967 treaty. For example, Secretary of State Rusk testified that "the treaty does not inhibit, of course, the development of an anti-satellite capability in the event that should become necessary."[14] In 1978, Secretary of State Vance reiterated that the treaty did not prohibit the development or deployment of anti-satellite systems, and that only the actual use of an antisatellite system against U.S. national technical means was prohibited.[15] Mr. Goldberg in his testimony also stated that the treaty in no way affected the manned orbiting laboratory[16] and did not include observation satellites or navigational satellites.[17] Speaking as the deputy secretary of defense, Cyrus Vance further indicated that military space programs concerned with communications, navigation, or observations are permitted, stating that these programs were peaceful uses of space, as were mapping and other observation satellite functions.[18] It should also be noted that Article IV, paragraph 1, speaks only in terms of placing weapons of mass destruction in orbit around the earth, and therefore intercontinental ballistic missiles or fractional orbital bombardment systems would not fall within the proscription of that paragraph.

Does the 1967 Outer Space Treaty or other international legal norms—or, for that matter, declared national policy—in any way limit the military activities of nations in space over and beyond the limitations contained in Article IV, paragraph 1?

As noted earlier in both Article I and Article III of the 1967 Outer Space Treaty, the use of outer space should be conducted in accordance with international law. These articles therefore incorporate other multilateral treaties, such as the Nuclear Test Ban Treaty, to which states parties to the 1967 treaty may also be signatories. They would also incorporate by reference legal norms that have been generally accepted by the international community. No customary international law further limits military activities in outer space. Article III, however, specifically refers to the Charter of the United Nations[19] and also makes reference to the maintenance of international peace and security. One of the purposes of the United Nations as expressed in the very first article of the charter is the suppression of acts of aggression or other breaches of the peace. Article II further requires that member states refrain from the threat or use of force in their international relations against the territorial integrity or political independence of any state. In the early days of space activities the Soviet Union considered the use of surveillance satellites to be a breach of the U.N. Charter, though the United States has consistently held that such activities are nonaggressive and not in violation of international law, including the charter. In recent times, however, particularly as a result of the verification provisions in the SALT and ABM agreements, the Soviets have recognized these national technical means of verification as a legitimate activity under the charter and international law. Such activities are also consistent with the maintenance of international peace and security as referenced in Article III of the 1967 Outer Space Treaty. Further, Article LI of the charter recognizes the rights of states to engage in individual or collective self-defense. Though the article is phrased in terms of self-defense against an armed attack, many writers in the field have suggested that a legitimate interpretation would include the traditionally recognized right to act in self-defense in the face of the threat of an armed attack; others have argued that anticipatory self-defense should be recognized, particularly when weapons exist that have the capability to destroy a nation within minutes of the launching of an attack.[20]

As to national policies, the policy of the United States has been clearly expressed in many ways. In 1958 President Eisenhower sent a special message to Congress concerning the establishment of NASA, stating that "a civilian setting for the administration of space functions will emphasize the concern of our nation that outer space be devoted to peaceful and scientific purposes."[21] The national Aeronautics and Space Act of 1958, Section 102, expressly provides that "it is the policy of the United States that activities in space shall be devoted to peaceful purposes for the benefit of all mankind."[22] It should be noted that the NASA act provides in the same section for the conduct of space activities by the Department of Defense and the Armed Services.

Where does all this lead? It appears that under the 1967 Outer Space Treaty, except for the limitations expressly set forth in Article IV, paragraph 1, no military activities are barred in outer space, but the U.N. Charter and the national policy of the United States suggest that limits may be observed. This leads to problems in definition. What is meant by "peaceful," by "aggression," and by "military"? What is meant by "nonmilitary"? The definitions are not clear. For example, the United Nations, after almost seven years of debate in its special committee on this question, defined aggression as follows: "Agression is the use of armed force by a state against the sovereignty, territorial integrity or political independence of another state or in any other manner inconsistent with the Charter of the United Nations as set out in this definition."[23] It also provides that the definition shall not be construed to enlarge or diminish the scope of the charter, including the charter's provisions concerning cases in which the use of force is lawful. Therefore, the resolution incorporates all the ambiguities of the U.N. Charter, in addition to clouding its own. The same can be said for the use of the terms "military" and "nonmilitary." Weather satellites contribute both to civilian and to military objectives, as do communications satellites, observation satellites, and navigational satellites. These activities by themselves are nonaggressive, and in the absence of a state of war are certainly peaceful and beneficial in nature, not only to the space powers but to the international community at large.

In summary, some conclusions can be reached as to the state of international law as it relates to so-called military activities in space. There are some specific prohibitions on the use of outer space for military purposes. They are contained in the Nuclear Test Ban Treaty, the Anti-Ballistic Missile System Treaty and the 1967 Outer Space Treaty. Beyond these expressed provisions there exists a quagmire of ill-defined terms, such as "peaceful," "military," "nonmilitary," "aggressive," and "nonaggressive," all of which are subject to the interpretation of parties to a treaty. Demilitarization of space is only a small part of the total problem of demilitarization. There is no way today that military activities in space can be separated from the broader problems of disarmament.

The United States did attempt through bilateral consultations with the Soviet Union to foreclose the development of antisatellite systems.[24] Those consultations were not successful, and today it is clear that the Soviet Union has in fact developed and tested an operational antisatellite system, thus escalating concerns in the United States about how best to meet this threat to national security. Past administrations have made it quite clear that an attack against American space assets would be considered an attack against the territory of the United States. This position appears to be legally correct under the provisions of the Outer Space Treaty and the U.N. Charter.

The discussion of the militarization of space at the United Nations Committee on the Peaceful Uses of Outer Space is a relatively recent phenomenon. In the author's service as a U.S. representative to the committee and to its legal subcommittee, which began in 1970 and continued through the 1979 session, the issue never arose until 1978, when it was mentioned as a concern by one or two delegations during the course of general debate. Since then, U.N. interest in military uses of space has increased and become more widespread. Proposals dealing with a U.N. Space Verification Agency have been suggested by France and Italy. Taking advantage of this interest, the Soviet Union has submitted to the U.N. General Assembly a "draft treaty on the prohibition of the stationing of weapons of any kind in outer space,"[25] which has been referred to the United Nations Committee on Disarmament.[26] Article IV of the 1967 Outer Space Treaty was a significant and major step toward reducing an arms race in space. Whether or not further steps in that direction will be successful will depend on the national security interests of states and their political will to come to an effective and verifiable agreement that will further limit the potential for armed conflict in space.

NOTES

1. 1967 Treaty on Principles Governing the Activities of States in the Exploration and Use of Outer space including the Moon and Other Celestial Bodies, 27 January 1967, 18 U.S.T. 2410, T.I.A.S. No. 6347, 610 U.N.T.S. 205 (effective 10 October 1967).

2. Treaty Banning Nuclear Weapons Tests in the Atmosphere, in Outer Space, and Under Water, 5 August 1963, 14 U.S.T. 1313, T.I.A.S. No. 5433, 480 U.N.T.S. 43 (effective 10 October 1963).

3. Treaty with the Union of Soviet Socialist Republics on the Limitation of Anti-Ballistic Missile Systems, 26 May 1972, 23 U.S.T. 3435, T.I.A.S. No. 7503 (effective 3 October 1972).

4. 1967 Outer Space Treaty.

5. Agreement on the Rescue of Astronauts, the Return of Astronauts,

and the Return of Objects Launched into Outer Space (1968), 19 U.S.T. 7570, T.I.A.S. No. 6599, 672 U.N.T.S. 119 (effective 3 December 1968).

6. Convention on International Liability for Damage Caused by Space Objects, 29 March 1972, 24 U.S.T. 2389, T.I.A.S. No. 7762 (effective 9 October 1973).

7. Convention on the Registration of Objects Launched into Outer Space, 14 January 1975, 28 U.S.T. 695, T.I.A.S. No. 8480 (effective 15 September 1976).

8. Agreement Governing the Activities of States on the Moon and Other Celestial Bodies, United Nations General Assembly Resolution A/RES/34/68.

9. See statements by the Indian delegate, A/AC.105/C.2/SR.66, p. 6; the Iranian delegate, p. 7; the Austrian delegate, A/A7.105/C.2/SR.71, p. 10; the Japanese delegate, p. 12; the Brazilian delegate, p. 17; and the Mexican delegate, p. 19.

10. A/AC.105/C.2/SR.66, p. 6.

11. Hearings on the Outer Space Treaty before the Senate Foreign Relations Committee, 90th Cong. 1st Sess. (1967), p. 76.

12. Ibid., p. 76.

13. Ibid., p. 100.

14. Ibid., p. 26.

15. "Compliance with SALT One Agreements," attachment to letter from the Secretary of State to the Chairman, Senate Committee on Foreign Relations (21 February 1978), in *Selected Documents*, no. 7, *The Department of State* 10.

16. Hearings on the Outer Space Treaty, p. 76.

17. Ibid., p. 77.

18. Ibid., p. 81.

19. Charter of the United Nations, 26 June 1945, 59 Stat. 1031, T.S. No. 993, 3 *Berans* 1153 (effective 24 October 1945).

20. DeSaussure and Reed, "Self-Defense—A Right in Outer Space," 7 *Air Force Judge Advocate General Law Review*, 38–45 (1965).

21. "Statements by Presidents of the United States on International Cooperation in Space," in *Senate Committee on Aeronautics and Space Sciences*, 21 September 1971, p. 12.

22. 42 U.S.C. Sec. 2451(a).

23. General Assembly Resolution 3314 (XXIX), 29 U.N. CADR, Supp. 142, *U.N. Doc.* A/9631 (1975).

24. "Announcement of Administration Review," 14 *Weekly Comp. of Pres. Document* 1136–37, 20 June 1978.

25. *UNGA Doc.* A/36/192, 11 August 1981.

26. *UNGA Doc.* A/36/192. The operative articles of the Soviet-proposed treaty appear in this volume in Appendix 3.

15

Arms Control, International Law, and Outer Space

HARRY H. ALMOND, JR.

> The theorizing mind tends always to the oversimplifica-
> tion of its materials. This is the root of all absolutism and
> one sided dogmatism by which both philosophy and
> religion have been infested.
>
> William James,
> *The Varieties of Religious Experience*

International law is, among other things, a future-oriented policy process that provides states with a framework for pursuing strategies in their search for noncoercive means of influence in their
relations with each other. Our present interpretations of international law support policies commensurate with the security of states:
all law is said to address order and the values of the social order alike.

Our expectations with respect to law, and in particular to international law, are associated with the broader goals of the United
Nations Charter: the maintenance of international peace and
security and the promotion of human dignity and human rights in
the social orders of states.

Strategies for shaping international law—particularly customary international law—are no less critical for rational and global
security than are strategies for framing and directing military policies

This chapter owes much to the warm support of the Commandant of the National War
College, Major General Lee E. Surut, USA; to Professor Uri Ra'anan, Professor of
International Politics at the Fletcher School of Law and Diplomacy; to the continuing
support of Professor Myres S. McDougal and W. Michael Reisman; to Colonel Robert
Thompson, Dean of Faculty at the National War College; and to countless others. It
reflects my respect for the courage of Gavriel Ra'anan.

None of the materials and positions set forth in this chapter should in any way be
attributed to the United States government or to any of its agencies. They are to be
attributed entirely to the author and are based exclusively upon his examination of the
published materials and sources.

and programs. Though the policies with respect to this larger strategy of nations are exceedingly complex and difficult to execute, the outcome of the policy processes is law, security, and order, which form a nation's goals and afford an economy of effort, burden, and expense in meeting them.

By seeking assiduously to establish, with like-minded nations, a firm body of general principles of law that are informed by the values we prize, effective and enforceable operating standards and principles, and guidelines for the conduct and behavior of states, we will be able to reduce the insecurity that prevails in the global community today.

If we attend to these matters, we have the opportunity of gradually phasing out our reliance on a balancing process with respect to weapons, continuously growing in destructive force, and replace it, as the exclusive basis for global stability, with a developing global social order. Such a shift, though it would unquestionably be gradual at first, would lead to a more secure global order, and the arms-control policies to which we are presently committed would fall naturally into place to serve the broader goals of community. At present, however, our arms-control processes and agreements are limited almost exclusively to maintaining the stability of weapons capabilites by checks and balances. This situation is the product of changing circumstances, wrought by an advancing military technology that cannot be controlled. The purpose of this chapter is to consider the arms-control process, and international law as it applies to this process, and to clarify the interaction between these policy-oriented activities. Emphasis is given to the changes imposed upon each of these by the external realities of state activities and relations. Further objectives of the chapter are to examine the Soviet proposed draft treaty of August 1981, intended by that country as a means to demilitarize and provide a weapons free zone in outer space, and to determine the extent to which that proposal is consistent with our own objectives and goals.

This chapter introduces a subject too large to be encompassed in this brief analysis. Accordingly, the introductory section, setting forth a framework of clarification of the arms-control policy of the United States, is much shorter than a thorough analysis would demand.

ARMS-CONTROL POLICY AND NATIONAL STRATEGY

Arms-control policy and the strategic policies of the nation overlap and interact. Arms-control policy is described in the Arms Control and Disarmament Act as a "component of our foreign policy"; it is expected, however, to be consistent with our national security. Our strategy for ensuring national security—identified also as "national power"—is described in an Army publication in the following language:

> National Power, the aggregate capacity of a state to achieve its national interests *and to influence the behavior of other states*, consists of several distinct yet interrelated elements—political, economic, socio-psychological, technical, and military. The attainment of national objectives such as peace among nations on terms not inimical to United States interests, necessarily involves simultaneous employment of these components of national power. Specific goals supporting any national objective are achieved through application of selected combinations of these elements of national power. Military and national goals are inextricably woven together. Application of one or all of the components of national power, including military power, may be required as the nation faces the broad sweep of international relations, ranging from free and harmonious mutual agreements between sovereign nations to unrestrained global military conflict. [my emphasis][1]

This quotation characterizes the nation's fundamental strategic and global policy, as the Department of the Army sees it. Stress has been afforded in the Army's interpretation to the matter of influence.

Power and influence are associated with one another by Harold D. Lasswell and Abraham Kaplan in their major work *Power and Society*. These authors declare that "it is the threat of sanctions which differentiates power from influence in general. Power is a special case of the exercise of influence: it is the process of affecting policies of others with the help of (actual or threatened) severe deprivations for nonconformity with the policies intended."[2] Klaus Knorr subsequently identifies influence as coercive or noncoercive, using the framework of inquiry established by Lasswell and Kaplan:

> Power can be used either to establish influence by means of coercion, or, without coercive intent to defend or change the status quo between actors. An actor (B) is influenced if he adapts his behavior in compliance with, or in anticipation of, another actor's (A) demands, wishes or proposals. B's conduct is then affected by something A does or by something he expects A may do. In consequence, B will modify his behavior if he would not have done so otherwise,

or he will not change his behavior if he would have altered it in the absence of external influence.[3]

The leading American jurist on international law, Professor Myres S. McDougal, in a work that he coauthored with Harold D. Lasswell, uses the same perspectives for identifying the power process in which influence among states is the critical and deciding factor that determines their standing in their relations and their standing in the global community. In their work entitled *The Identification and Appraisal of Diverse Systems of Public Order*, the two authors state:

> Within the vast social process of man pursuing values through institutions utilizing resources, we are especially concerned with the characteristic features of the power process. A social situation relatively specialized to the shaping and sharing of power outcomes is an "arena"; and it is evident that the world at any given cross section in time is a series of arenas ranging in comprehensiveness from the globe as a whole through great continental, hemispheric, and oceanic clusters to nation states, provinces, and cities and on down to the humblest village and township. The identifying characteristic of an arena is a structure of expectations shared among the members of a community. The assumption is that a decision process occurs in the community; that is, choices affecting the community are made which, if opposed, will in all probability be enforced against opposition. Enforcement implies severe sanction . . . . Whatever the type of participants—group or individual—the actual conduct of participants in the power process depends in part upon their perspectives, which are value demands, group identifications, and expectations.[4]

The national strategy of every state in peace and in war operates in the arenas associated with the power process. It provides a decision framework for a nation to establish, through power, the influencing capabilities that will ensure its survival, shape the policies and attitudes of its enemies or adversaries, and enable it to attain its fundamental goals.[5]

The term "strategy," however, like the term "law" or even the term "policy," is determined by the context in which it is used. It is ambiguous in nature. It appears as a strategy "in the books" for example, and as a strategy "in action." There are interactions and cross fertilization between these two arenas of strategy, as well as distinctions between them. Ambiguities arise because the term may be used, variously, to mean a strategy, a policy or policies, a strategic theory, strategic goals, guidelines, or the strategic process. It shares with law, the legal order, and legal processes the same problems of ambiguity, uncertainty, and lack of clarification.

Our fundamental strategic goal of the arms-control process must be to reach the decision process and decision flow associated with the use of force, and, through agreements and other enforceable policies, to stabilize our relations with the Soviet Union and other potential enemies so that the use of force between ourselves and them or with respect to our mutual interests is deterred. However, as long as the adversaries engaged in arms-control processes remain hostile to each other, in a state of readiness and preparation for confrontation or hostilites, or in competition that may lead to hostilities, arms-control policies, like foreign policy in general, must be conceived within the framework of influencing one's adversaries.

Configured in terms of the influence process, arms-control policy, during peacetime, is associated with the use of arms-control processes—that is, negotiations, initiatives outside the diplomatic forums, propaganda and ideological strategies, and the concluded agreements themselves—to establish influence. Such actions are undertaken by the Soviet Union, and such actions must be assiduously developed by the United States, or its security will be impaired.

Arms-control policy, though developed during peacetime, must be shaped against a future or potential armed conflict, unless, of course, there is such substantial disarmament that armed conflict may be considered as only a remote possibility. Arms-control policy inadequately pursued can impair readiness, military exercises, and preparation and lead to the use of force, when circumstances dictate that no other means of influence are available or appropriate. Our experience so far with arms-control agreements indicates that the agreements are enforceable, and enforced, and their deterrence power is dependent upon the use of force. It further shows that the very weapons that are to be controlled must be available for these purposes, and that disarmament of weaponry is nearly impossible to achieve under conditions in which adequate verification of compliance with disarmament is not possible.

Sun Tzu observed that "in war the best policy is to take a state intact; to ruin it is inferior to this." He observed later that "to subdue the enemy without fighting is the acme of skill." The arms-control process, when it is shifted to a deliberate part of the policy of influence and away from, for example, unrealistic assumptions that the policy will or does dispose of the hostilities between the United States and the Soviet Union, offers opportunities for tactics akin to those described by Sun Tzu.[6]

The arms-control process is the process, in short—along with other foreign policy processes that concern our relations with and influence on the Soviet Union and other states—wherein actions short of war but with all of the same objectives of war are pursued. This perception is the natural outcome of the Clausewitzian logic. But, as indicated more substantially below, the process operates along with and to support the use of other strategic instruments of national policy.[7]

The preceding discussion leads to a second dimension with respect to arms-control policy. The ultimate goals of arms-control policy and in fact the working premises of that policy relate to the use of force. Restrictively construed, arms-control policy would apply to each of the weapons actually covered in the arms-control agreements, and, more restrictively construed, it would apply to each of the agreements and their weapons *sui generis*. The breach of an agreement relating to the lesser weapons—such as, if they were controlled, to chemical or biological weapons—would not necessarily mean that the entire arms-control stabilization process for the other agreements and the other weapons would be affected. In fact, the agreements, if they do not imply this, could readily be worded to express that this is the understanding, thereby making the agreements operate more flexibly in a changing environment.

However, in applying to the use of force in general, at least by extension and by implication, it is apparent that nations give up their freedoms with respect to certain weapons, because they expect to be restraining the use of force and reaching those restraints through mutual agreement and understanding with other nations. If some other arms-control strategic goal is intended, then the stabilization process of arms control is limited to the discrete agreements associated with covered weapons. Moreover, because the arms-control agreements are inapplicable in time of war, they would be suspended at that time and would be inoperative even with respect to the covered weapons. The restraints on the use of force, at least between the United States and the Soviet Union, must necessarily be restraints on the use of force using nuclear weapons or weapons capable of escalating to nuclear weapons, or upon conflicts in which either party has an "interest" involving them in conflict.

To summarize this critical dimension, the effectiveness of arms-control policies is dependent upon their ability to restrain those uses of force in which the covered weapons might be used. This goal is usually identified with stabilization and deterrence. The enforceability of arms-control policies—and more specifically the arms-control agreements—is dependent upon force capabilities and upon the "putative military power," as identified by Klaus Knorr, operating to assure that the policies will not be violated. While enforceability may to some extent be imposed through the global community and its sanctioning processes, the primary means for maintaining enforceability at this time is by the parties threatening reciprocally to use force to enforce them.[8]

Ambiguities, then, repose between the opposing goals of the parties and between the opposing internal goals of each of the parties. Under present conditions, they will and must continue to engage in a process of power, seeking to influence each other, and to shape the policies of each other toward their respective goals. The Soviet Union seemingly is committed to a global community divided amongst communist states, probably under the direct control or at least the hegemony of the Soviet Union. The United States, under the United Nations Charter and by extension of its fundamental instruments and traditions, is firmly committed to a global community associated with a democratic process and the pursuit of human dignity. These are competing goals, and the instruments to be used in such a competition include, where appropriate, resort to military measures.

Accordingly, the third dimension of arms-control policy, for the United States, at least, is associated with another set of outcomes. The United States would like to see the arms-control process contribute to the reduction of the unknown factors that influence the outbreak of warfare. This would fall short of preventing the use of force, but would strengthen the processes of deterrence. It would like to see its own security, and if possible the mutual security of itself and the Soviet Union, enhanced and their relations stabilized. This was perhaps the expectation that proved so confused in the policy of detente. It would like to see a reduction in the costs of maintaining its security through armaments, military forces, and so on. It would also like to see an improved environment with the Soviet Union and other states for relations based on the noncoercive processes of influence.

These expectations appear in the form of policy and strategic goals. While the preambles of the arms-control agreements and the language of the United Nations Charter support such expectations, relations with the Soviet Union and the actions of that country, as perceived by the United States, have compelled a different, more realistic assessment of its goals. It is evident that that country has not relinquished its own fundamental goals, nor the means to achieve them.

A realistic assessment compels us to stress the processes of influence between the states and to recognize that coercive processes remain largely unchanged. Such an assessment also requires a much more realistic appraisal of which weapons should be covered in arms-control agreements, how they should be covered (that is, the detailed provisions that would fit with such an appraisal), how long the agreements should run, what actions can and must be taken when the agreements are not subject to compliance, what measures can be developed to establish verification of compliance (because this is the critical security element of each of the agreements and must operate at the conclusion of the agreement and during its entire term of application), and so on.

Because arms-control policy is a part of the process of influence and operates in the world power process in which we and the Soviet Union and other states participate, the arms-control process and arms-control agreements must be perceived as instruments of influence. That influence will extend to the Soviet Union, to its conduct, to our allies, to third states, and to allies or states associated with the Soviet Union. If successful, it, more than arms-control policy, can assure us of deterrence of a major war. If unsuccessful, the arms-control agreements may fall apart; as suspicions develop and deception and measures of surprise are pursued, military measures and other measures of influence short of war or perhaps involving a limited war, will be used to achieve the objectives of one of the adversaries. The strategies, strategic goals and process, and policies associated with arms control (and disarmament) must be those of influence, measured by the effectiveness of our influence, strengthened where the means are too weak, and backed by force capabilities and the will to use them.[9]

INTERNATIONAL LAW, POLICY, AND ARMS CONTROL

International law is shaped toward policy goals of the states in the global community and toward their own perceptions of a global legal order and legal process; it is also shaped, and reshaped, through practice that involves the process of influence. International law, when deliberately shaped by deliberate policies, can strengthen our arms-control policy goals. However, while the arms-control policy develops primarily through undertakings that have some similarities (though limited) to contractural obligations of the domestic law, international law develops and secures its sanctions through the reciprocal tolerances among the states. Because it is oriented toward future policy goals, it is clarified by an examination into the policy functions associated with the legal process itself.[10]

The policy functions, according to the studies of Harold Lasswell and Myres McDougal and their associates, commence with an identification of the values or base values, such as power, wealth, and so on. Because law is a policy-oriented decision flow, it is possible to identify separately the functions relating to the procedures that will be adopted for making law develop through the appropriate legal processes and the structures of authority that identify the authoritative decision makers who have the competence and access to the capabilities of sanction and enforcement.

Briefly, these policy functions encompass the prescription (legislating, lawmaking) activities, intelligence (or the sharing of information concerning the decision process) and the functions of recommending, invoking the law, applying, appraising, and terminating it. For each there are various strategies that have developed. An inquiry, in depth, into the arms-control agreements with respect to each of these functions—and with respect to developing and negotiating the agreements, their application, and their termination—leads to clarification of the policies that such agreements are establishing for us and, with adequate information, for the Soviet Union. Moreover, by clarifying the legal process in terms of the policy functions, we are enabled to establish arms-control policies through agreements that have more extensive effects.[11]

However, it is apparent that the policy approach cannot be used by only one state to impose its will upon the others. The approach depends upon a realistic appraisal of what states expect when they turn to shaping what they believe is international law and what they believe are the restraints of undertakings of international law. The Soviet Union, curiously, combines a policy approach of its own— seeking legal and policy principles associated with "peaceful coexistence," such as positions concerning legitimacy of intervention, self-determination, wars of liberation, the obligations of states with respect to expropriation of private property, and so on—with such traditional fixtures as a rigid adherence to "sovereignty." It has little respect for customary international law except insofar as law furthers Soviet policies.[12]

It is apparent, by comparing the work of Tunkin and the work of Lasswell and McDougal, that the policy orientation in Western law is informed by different values and attitudes toward values in the two communities of the West and East. In the West, the stress is on human dignity and the rights of human beings. In the East, the stress is on the values associated with state power, so that wealth, enlightenment, and skills are bent toward the power of the state. The law that supports and shapes these policies, clearly, is vastly different from the law that would support policies associated with the claims of human beings to their rights, including their participation in the governing and legal processes. As long as arms-control policies are narrowly confined to weaponry and to the weapons actually covered by the arms-control agreements, it is unlikely that they will extend beyond a balancing of "power" in the weapons sense.

A second aspect of international law is associated with the strategic instruments of policy themselves. Because law is the outcome of policy choices, the development of such instruments, and their application, is of substantial importance to the shape that international law will be taking. Here, too, the challenge from the Soviet Union is in large measure a challenge of more effective strategic instruments than those that we are wielding.

Foremost among these instruments is that associated with military measures and means. These of course may be refined (in a separate analysis) into force and military capabilities designed for all kinds of objectives. Those required for urban activities differ from those for rural actions, and so on. The differences are of major importance when the logistics dimensions are introduced, because the cost and difficulty of moving major force components are self-evident.

In addition to the military instrument as a strategic instrument of policy, there are those identified as the ideological, economic, and diplomatic instruments. Adam Ulam, in his book *The Rivals*, describes how the Soviet Union almost from its inception successfully used diplomatic measures to secure its objectives against the West.[13]

The economic instrument as a strategic instrument of national policy depends upon the economic environment; that is, the economic conditions of the attacking state and the target state. It may, like the other strategic instruments, depend upon military measures—putative and actual military power—to ensure its effectiveness. Klaus Knorr discusses the separate question of establishing a very substantial economic base as critical to the nation desiring to use such measures either offensively or, in a sense, defensively (for example, through substitutes, alternatives, or new developments, as in the oil and energy crisis).[14]

The ideological instrument as a strategic instrument of policy appears in the general policies of the Soviet Union. This instrument goes directly to the people to encourage them to overthrow their governments and replace them with communist governments, or it works through pacifist or other movements that are supportive of Soviet policies. The Stockholm Appeals, the efforts to secure popular resistance to the neutron bomb and to American troops in Europe, and the movement for unilateral disarmament of nuclear weapons are familiar examples that do not need elaboration here. The effectiveness of this instrument with respect to the "peoples" depends on access to them; application of this instrument is clearly asymmetrical between the Western democratic, "open" societies and those of the East.[15]

These strategic instruments are aimed at establishing order, and the order is established, through their use, as part of the sanctioning process. The development of such instruments and the strategies associated with them is critical to establishing a global legal order and legal process that is commensurate with our policies and policy goals.[16]

Accordingly, while the four instruments are used and strengthened by the addition of technology (actually a form of enlightenment and skills) and by wealth and resources, the military capabilities are critical to great-power status even in an "enlightened age" such as we are experiencing today. With effective military power, each of the instruments is enhanced in its actions. Without it, they are almost impotent. They may be used together and in various combinations. But, apart from the significance of the military instrument, the determining elements are how effectively they have been fashioned, how effectively used, and the timing in their use.

Our applications of international law and the associated legal processes and means for clarifying that law must be, with respect to proposals such as the Soviet proposal for a weapons-free zone in outer space, to ensure that the proposal is consistent with our goals, particularly our security goals, that our freedom with respect to the use of noncoercive influence measures remains intact, that our freedom to use force and military measures for legitimate objectives is unaffected, and that our force capabilities essential for maintaining deterrence and a checks and balances process with the Soviet Union on the covered weapons (that is, primarily the major nuclear weapons) remain in effect.

Our primary tactical concern is to shift from excessive attention to arms control to the processes of influence. In shifting this attention we become concerned with military measures and capabilities as part of this process, rather than as part of the seemingly concluded product in the form of a shared global order by states engaged in shared responsibilities. Our goals in influencing the Soviet Union, while ultimately concerned with establishing the global order along policies that are congenial to us, must be more specifically identified with forcing the Soviet Union away from policies of aggression, from threat, from hostile and coercive competition, and from worldwide confrontation. These are not easily achieved, and it is doubtful that the arms-control process as it presently has evolved will assist us in pursuing them.

Arms-control processes can be used by either the United States or the Soviet Union for a variety of goals that are not usually associated with arms control in general. In place of stabilized and improved relations, they can be used for strategic advantage. Beyond the scope of this chapter are such goals as moratoriums to enable research and development to catch up with the other side or to overtake and surpass it; deception through clandestine conduct or other conduct violating the undertakings and understandings; disagreements with respect to the language of the agreements to compel the agreements to support an exclusive policy of one side to its strategic advantage; using the negotiations and the agreements to support ideological campaigns attacking the other negotiating party; and so on.[17]

The "controls" imposed by arms-control agreements, according to some, include those established by customary international law or the treaties associated with restraints on use during wartime. These, however, have traditionally been applied under the law of war, and a distinction must be made between use controls and arms controls. Some believe that arms-control agreements should include prohibitions on the use of the covered weapons during wartime, and this of course, if respected during combat, would reduce the freedom and legal right of the belligerents to use force based on those weapons.

However, the distinction is between establishing controls in peacetime that are operative in peacetime and suspending them or even terminating them in time of war. Moreover, there is a further distinction based upon how the prohibitions and undertakings are enforced among states. The undertakings of the arms-control agreements are enforced through the measures and procedures associated with treaty law and also through the threats of the parties themselves to use force to enforce them (which is rare), to return to an arms race, or to engage in other acts of unfriendly relations (such as suspending ongoing or future negotiations, imposing embargoes, breaking off relations, and so on).

The law of war that is directed to restraints on the use of weapons is enforced through reprisals, through claims by the victors for compensation, reparations, or justice at war crimes tribunals, and, in part, through appeals to the international public opinion in the appropriate forums, through the United Nations, or through the communications media. None of the arms-control agreements, except perhaps the biological weapons convention and the environmental modification techniques convention, attempt to deal with controls on the use of weapons.

In the event that parties seek to achieve the same results attained by the arms-control agreements, they may resort to outlawing a weapon entirely, as was done with the dum-dum bullet. It is unlikely, however, that such an effort would succeed because it is easily violated, and verification could occur only at the point of prohibited use.

This brings up the third distinction between prohibitions on the use of weapons and the arms-control undertakings. Arms-control agreements must be subjected to continuing and strict compliance or they will erode, in which case the arms-control process in general, with respect to future or other agreements, would be affected. Compliance is identified with verification. But "verification" of violations of the law of war are made during combat, and they raise the separate, but complicating, element that the act of verification is probably more difficult in combat and must be resolved when the alleged misconduct occurs.

The usual wartime enforcement measure is through reprisal, or response to ensure correction and remedy by an act in kind, such as using the same illegal weaponry or engaging in the same illegal attacks against the adversary, but under closely controlled legal constraints. There is a controversy whether reprisals by measures that are not reprisals in kind are as effective: some believe that self-denial of the capability and will to respond in kind probably reduces the deterrence a state can command against attacks or weapons that are illegally made against it, and it certainly reduces the options.

A number of strategic implications arise from these distinctions in policy, because they lead to differing expectations as to what parties develop with respect to each other, and therefore extend to their strategies and policies concerning readiness, preparation, and the overall development of capabilities.

If the parties genuinely expect the controls on use to be effective, they must also expect that they will be effective either because war itself can be managed and regulated along use constraints, or because war as a form of influence in the relations among states can be limited. The practice of states during combat in the past shows that in major wars the violence escalates and the principles of moderation are loosened. It seems clear that for the purposes of restraint the more effective measures would lie in the arms-control process, and, though that process has been criticized for other reasons in this chapter, it would lie in an effective and enforceable process. In that case, we must direct our attention to the environment that assures an effective arms-control process.

At this point in our relations with the Soviet Union we are compelled to conclude that the legal order established through the arms-control agreements is minimal, while the agreements themselves refer primarily to controls on the development, deployment, testing and production of weapons. None of the agreements limits the use of weapons as such, and, even if they attempt to do so by implication, parties that tried to enforce this interpretation would be subject to retaliation for breach or alleged breach, to denunciation, or to erosion if the underlying circumstances that led to the agreement had changed. The agreements are cast as legal instruments—as international treaties or international agreements—but they provide little to bolster the global legal order, or even to assure us that their prohibitions will be respected. What gives the agreements their enforceability is the military capability of the parties and their will to enforce the terms of the instrument.

To move toward a global order, the attitudes, policies, and positions of the adversaries—the United States and the Soviet Union—would have to change substantially. While their relations continue to show little change, there is little the United States can do to influence the Soviet Union through arms-control processes, unless those processes are converted to processes for establishing influence on or shaping the policies of the Soviet Union. Even though the framework of international law indicates which policy functions operate through that system of law and how they operate, it is evident that an effective, shared, and enforceable law between these two countries would require a trustworthy flow of communications between them concerning aggression and the use of force, reliable institutions and procedures in which they and other states would share in conducting their affairs, and, in particular, a common perspective concerning the claims, rights, demands, and interests of their citizens and of human beings in general.

For these reasons, the Soviet proposal of August 1981 is thought to be unlikely to support even the minimal arms-control objectives, because it would perpetuate a destabilized environment in outer space; it does not affect the hostile relations between the space powers, but maintains instead a realpolitik with respect to their positions; and it neither affects their competition in space in military matters nor prevents them, under wide areas of individual discretion, to use armed force. More than other arms-control agreements, it is a proposal that simply legitimatizes certain uses of force, rather than restraining them.[18]

THE SOVIET PROPOSAL FOR A WEAPONS-FREE ZONE IN OUTER SPACE

The Soviet proposal of 1981 purports to be an arms-control agreement, to be established on a multilateral basis, establishing a weapons-free zone and some demilitarization of outer space.[19] It contains provisions that prohibit some uses of antisatellite weapons, but it does not prohibit the development, testing, or deployment of these weapons. The weapons-free provisions apply to all weapons, and the proposal, in this respect, would therefore enlarge upon the existing undertakings of the 1967 Outer Space Treaty, whose limita-

tions extend exclusively to the orbiting of weapons of mass destruction. The provisions, however, do not apply to weapons that might be
deployed into outer space from earth.

The questions with respect to the stabilization of outer space
against the future use of weapons or the conduct of hostilities, the
lessening of the competitive arms race associated with activities in
outer space, the rights of self-defense to which all states are entitled
under Article 51 of the United Nations Charter, the establishment of
a peaceful regime in outer space, and the issues concerning the
protection of the terrestrial assets of states through appropriate
weapons systems deployed in outer space are all involved in this
proposal and the strategic context that it seemingly addresses and
seeks to shape.

Similarities with earlier weapons-free proposals should be
noted. The Rapacki Plan proposed on 4 November 1958, called for a
nuclear-weapons-free zone in central Europe, but was opposed by
the United States in large measure because the states at the perimeter
of the zone could easily introduce their armed forces and their
weapons and weapons systems into the zone. Zones differing in some
of the details have been proposed for the Indian Ocean, the Middle
East, and Africa. The MBFR negotiations for a mutual and balanced
force reduction in central Europe have some similarities, but call for
more substantial verification and continued phasing down of weapons deployments; these, in turn, are similar to the zero option
proposals of the present administration. There are also some similarities with the demilitarization of Antarctica, except that there is
ample provision for verification, and access to the means of adequate
verification of that continent is reasonably assured.[20] The same can
be said of the Nuclear Free Zone of Latin America where the International Atomic Energy Agency (though partially discredited by its
current spokesmen) is to undertake monitoring of compliance. With
regard to outer space, the Outer Space Treaty for 1967 provides for
partial demilitarization.[21]

The letter of submittal of the Soviet Treaty Proposal by Foreign
Minister Andrei Gromyko, dated 10 August 1981, and the proposal
itself appear in this volume as appendix 3. The letter notes the
expectation that outer space might be limited to peaceful purposes,
but it also notes that the 1967 treaty needs to be supplemented by
reducing the "danger of the militarization of outer space." It does not
suggest the amendment of that treaty for this purpose, because the
Soviets are, with the letter, proposing an entirely new treaty, not an
amendment to the old one. This approach in itself has risks because,
even if adopted, it would not be clear how far the proposal amends
the 1967 treaty or how to account for the new state of affairs where

some *states* conceivably might be party to the 1967 treaty but not to the proposed Soviet treaty.

The submittal letter further states that "outer space should always remain unsullied and free from any weapons and should not become a new arena for the arms race or a source of strained relations between states." This end would be served "by the conclusion of an international treaty on the prohibition of the stationing of weapons of any kind in outer space."

The preambles of this treaty, like those of other treaties, are useful in setting the environment in which the treaty is expected to apply or the environment that it is expected to shape into being. The proposal does not include preambles referring to peaceful purposes, uses, or applications of outer space and does not refer to the earlier treaties on outer space (as has been the case in the past), but it mentions that one of the objectives of the treaty is the same as that of the United Nations Charter: to strengthen peace and international security. They also repeat Article 2(4) of the charter, concerning the obligations of states to refrain from the threat or use of force "in any manner inconsistent with the Purposes of the United Nations."[22]

The first four articles are the operative articles of the Soviet proposal, and for the purposes of this analysis deserve the closest attention. The four articles should be read together, because together they provide the total context of the weapons-free zone. Article 1 limits the placing of weapons in orbit, the installing of weapons on celestial bodies, the stationing of weapons in outer space, and the assistance, encouragement, or inducement of other entities to do these things. It does not specifically refer to or limit the launching of weapons into outer space; launches that are treated separately or that fail to place weapons in orbit would not be included. It limits these matters with respect to "reusable manned space vehicle of an existing type or of other types which States Parties may develop in the future."

A number of unresolved ambiguities arise out of this provision. The term "weapons" is not defined, and the term by itself is too ambiguous to establish a reliable prohibition. A variety of agents under the Geneva Protocol of 1925 could not be identified as "incapacitating gases," and therefore disputes, still unsettled, abound concerning the term "riot-control agents." A similar ambiguity would arise with respect to the term "weapons" as proposed here. Moreover, further problems arise because there may be a future need to have armed enforcement officers on spacecraft or to convey such officers to space habitats in outer space, where they would also be armed for policing purposes.

Moreover, the article implies that if the Space Shuttle were armed there would be problems in determining whether a given shuttle or space object was armed simply because a predecessor had been armed in the past. The approach under the SALT agreements has been to identify as weapons systems launchers that have carried, even once, weapons to be limited. That approach might readily be applied, under this proposal, to the Space Shuttle.

Linked to this problem is the language in Article 3. This is a provision limiting antisatellite missiles (ASATs), which in itself causes confusion because the United States and the Soviet Union are engaged in bilateral negotiations with respect to such missiles. Article 3 read with Article 1, however, would enable the contracting states to use ASATs against space objects that contravened Article 1. This would mean, of course, that the ASATs must be tested, deployed, and available for such use, and that such use would be a permissible use of force not constituting an act of war, to be exercised by any contracting state largely at its discretion with respect to use, notification or warning, and so on.[23]

The draft, particularly in these articles, also limits the right of states to self-defense. By implication a space object violating Article 1 because it is armed would not have a legitimate right of self-defense; this represents an amendment of Article 51 of the United Nations Charter and a modification to the same end the customary international law regarding self defense. In effect,the violation of Article 1 would constitute a form of aggression, and the space object that engaged in such a violation—like pirates and international criminals—would be fair game for any state under this new international law. Finally, the provisions on self-defense in the Outer Space Treaty of 1967 would also be amended by the entry of this draft treaty into force.

With respect to entry into force, only a limited number of states might be induced to conclude the treaty. The Soviet Union has insisted under the so-called Brezhnev Doctrine that a separate body of international law controls the relations in the socialist commonwealth of states, and that this body of law legitimatizes Soviet intervention—including the use of armed forces by the Soviet Union or by other members of the "community" that the Soviets choose to involve—whenever a member of the socialist commonwealth is threatened with respect to its communist form of government either internally or externally. This doctrinal position, coupled with its extension through the permissive clauses for intervention of a security treaty as in the case of Afghanistan, and further coupled with the Soviet Union's conclusion of an outer space treaty with Warsaw Pact members limiting remote sensing, suggests the possibilities that can be exploited to reshape international law in general, the outer space treaties, and the accepted principles relating to aggression.[24]

Article 2 of the proposal declares that space objects shall be used "in strict accordance with international law, including the Charter of the United Nations, in the interest of maintaining international peace and security and promoting international cooperation and mutual understanding." Such a provision is redundant of existing obligations of states, but, because it is introduced into this proposal, it has the effect of making the proposal a part of that international law. The implications of this challenge to the legal order have just been mentioned; and the strategic implications include those associated with the future use of ideological instruments of strategic policy, as well as diplomatic and military instruments.

Moreover, Articles 1, 2, and 3 have further implications for the right of self-defense. The right to test ASATs and deploy them has been preserved. But the right of self-defense—of space objects and other interests and activities—includes the rights to conduct research and testing, to make modifications in armaments, and to development, readiness, military exercises, and so on. These are critical to give the right of self-defense real effectiveness, particularly in an age dominated by rapidly advancing military technologies.

The strategic implications of this provision are that these rights of self-defense would be denied, while the rights of states concerned with using ASATs for violations of Article 1 remain intact. Yet, even assuming that states would accept this provision and its implications, it would run into difficulties because it could not be monitored for compliance. It is unrealistic to build a treaty around provisions whose enforceability and effectiveness are almost certain to be illusory. While there are disagreements over what constitutes adequate verification, and hence over the adequacy of monitoring processes and their effectiveness, those disagreements must be resolved against the realities of state behavior: adequacy of verification in a world of secure states and in a secure world order is not the same kind of problem as adequacy for a destabilized order.

Other implications might also be mentioned. For example, states that assist other states (whether contracting parties or not) with respect to arming their space objects are subject to the same forcible measures in the use of ASATs as are the offending states. While the treaty does not clarify how such enforcement would be imposed, presumably it would be grounds for a form of reprisal or other correcting measures.

The language of Article 3 needs separate attention. The prohibition on the uses of ASATs extends to those that might "destroy, damage, disturb the normal functioning or change the flight trajectory of space objects of other States Parties." Such a prohibition is not all inclusive, but it is also ambiguous. It might affect monitoring if a space object of one state passes close to the space object of another for purposes of adequate verification of compliance; there may be no other means for monitoring its activities. But then the complaint may be raised that the "normal functioning" of the monitored space object has been affected.

Article 3 of course denies states, other than the launching state, the right to destroy space objects. This means that if a space object is bent on a destructive course it cannot be diverted or destroyed by the state that might be struck by the object, at least not without the consent of the launching state. Article 3, it appears in light of the above observations, covers a matter that has little to do with the weapons-free zone and, in effect, impairs the effectiveness of such a zone.

Because Article 3 permits ASATs, it would substantially modify the expectations with respect to any treaty seeking to control or deter the development of ASATs. It not only permits such weapons systems, but it says nothing about verifying them as such. Unlike the SALT, particularly SALT II, no effort has been made to deal with the difficult business of verifying that tests, development, or other ASAT activities are taking place. Such actions need not be identified, because Article 3 expressly permits such weapons, and therefore permits their testing and development for the purposes specified.

Article 4—the provision relating to verification—falls short of the more extensive provisions in the ABM and SALT agreements, changing the effectiveness of that precedent and failing to build upon it. The ABM treaty, in Articles XII and XIII (see appendix 3), makes verification of arms-control agreements—and the ASAT provision of Article 3 is such a provision—dependent upon access to the critical data concerning compliance, opportunities to verify the actions or activities of the other side to ensure compliance, and also confidence-building measures structured into the compliance procedures. For this reason the ABM and SALT treaties adopted an approach that combines direct undertakings or obligations that include respect for reconnaissance and commitments not to interfere and not to use deliberate concealment measures. Article 4 of the Soviet proposal has changed these as the language of this provision indicates.

The provisions of Article XIII of the ABM treaty are in reality a confidence-building measure. They enable the parties to air their complaints, establish a forum for that purpose, develop the means of establishing what data will be included or excluded, establish eventually certain rules of the road in their relations, improve on their confidence and trust in each other, and of course resolve disagreements and disputes. Each of the various functions of the Standing Consultative Commission of Article XIII might have been useful in the context of the Soviet proposal, but they may have been omitted because that country believed they would be unworkable—or not in its interest—in a multilateral treaty.

The Soviet draft, however, fails to provide measures and procedures for ensuring adequate verification, and it has taken no steps to ameliorate the deficiencies of self-monitoring by the parties. The entire checks and balances process of the arms-control elements of a weapons-free zone quickly falls apart when that process is made to operate in such complex activities as those involving outer space. At best, they can and do operate in the simple agreements.[25]

The problems of verification are compounded by the nature of our activities in outer space. Those activities depend upon exploitation of advanced technologies. The technologies themselves may be used for peaceful, military, or aggressive purposes or for warfighting, because they are "neutral" with respect to these matters. Exploitation of outer space involves the technologies concerning launching, orbiting, transiting, maneuvering, reconnaissance, survivability, and so on; and these are applicable to all of the activities of states. Furthermore, such technologies are dependent upon research and testing. While some of these can be monitored, many of these activities cannot.

In a real sense, even the SALT agreements are vulnerable to erosion and breakdown because the technologies can neither be verified nor controlled, because they can lead to weapons systems that may prove even more formidable than any we presently have for "offense" or "defense," and because the parties cannot or are unwilling to share in them. The modernization provisions permitting the states party to those agreements to improve their weapons systems are provisions that built into the agreements asymmetries that would upset their balance. The same can be said for this attempt at a weapons-free zone.

CONCLUSIONS

The Soviet proposal for a weapons-free zone in outer space fails to meet the major arms-control policy goals. Instead of stabilizing outer space, it tends to destabilize and to legitimize the process of destabilization. While it purports to limit arms, it limits only some of them. It fails to provide for adequate monitoring of the activities that are associated with compliance. Weapons deployed outside the zone, or the weapons systems of states that refuse to become parties, will erode the system and make it illusory. The resulting public "order" is an order of insecurity among the contracting states. Moreover, a number of provisions are peculiarly oriented to Soviet policies that would substantially modify the global social and legal orders and the processes associated with those orders.

However, the proposal and an analysis of the proposal enable us to clarify what we should expect from arms-control agreements. In addition to the policy goals just mentioned, we will need to have either measures designed to improve the communications processes among states or a development in their order and relations that lead to such improvement, or both. Through this, we have the opportunity to establish or constitute a more secure order, a process that bears resemblance to developing constitutions for a domestic order and is perhaps most closely associated with the long but firm adherence of the English peoples in developing their own "unwritten" constitution.

Moreover, through improved communications processes a number of elements that go into security and insecurity are addressed. Among these, in the strategic sense, are those that involve deception, surprise, clandestine activity, excessive secrecy, and insecurity in general. To move in this direction is essential, even though the velocity of such movement toward improved relations will be extremely slow. It would mean that the Soviet Union would be opening its own social order to the outside world, and freeing its own people from the shackles of a totalitarian control. Regrettably, much of arms-control thinking is premised at least tacitly on the belief that the Soviet Union behaves like an open society, or can be induced to do so through such measures as arms-control itself or detente.

The current checks and balances system that characterizes arms control is a fragile system because it is dependent upon mutual policing against severe outbreaks of aggression. It is evident that our tolerance for limited aggression has grown and that some testing of that tolerance continues.[26] It is also evident that with respect to outer space we may, unless our relations can be shifted to other terms of reference and behavior, be pursuing in space much the same process that we pursue with military and other stategic measures on earth or on the high seas.[27]

Former Secretary of State Haig has noted that the arms-control process wherever it is to be in effect depends upon deterrence. While deterrence itself is a complex decision and policy flow, it "does not rest upon a static comparison or the number of size of nuclear weapons.... Deterrence... rests upon a military balance measured not in warhead numbers but in a complex interaction of capabilities and vulnerabilities."

The interaction of law, policy, arms-control measures, and the strategic instruments of policy continues to grow in complexity. However, our most urgent task is to clarify these is such a way that through the principle of "simplification" (that is, drawing upon one of the principles of war), we may be able to avoid being the victim of our own complexities: those imposed upon us by our size, our technologies, and our knowledge that exceeds our capacity to control it or its outcomes.

The road in this direction lies through a full understanding of what the trends associated with our development in terms of our major instruments and perspectives mean. International law is part of that heritage and provides us access to firm principles, to means for shaping our future, and, through sharing common goals in human dignity, to enlist the support of peoples everywhere.

NOTES

1. Department of the Army Publication, FM 100-1, August 1981, p. 4.
2. Harold D. Lasswell and Abraham Kaplan, *Power and Society*(New Haven: Yale University Press, 1950).
3. Klaus Knorr, *Power and Wealth* (New York: Basic Books, 1973), pp. 3–4. This quotation continues: "Influence can be noncoercive as well as coercive. It is coercive when B's conduct is affected by his fear of sanctions of one kind or another: that is, some threat, actual or imputed, to his goal achievement. B's choice of behavior is consequently restricted by A's influence. On the other hand, influence is noncoercive, if B's choices are enriched rather than limited by A's influence, for example—if A persuades B that a proposed cooperative venture is mutually beneficial. In the event of coercion, B loses, or expects to lose, something of value while A gains, or expects to gain, something of value. When influence is noncoercive, both A and B gain, or expect to gain, something valuable. Some writers use the term 'power' to designate all influence, whether coercive or noncoercive." Knorr prefers to designate only coercive influence as power. While power is not equated exclusively by Knorr with military power, that power is not simply military capabilities. In *Military Power and Potential* (Lexington, Mass.: Heath Lexington Books, 1970), p. 21, Knorr declares: "In large part and indispensably, nations become military powers of consequence, globally or within a region, because they have a superior military potential, which even with a moderate rate of mobilization generates commanding ready military strength, or because, though endowed with a moderate potential in terms of manpower and other resources, they mobilize to a greater extent than do states of comparable military potential.... Military potential has a bearing on a nation's putative military power. This power results from ready military forces, from the ability to augment these forces, and from a nation's reputation for employing military force in the event of a serious international dispute. The first two factors—ready, mobilized forces and military potential—may be regarded as a nation's military strength which figures in the

equation of putative military power. Indeed, military potential may be a factor even in actualized military power." Knorr separately defines "putative power" as "something that powerful states have and can accumulate," that is, power as a means. Actualized power "is an effect, that is influence actually enjoyed." See *Power and Wealth*, p. 14.

4. Cited in Myres S. McDougal and W. Michael Reisman, *International Law Essays* (Mineola, N.Y.: Foundation Press, 1981), p. 21. Lasswell and Kaplan (*Power and Society*, p. 75) declare: "The concept of power is perhaps the most fundamental in the whole of political science: the political process is the shaping, distribution, and exercise of power (in a wider sense, or all the deference values, or of influence in general)."

5. In the current environment the strategies of arms control must be coordinated with the strategies associated with warfighting. A nation totally disarmed with respect to particular weapons will be unable to practice with those weapons and establish the necessary readiness, preparations, organization, military and logistics structure, and discipline in exercise that would enable it to operate effectively during combat. However, even a nation under arms control, where the weapons are not eliminated but are subjected to "controls," may impose upon itself the same outcome. It can cripple its own use of such weapons, or defense against such weapons, by persuading itself that the arms controls it has established with a potential adversary are tantamount to a nonuse of the weapons in combat. More insidiously it can impair its own will so that others will perceive, both as to the covered weapons and as to others that are not covered by arms-control agreements, that it will choose, or be perceived to have chosen, to refrain from the use of force even to protect its extraterritorial interests, reserving that use, presumably, only to protecting the homeland. If arms-control strategies move into this direction before a global order has made arms controls less important for the checks and balances of weapons, they would clearly be contrary to a nation's security interests and enable an adversary to turn to the other strategic instruments of policy to achieve goals that might otherwise have required the use of force, reserving its weapons solely for the purpose of threat. Democratic societies, seemingly, are vulnerable to this use of strategy and particularly vulnerable during peacetime when they cannot perceive a combat in being.

6. Sun Tzu, *The Art of War*, trans. Samuel B. Griffith (New York: Oxford University Press, 1981, reprint).

7. McGeorge Bundy, George F. Kennan, Robert S. McNamara and Gerard Smith, in a joint article in *Foreign Affairs* (Spring 1982), cited in *New York Times*, 8 April 1982, p. A14, argued that the deterrence associated with arms control over nuclear weapons could be established under a "no first use" policy that they were recommending. But they required massive development of conventional forces to offset this deterrence equilibrium and could only conclude that if such a policy were adopted we might find that we could "escape from the pressure to seem willing and able to use these weapons" and would then "find that our requirements are much less massive than is now widely supposed." Their observation that "as long as the weapons themselves exist, the possibility of their use will remain" ignored the fact that even with their proposal there was no guarantee the weapons would no longer exist, no agreement to that end, and clearly none that was verifiable. Accordingly, by their own words they recognized that at best the policy they proposed could only establish a hoped for "psychological set" on the policy-makers, but that there was no guarantee they could have that.

8. In an early attempt to clarify the nature of the arms-control process

and the operation of arms-control agreements, Thomas C. Schelling proposed a strategy described in his book *The Strategy of Conflict* (Cambridge, Mass.: Harvard University Press, 1960). He used the term "strategy" as a term taken from the games of strategy "in which the best course of action for each player depends on what the other players do." He further noted (p. 3 n.) that "the term is intended to focus on the interdependence of the adversaries' decisions and on the expectations about each other's behavior." This he noted "is not the military usage." He studied the entire subject in terms of bargaining situations and noted that the parties were not concerned with "the efficient application of force" but with "the exploitation of potential force." His conception is based on a series of threats; on the capability to carry out the threats; on the minimal level of communications to avoid surprise, deception and so on; the rational behavior of adversaries capable of determining the costs, risks, and benefits of using force, or more specifically, of violating the agreed strategy; it is not dependent upon confidence, trust, or even good will between the parties. It is in effect a balancing of weapons capabilities and wills into a mutual deterrence equilibrium.

9. This analysis does not examine the interdependence of effective arms-control measures with effective measures regarding aggression, but brief mention must be made as to this. The United Nations Charter vested the Security Council with what appears to be exclusive competence concerning agression in Article 39. An attempt to overcome some of the weaknesses in working with aggression was made by the General Assembly, which recommended adoption of a definition of aggression. The following language from that definition is pertinent: "The first use of armed force by a State in contravention of the Charter shall constitute prima facie evidence of an act of aggression although the Security Council may, in conformity with the Charter, conclude that a determination that an act of aggression has been committed would not be justified in the light of other relevant circumstances including the fact that the acts concerned or their consequences are not of sufficient gravity." The weaknesses in such a definition are self-evident: the Security Council retains its competence, and the permanent members retain their right to veto acts alleged to be aggression on behalf of themselves and their clients. Accordingly, aggression remains an area of danger and risk for the stabilization associated with the arms-control processes. The relationship of aggression with arms-control measures is borne out in the fundamental goals usually asserted as to arms-control policies; that is, that the parties shall refrain from using the covered weapons (implied and enforced by mutual threat), and, in the more liberal expectations, that the parties are to refrain from using force in their relations. This larger expectation is of course what is expressed in Article 2(4) supported by Article 2(3) of the United Nations Charter, but it is given specific content with respect to the weapons covered in the arms-control agreements. The weakness of arms control in part derives from aggression itself—the impermissible use of force as measured by community standards—and because such states as the United States and Soviet Union find themselves compelled (or deliberately choose) to use force in their competitive struggle in a power process environment. For these reasons the arms-control process must be cautiously appraised because, once outside the controls of those who are informed in such matters, and once disassociated from warfighting needs, it may lead to an illusory expectation that because arms-control agreements cover the use of force (only an implication or weak inference) at least by the weapons covered in the agreements, the matter of aggression has been resolved. A more careful appraisal suggests

that the broader arms-control policies in the limited ways in which they can effectively operate today may indeed help us to identify certain acts that might be considered aggression, but that such aggression cannot be countered because to do so would impair the relations and undertakings associated with a foreign policy that is derived from an arms-control policy. This situation could occur in the future with respect to chemical or nuclear weapons and their use. For a review of the matter of aggression, and the stages leading to the "definition" in the General Assembly, see the two-volume work of Benjamin B. Ferencz, *Defining International Aggresson: The Search for World Peace: A Documentary History and Analysis* (Dobbs Ferry, N.Y.: Oceana Publications, 1975). Ferencz, however, pins high hopes on the effectiveness of this "definition," even though its enforceability is sadly lacking.

10. The policy orientation of international law is not considered in depth in this chapter. However, the orientation is that which stresses the policy functions and policy values associated with an emerging law. Under these perspectives we draw upon the strategies associated with the policies of governments—their decisions and choices—that shape the future law into existence so that it is congenial to their policies and values, strengthen and maintain it, and, where law no longer serves their policies, terminate it. The difference in approach is in part the difference between those concerned with the law in books and those concerned with the law in action. The traditional legal approach is rigid and often authoritarian. Under this approach the tendency is to view the judgments of authorities—especially the judgments of courts—as final "decisions" that can never change. A policy-oriented law approaches law in terms of the changing realities, circumstances, and environment and stresses a legal process that adapts to such change rather than rule. The rules of law are incorporated in the processes and given the flexibility to enable them to apply over longer periods of time (the same approach is used with our own Constitution). International treaties drawing upon this perspective tend to use ambiguities or general principles and guidelines, and, even when the language is not ambiguous, there are, for the above reasons, tendencies of states to treat the language as ambiguous. A more extensive review of these matters can be found in the writings of Professors Harold D. Lasswell, Myres S. McDougal, and W. Michael Reisman and their associates, as well as in the writings of constitutional lawyers in general.

11. This analysis can be pursued in far greater detail by considering the essays of McDougal and Reisman, *International Law Essays*. One of the policy functions, that of termination, had had relatively little analysis until Arie D. David's *The Strategy of Treaty Termination* (New Haven and London: Yale University Press, 1975). David's text is an excellent example of the use of the policy approach, because it moves from the automaticity of the traditional international law to that in which the policies and shaping of policies belong to the participants. He notes that "rules of law were not formulated (in the traditional approach) in terms of policy choices, but rather in mechanical terms that narrowed the freedom of choice of decision makers. They were presumed to apply 'automatically' whenever the conditions called for their application, however fair or unfair the decisions might be. The goal, either actual or verbal, was to return to status quo ante, in other words, normalcy, balance, and so on" (p. 5).

12. Soviet legal theory is presented in detail by Grigori I. Tunkin, *Theory of International Law*, trans. and with an introduction by William E. Butler

(Cambridge, Mass.: Harvard University Press, 1974). The views of Tunkin must give pause to those who seek with the Soviet Union a shared legal order. Customary law is only that law that embodies "tacit consent" (p. 123); self-determination applies only with respect to peoples not subject to communism (p. 8ff.); the socialist commonwealth of states has its own and applied interstate law, a higher law than that of international law under the Brezhnev Doctrine; and so on.

13. Adam Ulam, *The Rivals: America and Russia Since World War II* (New York: Viking Press, 1971); see also his collected papers, *Ideologies and Illusions: Revolutionary Thought from Herzen to Solzhenitsyn* (Cambridge, Mass.: Harvard University Press, 1976). In the first book, Ulam notes that during the Suez crisis the Soviet Union deflected much of world opinion from its actions in Hungary, and, insisting that France, Israel and the United Kingdom were "imperialists," shaped the Suez crisis toward the American decision. It became for NATO, he argued, a crippling blow, and "much of the underlying spirit of cooperation, of the Europeans' readiness to shoulder a proportionate part of the burden, was bound to evaporate" (p. 261). He also argued that wars of liberation were a Soviet diplomatic triumph: "for the Soviet Union the wars of national liberation presented an opportunity to weaken the opposition (i.e., at home) and to expand Russian influence without the risks and inconveniences involved in outright Communist expansion" (p. 274).

14. Knorr, *Military Power and Potential*, pp. 54ff.

15. Cf. Tocqueville: "Foreign politics demand scarcely any of those qualities which are peculiar to a democracy; they require, on the contrary, the perfect use of almost all those in which it is deficient. Democracy is favorable to the increase of the internal resources of a state, and fortifies the respect for law in all classes of society: all these are advantages which have only an indirect influence over the relations which one people bears to another. But a democracy can only with great difficulty regulate the details of an important undertaking, persevere in a fixed design, and work out its execution in spite of serious obstacles. It cannot combine its measures with secrecy or await their consequences with patience. These are qualities which more especially belong to an individual or an aristocracy; and they are precisely the qualities by which a nation, like an individual, attains a dominant position." *Democracy in America*, vol. 1 (New York: Alfred A. Knopf, 1945), pp. 234–35.

16. For a review of these see Myres S. McDougal et al., *Law and Public Order in Space* (New Haven and London: Yale University Press, 1963), pp. 404ff. The authors in this and other texts refer to sanctioning goals that we can associate with, for example, the use of force as the goals of prevention, deterrence, restoration (that is, of minimum order), rehabilitation (of those involved in misconduct), and reconstruction. See also Myres S. McDougal and Florentino P. Feliciano, *Law and Minimum World Public Order: The Legal Regulation of International Coercion* (New Haven and London: Yale University Press, 1961), pp. 287–96. In this text the authors indicate that the primary goal is that of minimum public order, because that goal must be reached at an early stage and maintained to provide for the communications essential for processes of noncoercive influence. The goals described above are described as stages toward reaching and maintaining the minimum public order. The devlopment of the public order and the legal order concurrently is described by the authors in detail in the two texts.

17. As in wartime, the peacetime conduct of states engaged in competi-

tive activities and in competition for power can be identified against general "principles." The "principles of war" are identified in the Department of Army Publication, FM 100-1, August 1981, as those of objective offensive, mass, economy of force, maneuver, unity of command, security, surprise, and simplicity. Harry G. Summers, Jr., in his book *On Strategy: The Vietnam War in Context* (Carlisle Barracks, Pa.: U.S. Army War College, n.d. [1980?]), follows the Vietnam War by applying the principles. The same analysis could be used with respect to the use of arms-control agreements employed as instruments of influence and manipulation. The objectives of the agreements can be identified in terms of the weapons to be covered, the tactic being to identify and expend time on weapons that have no military utility (compare the agreement relating to environmental modification techniques) or to identify weapons more useful to one's adversary. The principle of "economy of force" might refer to arms-control policies designed to favor one's weapons generally against those of one's adversary; for example, the Soviet Union at the outset favored its conventional weapons and sought only controls on the weapons that were part of the strategic advantage of the West, the nuclear weapons. The arms-control negotiations may be subject to surprise and maneuver.

18. Henry A. Kissinger, *A World Restored: Metternich, Castlereagh and the Problems of Peace 1812–22* (Boston, Mass.: Houghton Mifflin, 1957) pp. 1–5, provides his insights into states that seek to revolutionize the world order. Ulam (*The Rivals*) and other writers, such as George F. Kennan (see especially *Russia and the West Under Lenin and Stalin* [Boston, Mass.: Little, Brown, 1961]), suggest that the Soviet Union has a firm policy to replace the global order with an order shaped according to its own goals and values. Where this is the fundamental challenge between the United States and the Soviet Union —between the East and West—diplomacy becomes part of the confrontational mechanism. Kissinger declares that "diplomacy, the art of restraining the exercise of power, cannot function in such an environment," and attention must be turned to what the environment requires. Stability is eroded with the weakening of a "generally accepted legitimacy" among states. Kissinger notes with respect to the political environment: "But the attainment of peace is not as easy as the desire for it. . . . Those ages which in retrospect seem most peaceful were least in search of peace. Those whose quest for it seems unending appear least able to achieve tranquility. Whenever peace—conceived as the avoidance of war—has been the primary objective of a power or a group of powers, the international system has been at the mercy of the most ruthless member of the international community. Whenever the international order has acknowledged that certain principles could not be compromised even for the sake of peace, stability based on an equilibrium of forces was at least conceivable" (p. 1). If it is assumed that the Soviet Union is insecure as a revolutionary power in this environment, then, according to Kissinger, "only absolute security—the neutralization of the opponent—is considered a sufficient guarantee, and thus the desire of one power for absolute security means absolute insecurity for all the others" (p. 2). For a review of the extended efforts of states to bring community standards to bear on aggression and the failure of those efforts for reasons such as those just cited, see Ferencz, *Defining International Aggression*.

19. The term "demilitarization" during peacetime raises questions of monitoring compliance. Demilitarization during armed combat is more troublesome. The Geneva Protocols of 1977 supplementing the Geneva Conventions of 1949 extend to rules regulating the conduct of hostilities, and

they contain the following proposed provision to govern demilitarization during armed conflict or warfare:

Article 60—Demilitarized zones

1. It is prohibited for the Parties to the conflict to extend their military operations to zones on which they have conferred by agreement the status of demilitarized zone, if such extension is contrary to the terms of this agreement.

2. The agreement shall be an express agreement, may be concluded verbally or in writing, either directly or through a Protecting Power or any impartial humanitarian organization, and may consist of reciprocal and concordant declarations. The agreement may be concluded in peacetime, as well as after the outbreak of hostilities, and should define and describe, as precisely as possible, the limits of the demilitarized zone and, if necessary, lay down the methods of supervision.

3. The subject of such an agreement shall normally be any zone which fulfills the following conditions:

    (a) all combatants, as well as mobile weapons and mobile military equipment, must have been evacuated;

    (b) no hostile use shall be made of fixed military installations or establishments;

    (c) no acts of hostility shall be committed by the authorities or by the population; and

    (d) activity linked to the military effort must have ceased.

The Parties to the conflict shall agree upon the interpretation to be given to the condition laid down in subparagraph (d) and upon persons to be admitted to the demilitarized zone other than those mentioned in paragraph 4.

4. The presence, in this zone, of persons specially protected under the Conventions and this Protocol, and of police forces retained for the sole purpose of maintaining law and order, is not contrary to the conditions laid down in paragraph 3.

5. The Party which is in control of such a zone shall mark it, so far as possible, by such signs as may be agreed upon with the other Party, which shall be displayed where they are clearly visible, especially on its perimeter and limits and on highways.

6. If the fighting draws near to a demilitarized zone, and if the Parties to the conflict have so agreed, none of them may use the zone for purposes related to the conduct of military operations or unilaterally revoke its status.

7. If one of the Parties to the conflict commits a material breach of the provisions of paragraphs 3 or 6, the other Party shall be released from its obligations under the agreement conferring upon the zone the status of demilitarized zone. In such an eventuality, the zone loses its status but shall continue to enjoy the protection provided by the other provisions of this Protocol and the other rules of international law applicable in armed conflict.

(From U.N. Document A/32/144 of August 15, 1977. Annexes I and II.)

These provisions were hammered out in numerous sessions leading to the conclusion of the Geneva Protocols of 1977. They have not yet been ratified by the United States or other major military powers. Stress should be given to the fragility of the zone; it requires a common interest of the parties in keeping it demilitarized.

20. For an extensive study of militarism see Alfred Vagts, *A History of Militarism* (New York: Meridian Books, 1959). The proposals for demilitarization tend to draw in these emotional and associated elements. Vagts states that "militarism is thus not the opposite of pacifism, its true counterpart is civilianism. Love of war, not bellicosity, is the counterpart of the love of peace, pacifism; but militarism is more, and sometimes less, than the love of war. It covers every system of thinking and valuing and every complex of feelings which rank military institutions and ways above the ways of civilian life, carrying military mentality and modes of acting and decision into the civilian sphere" (p. 17). He further declares that "every war is fought, every army is maintained in a military way and in a militaristic way. The distinction is fundamental and fateful. The military way is marked by a primary concentration of men and materials on winning specific objectives of power with the utmost efficiency, that is, with the least expenditure of blood and treasure. It is limited in scope, confined to one function, and scientific in its essential qualities. Militarism, on the other hand, presents a vast array of customs, interests, prestige, actions and thought associated with armies and wars and yet transcending true military purposes. Indeed, militarism is so constituted that it may hamper and defeat the purpose of the military way. Its influence is unlimited in scope. It may permeate all society and become dominant over all industry and arts. Rejecting the scientific character of the military way, militarism displays the qualities of caste and cult, authority and belief" (p. 13).

21. Partial demilitarization is provided by Article IV, prohibiting "the establishment of military bases, installation and fortifications, the testing of any type of weapons and the conduct of military maneuvers *on celestial bodies*." (Outer space itself is not mentioned nor are artificial or manmade space objects not located on celestial bodies. Ambiguity perhaps resides in the term "celestial bodies." It may not include asteroids. However, for obvious reasons, inspection and monitoring of compliance of such activities will not be easy tasks; and if these fail, the provisions in Article IV could die through a "fundamental change of circumstances" (clausula rebus sic stantibus).

22. Note that Article 2(4) reads: "All Members shall refrain in their international relations from the threat or use of force against the territorial integrity or political independence of any state [that is, not "any member"] or in any other manner inconsistent with the Purposes of the United Nations." Note also the related Article 2(3): "All Members shall settle their international disputes by peaceful means in such a manner that international peace and security, and justice, are not endangered."

23. Arms-control agreements and disarmament agreements do not provide for restraints, prohibitions, or undertakings to refrain from the use of force. Such restraints are usually regulated under the law of war, and if specific rules are not applicable to the particular weapons involved they are then subject to the principle of military necessity. That principle restrains excessive uses of force; that is, uses of force that cause unnecessary suffering, disproportionate to the attainment of the legitimate military objectives. Only a few weapons are outlawed entirely: even the lethal chemical weapons under the Geneva Protocol of 1925 are prohibited with respect to a first use, so that any contracting state can respond with such weapons when they are first used against it. The difficulty of making restraints on use and arms-control undertakings arises first because the arms-control agreements are suspended or terminated once war breaks out. Second, verification of a pro-

hibited use is usually part of armed combat, or part or a process concerned with aggression (to which arms control is however closely related). Third, the rationale of arms contol in this context is that if the weapons are balanced, controlled, and stabilized, the parties will be induced to refrain from use; thus, the restraints on use are indirect, not direct. Attempts to suggest that there are restraints on use in such arms-control treaties as those relating to biological weapons and to environmental modification techniques are likely to prove illusory.

24. See Convention on the Transfer and Use of Data of the Remote Sensing of the Earth from Outer Space, dated 19 May 1978, Moscow, from United Nations Document A/33/162, 29 June 1978, and signed (ratified?) by Cuba, Czechoslovakia, the German Democratic Republic, Hungary, Mongolia, Poland, Romania, and the Soviet Union. Article IV requires the consent of the subjacent state to secure or possess data from remote sensing in outer space "with a better than 50 metres resolution on the terrain." The consent extends to transfer of such data. Data with respect to "natural resources of the economic potential" of the contracting parties must also be withheld from all parties including the acquiring State unless consent is obtained. (This is an extension of the "sovereignty" principle to data and to the data process and acquisition system.

25. Schelling, *Strategy of Conflict*, has argued that a checks and balances process effective in an arms-control environment could be established as part of his "strategy of conflict." However, such a process, perhaps workable for bilateral arrangements, would become extremely unworkable in a multilateral context. It might be aided by the use of international means for reconnaissance, such as those recently proposed by the French, but that proposal, which I have analyzed separately, is weak because it presupposes strong cooperative relationships among adversaries.

26. The development of international law must account for these changing perspectives. It is shaped and reshaped by the claims and counterclaims, demands, and reciprocal tolerances of states, being gradually molded into shape, but never reaching a "final" stage. Law being conceived in terms of policy and process, this of course is understandable. But the point should be made that if we acquiesce in changing practices of states, we also acquiesce in changing policy and law. We must accordingly be firm in those principles that are of importance to us, or we will lose them. In this connection, note that our legislation in the Arms Control and Disarmament Act currently requires that the director of ACDA report to the Congress that we have and are maintaining on a continuous basis our verification and monitoring capabilities with respect to compliance by other states with respect to our arms control agreements. This is intended to avoid acquiescence in loose practices and eventually the loss of our legal position in those treaties. The gradual erosion of the system of the International Atomic Energy Agency should be cited as one where states have gradually lost interest in the policies associated with enforcing nonproliferation. Both the policies and the law are thereby affected.

27. It is arguable, for example, that the military requirements for militarized space objects for outer space will bear certain similarities to those required on the high seas from our naval forces, to wit: (1) we may require military capabilities as part of our *peacetime presence*, for the purposes of influence to support our foreign policy in peacetime and to establish our strength and capabilities among allies, adversaries, and the noncommitted; (2) we may require some capabilities for *strategic deterrence*, either through arms-control agreements or without them, to maintain the strategic

capabilities to ensure that there is a stabilized regime for both outer space and terrestrial purposes; (3) we may require such capabilities for *denial and interdiction*, to deny the Soviet Union control over outer space as would impair our security or affect our position during warfighting; (4) we may need them for *power projection in outer space*, to project and make effective our military and protective powers against an adversary, his assets, or what he is using to attack our interests wherever located; and (5) we may need some for *space control*, for capabilities sufficient or adequate to maintain control over areas of space so that we are not hindered in undertaking military activities in space or on land, particularly where the use of outer space is needed to provide the area from which that control must be asserted. We cannot in any event assume on the basis of hopes and expectations of our own, unsupported by empirical evidence, or upon trends from past experience, or upon the well-established predispositions of ourselves and our adversaries, that outer space will be peaceful and free of future combat simply because we believe the outcome would be in all of our interests. This flies in the face of reality. As former Secretary of State Haig, in response to McGeorge Bundy et al., has indicated (see *New York Times*, 7 April 1982, p. A8), "At the heart of (our) deterrence strategy is the requirement that the risk of engaging in war must be made to outweigh any possible benefits of aggression. The cost of aggression must not be confined to the victims of aggression .... Deterrence has been supported because deterrence works. Nuclear deterrence and collective defense have preserved peace in Europe .... Clearly neither improvement in the nature of man nor strengthening of the international order have made war less frequent or less brutal." On the discussion above, see Stansfield Turner, "Missions of the United States Navy," *Naval War College Review*, March–April 1974, p. 1ff., for the naval missions used as analogies.

6

Policy Implications

16
Space and Security: Policy Implications

ROBERT L. PFALTZGRAFF, JR.

Technology has always exercised a direct influence upon the conduct of warfare and the development of commercial activity. As long as technology favored the projection of power over the oceans, those states most fully able to build and deploy naval forces were preeminent. The advent of the technological means for rapid movement of large forces over land, and subsequently for flight through the earth's atmosphere, transformed not only the ways in which war could be waged, but also the hierarchy of states possessing the requisite military means. The Industrial Revolution altered drastically the conduct of warfare as well as the economic structures of states. Those states possessing the most advanced technologies and industrial-economic systems became also the great military powers of the twentieth century. Thus there has existed an inextricable relationship between technology and the utilization, both for military and civilian purposes, of the earth's surfaces—maritime and land—as well as the surrounding atmosphere and exosphere. Such a frame of reference emerges from the analysis of historic technological-geo-strategic-economic relationships. Clearly, the existence of technologies for the transport of formerly earthbound objects, human and physical, into outer space has implications for both military and civilian activities at least as great as those changes that accompanied the great technological innovations of the past.

Although the authors of preceding chapters furnish ample evidence of the extent to which space has already become vitally important, especially for surveillance, communications, reconnaisance, and verification, much of our focus has been on its emerging and future potential. Hans Mark distinguished between the present use of space for a variety of national security activities, including communication and warning in, for example, crisis management, as well as the highly profitable commercial enterprise in space associated with communications satellites. Beyond its military utility for terrestrial defense, space will become an arena for defense and for commercial-industrial activity on a far more extended scale. Numerous advantages were cited in preceding chapters: the lack of gravity, sterile conditions, virtually inexhaustible supplies of minerals, and solar energy. As in previous eras of technological advance that ushered in wholly new commercial-industrial activities and military needs and capabilities and enhanced the importance of certain geographical areas, so will space make necessary adjustments of radical proportions in our thinking about military doctrine, geopolitical relationships, defense capabilities, arms control, government-industry relations, access to resources, and possibly the colonization of space. Throughout the volume an effort has been made to address such issues and to assess their broad implications for public policy and for political relationships and defense.

In this respect, preceding chapters have addressed the likely impact of space upon military doctrine. It was held to be necessary to develop a military doctrine to take account of space. The prerequisite for such a doctrine is an understanding of the particular sectors in space that will be strategically of the greatest importance. In the United States there has been an absence of serious doctrinal discussion of the utilization of space. Instead, technology has been the determining influence upon whatever space doctrine now exists in the United States. Addressing this question, Marc Vaucher set forth the concept of gravity wells—zones of least resistance—which will provide the greatest potential for maneuver, for the location of space structures, and for movement in space. If this analysis is correct, the key to the control and utilization of space, in geopolitical terms having direct antecedents in, for example, the terrestrial maritime chokepoints, would in the future lie in the ability of one state or another to place its spaced-based assets in positions to control the lines of communication in cislunar and translunar space.

Although several contributors addressed specifically the role of the Soviet Union in space, a pervasive theme of this volume is the importance attached by the Soviet Union to the utilization of space for military purposes. Because the Soviet Union emphasizes the primacy of the military applications of technologies in space, it follows that the program of the Soviet Union falls within a military organizational framework. The Soviet space establishment, sharply in contrast with that of the United States, consists of military personnel from top to bottom. If the Soviet space program were not a part of its military policy, it would probably not have access as it does to resources on a preferential basis. The Politburo has ultimate responsibility for the establishment of goals and priorities, the funding, and the overall organizational framework for the Soviet space program. Within the Politburo, the minister of defense is given primary control over space programs as a necessary component of defense. To assess the space program of the Soviet Union in organizational terms is to examine in a broader sense the Soviet structure for the conduct of scientific research and the application of technology to needs determined by the state to be important.

Although there are substantial gaps in our knowledge of the Soviet space program, efforts are known to have been made to achieve greater coordination within and among the various state ministries, industries, and technologies engaged in space activities. While the Russian penchant for secrecy may have had a detrimental effect to the extent that it has impaired the flow of scientific information among the various institutes and other organizations engaged in research in the Soviet Union, there is nevertheless no lack of coordination between the space program of the Soviet Union and its overall national security policy, and the Soviet Union appears to be pursuing a major program in space research designed to produce maximum gains in the military sector. The Soviet Union launches more satellites per year than does the United States, and most of them have military missions, although Soviet satellites have shorter lives and therefore must be replaced more frequently than their American counterparts. Whatever its military and scientific purposes, the Soviet space program has as an important political purpose to produce spectacular and highly visible results to convey the image of the Soviet Union as a state on the frontier of high technology. As Marcia Smith suggested (see appendix 2), the Soviet Union is engaged not only in earth orbital projects, with which the world has become familiar since the first Sputnik in 1957, but also in research for eventual manned planetary exploration. In the military sector, the Soviet Union has developed space programs such as a fractional orbital bombardment system, radar ocean surveillance satellites, and an antisatellite device, in which the United States presently has no comparable program. Elaborating upon the military focus of the Soviet space program, Clarence Robinson pointed to the testimony of the undersecretary of defense for research and engineering in early 1982 that the Soviet Union could have in operation by 1990 a permanently manned orbital space station capable of striking ground, sea, and airborne targets from space. Moreover, the Soviet Union is said to be more advanced than the United States in the development of directed energy weapons, including particle beam and high-energy laser devices, which could have military uses in space and in terrestrial warfare. Their initial purpose would be the destruction of satellites, but they could eventually be deployed against such targets as ballistic missiles, high-flying aircraft, and fleets at sea. Addressing the broader frameworks and assumptions, respectively, of the United States and the Soviet Union, Colonel Frederick Giessler suggested that the fundamentally different approaches of the superpowers to technology are derived from deeply rooted societal asymmetries. Moreover, the Soviet Union integrates intelligence gathered from the "open society" with intelligence gained by technical means. The Soviet Union designs capabilities, for space and other uses, in order to achieve specific goals. As Uri Ra'anan pointed out, there has emerged in Soviet military writings a doctrine on space, which will be used increasingly for the defense of the Soviet Union and its allies. From the Soviet perspective, clearly, future military operations will have space as an important arena. Therefore, Soviet programs encompass: the building of strategic offensive systems both to conduct warfare in space and to attack terrestrial targets; the neutralization of the space systems of other countries; and the building of space weapons as an adjunct to the existing military services. Given the importance attached to the achievement of surprise in warfare—a recurrent theme in Soviet military literature—the deployment of a Soviet antisatellite system since the late 1970s may represent only the prelude to a far more extensive space effort to be mounted by the Soviet Union in the years ahead.

In this volume, an assessment of Soviet antisatellite capabilities furnished the basis for an examination of problems of space-based asset vulnerabilities. It was generally acknowledged that the question of the survivability of systems deployed in space must be addressed. According to Robert B. Giffen, space system survivability could be enhanced by a mix of approaches, all of which have their analogies, counterparts, and antecedents in the techniques available for the protection of terrestrial capabilities: hardening; proliferation, and deception; mobility and maneuver; and the ability to replace rapidly those systems destroyed. The need for a comprehensive strategy for space system survivability was said to be sufficiently important that the United States should establish, within the Department of Defense, an Executive Agency for Space.

Central to the utilization of space both for military and civilian purposes is the deployment of technologies for communications, intelligence, and verification. Without satellite systems in orbit, the United States would find it impossible to maintain existing strategic nuclear capabilities. The destruction of surveillance, communications, and early warning satellite systems would render unviable American strategic nuclear forces within prevailing doctrinal principles. By the same token, the deployment of new generation satellite systems can enhance greatly the ability of the United States to track Soviet MIRV reentry vehicles and augment intelligence collection capabilities, perhaps as an alternative, if not a supplement, to ground-based monitoring stations. According to Patrick Friel, the deployment of a space-based sensor system could provide the basis for a limited ballistic missile defense of the United States. Moreover, data obtainable from the active and passive sensors on environmental satellites could enhance our means for monitoring the earth's resources and environment. It was suggested that such technologies, in their environmental monitoring functions, might be made available either on a national basis or as part of an international organization. A worldwide monitoring system to provide information on environmental problems would be less controversial, of course, than one that observed and disseminated information on military buildups and potential international crises. The general principle that may be adduced from the emergence of space-based technologies is that information about earthbound activities is likely to be more available, although not necessarily in the kinds and amounts of data that would keep pace with developments in military technologies.

Strategic defense was held to constitute one important dimension of technologies for space. This includes the potential afforded by the utilization of technologies deployed in space for the destruction of a ballistic missile. The ability of either superpower, it was suggested, to destroy a ballistic missile in the boost phase of its launch, and only less so in midcourse, would afford the means to protect all or at least a large portion of its homeland from nuclear attack. In his chapter, Wallace E. Kirkpatrick pointed to the feasibility of, and the need for, a coherent offense/defense strategy based upon an evolutionary approach that would include conventional low-altitude terminal systems in the present decade, as well as layered, nonnuclear systems to operate in the endosphere and the exoatmosphere in the 1990s, with space-based directed energy weapons to be deployed early in the next century.

Barry J. Smernoff held that, as a result of technologies that are presently available or that will soon be feasible, the United States and the Soviet Union will have the means to deploy a defense against strategic weapons. The present offense-dominant strategic environment could be transformed by the building of strategic defense capabilities, together with superpower agreement, as envisaged in the arms-reduction proposals of the Reagan administration, to cut substantially on a symmetrical basis the strategic forces of the United States and the Soviet Union. Thus it was suggested that a coherent U.S. strategy for space, together with the establishment of a lasting position of technological superiority in space, could enhance greatly the national security of the United States and make a major contribution to the global strategic-military environment. Among those who addressed strategic defense and space-based systems, there appeared to be a high level of consensus on the concept itself, with disagreement only on the time and level of technological effort that would be needed to build them.

To what extent, it was asked, are space operations likely to differ militarily from air operations, just as man's ability to use the earth's atmosphere for defense represented a sharp departure from the needs and characteristics of land and maritime warfare? Closely related was the question of whether space constitutes a set of military missions in its own right, or whether space is simply another medium to augment existing roles and responsibilities. To answer such a question is to set forth criteria for evaluating the doctrines and capabilities, as well as the organizational structures, to be evolved for the U.S. military space program. Closely related to the function of the organizational structure for the overall U.S. program for the military uses of space is the Space Command created in 1982 to integrate the space activities of the United States Air Force. Major Joseph E. Justin suggested that if the long-term objective of the United States is the utilization of space for its own value, the command requirements are likely to differ from those that would be appropriate if space were viewed simply as an adjunct to terrestrial security needs.

Among the contributors there seemed to be general agreement that manned space vehicles would be necessary for the U.S. space program, especially as it evolved beyond simply the support of terrestrial military and civilian functions, such as communications, navigation, reconnaissance, and surveillance. In complex operations in space, as on earth, there is no substitute for human judgment. We were said to be entering an era in which largely passive systems will eventually be replaced by the means to initiate hostile action in space. Although it is widely acknowledged that space-based systems, like most other technologies located elsewhere, will be vulnerable to various forms of attack, nevertheless it will become both possible and necessary to deploy space defense systems to protect space assets and counter hostile actions. Although we are on the verge of remarkable breakthroughs in electronic technologies, the role of human beings in space will increase. According to David Leinweber, the tasks best suited for crews are those that can be conducted in relatively safe environments. Such tasks should be nonrepetitive and relatively complex, calling for decisions and intuitive ability not easily accomplished by machines. The greater the degree of involvement in space, the greater the likelihood that manned vehicles in space will be used. This, in turn, it was suggested, will provide the need for the acquisition of a broader base of knowledge than now exists about such questions as the relative economics and abilities of crews performing construction and heavy maintenance tasks in space, together with other problems associated with prolonged human activity outside the earth's atmosphere and gravitational field.

To a greater extent than any other nation, the United States has pursued programs for both civilian and military uses of space. On a scale that included, on the one hand, the principally civilian programs of Western Europe and Japan and, on the other, the military-oriented Soviet program, the United States would fall perhaps at midpoint. This condition, reflected in the U.S. organizational structure for space policy, is manifested in other ways that were examined in this volume. These include the potential for private-sector exploitation of space, leading in turn to a review of issue areas that may be analogous to the problems of the present Law of the Sea Treaty negotiations. Issues such as the rights of users to physical space resources based upon the mechanisms of a free market, together with an alternate approach to space as a "common heritage of mankind," will arise. Clearly, the incentives to explore and exploit space-based resources, determined not only by opportunity costs set by the market but also by the actions of governments, will have a profound effect upon the role of private enterprise in space.

Within the United States, there exist numerous organizational relationships between government and industry. In general, the private industrial sector in the United States is responsible for providing technologies and know-how to the government under contract for military and civilian space programs. In addition, official organizations, such as NASA, have provided services to private industry, and the U.S. government has entered into joint ventures with U.S. companies. Last but not least, as John B. Gantt suggests, the Communications Satellite Corporation (COMSAT) furnishes an example of a privately owned company established under federal legislation in 1962 for the establishment of a global communications satellite system. Given the complexity of space technologies and other factors of a scientific and political-economic-military nature, the experience of COMSAT may be instructive in assessing the need and the prospects for a future industry-government collaboration in space-related activities.

The history of the American space program, surveyed by Bruno Augenstein (see appendix 1), revealed numerous changes in organizational structure and, in particular, the emphasis that successive administrations have placed upon separate efforts for the military and the "peaceful uses of space." While the military programs for space were lodged in the military services, the National Aeronautics and Space Administration (NASA) was established in 1958 to pursue the peaceful space program. The question that remains unresolved is the appropriate structure for the conduct of U.S. space activities in the late twentieth century. Technological opportunities are said to have outstripped our organizational framework for exploitation. In this perspective, the most pressing need is for the formation of a national space plan which, in itself, should make possible the evaluation of the relative merits of one or another technology and mission. The question of appropriate organizational structures for space programs was addressed by John M. Logsdon, who concluded that the Space Act of 1958, which separated civilian and military programs, remains valid in the 1980s. In this view NASA should not be linked more closely to national security efforts in space. Instead, NASA should be revitalized in order to assure a separate and vigorous governmental space program outside the immediate national security arena.

The legal implications of the use of space for civilian or military purposes are apparent. These include the potential role, as well as likely problems, of arms control in space. Although several proposals and draft treaties have been developed, Harry H. Almond, Jr. concluded that the idea of a weapons-free zone and the demilitarization of outer space appear to be infeasible because outer space provides a major strategic environment for enhancing the security of a nation. Outer space, no less than the terrestrial environment, cannot be clearly separated from national security. The relative ease of movement and the utility of space for reconnaisance and other national security functions will make the conclusion of arms-control agreements on space at least as difficult as those associated with the limitation of weapons on the earth's surface have been. For these reasons, as well as the fact that demilitarization and weapons-free zones have not proven to be feasible in the past, the exclusion of weapons from space is not seen as promising. Thus, it is possible to set forth several categories of space-related arms-control issues, all of which will present formidable, if not insurmountable, problems: (1) weapons launched into space from earth; (2) weapons launched within space from platforms located in space; and (3) the verifiability of the foregoing kinds of systems in any arms-control agreement. To the extent that space is seen either as an extension of the terrestrial conflict arena or as a conflict arena in its own right, the problems of arms control in space will be magnified. Conversely, the lower the priority attached to space as a dimension of national security, the easier would be the conclusion of an arms-control agreement which, by definition, would be peripheral to a nation's security needs.

At least as complex is the state of international law as it relates to military activities in space. According to S. Neil Hosenball, except for some specific prohibitions on the use of outer space for military purposes, there is a lack of agreed understanding of what is peaceful, military, nonmilitary, aggressive, and nonaggressive. Moreover, certain technologies for space have both military and civilian applications. Activities that are nonaggressive in peacetime suddenly acquire aggressive dimensions during wartime. Thus it will be difficult to separate military activities in space from the broader dimensions of arms control and to distinguish always between the civilian and military dimensions of space programs. The development of an acceptable body of space law will confront difficulties, it would seem, at least as formidable as those facing international law in its terrestrial manifestations.

Although the principal focus of this volume is on the space programs of the superpowers, both Western Europe and Japan have embarked upon active programs, especially for the commercial exploitation of space technologies. Having accepted French leadership in the development of launch vehicles, Western Europe is concentrating its collective efforts on satellites for navigation, communications, meteorology, and related sectors designed to provide commercial benefits. As John Hoagland suggested, the European Space Agency represents a viable multilateral framework that has already made possible the achievement of an impressive level of technological collaboration within Western Europe and, to a lesser extent, between this European entity and the United States; Skylab, in which Western Europe has invested more than one billion dollars, is now the most tangible evidence of such joint transatlantic action. Nevertheless, the gap between the United States and its allies in the military uses of space holds the potential of creating a new doctrinal divergence on, for example, strategic defense, as the superpowers increase their use of space for military purposes.

Similarly, Japan has launched a modest, but promising, space program whose purpose is to exploit commercial opportunities associated with the utilization of space for such purposes as land utilization research; agricultural, forestry, and fisheries resource surveillance; and environmental monitoring. From such an analysis, it may be inferred, Japan is likely to make use of space in the generation ahead in its quest to place itself at the forward edge of the technological frontier, as it has in the building of semiconductors and diversification of energy supply.

Numerous policy implications flow from the preceding chapters. Here it is possible only to synthesize some of the many proposals that were stated in explicit form or were implicit in the analysis and conclusions of the various authors, without suggesting that all policy implications were endorsed by all contributors.

1. Because both the United States and the Soviet Union can be expected to regard space as an arena for competition, the United States must give greater attention to the development of a space doctrine and a set of long-range objectives, together with a program for space, than it has thus far. The United States should make a renewed commitment to world leadership in space technology. The United States should build upon the present technological advantage demonstrated in the successful missions already conducted by the Space Shuttle.

2. The United States should develop a balanced military space program containing a mix of shuttle fleet and expendable launchers, manned and unmanned space systems, and survivable systems, as well as an antisatellite deployment capability.

3. In the U.S. space program, high priority should be attached to the pursuit of an active program in research for space-based ballistic missile defense and its deployment as soon as it becomes feasible.

4. Major attention should be given to the development of technologies designed to protect U.S. space-based assets and to counter hostile actions. The survivability of U.S. space-based assets could be enhanced by technologies designed to increase satellite maneuverability; the deployment of decoys; and the reduction in the radar and infrared/optical signature of satellites. Space-based systems employing large numbers of less sophisticated vehicles were said to be less vulnerable than those employing small numbers of more sophisticated satellites.

5. The United States should consider the adequacy of its bureaucratic-administrative structure for space programs. This includes the organization of space-related programs within the military services and the relationship between each of the components of space and the overall long-term objectives of the United States in space. Separate programs for military and civilian uses of space should be maintained, although the defense of space-based industrial assets may

eventually become a military security concern of the United States and other powers with such infrastructures.

6. The United States should make use of existing experience in industry-government collaboration, as in COMSAT, to promote peaceful space activities and to encourage the development by the private sector of a major role in space activities.

7. An effort should be made to evolve an international framework for the commercial-industrial exploitation of space. In such an organization, member states might hold shares and receive income from the auctioning of user rights to the space resources to the highest bidders. Such a framework could offer the prospect for efficient utilization of space resources and the potential satisfaction of any agreed upon equity principle.

8. Attention should be given to the development of collaborative mechanisms and practices between the United States and Western Europe and encompassing other states, especially Japan. The United States should develop space programs, on an international basis, with our allies. If future generations of U.S. strategic systems based in space can offer benefits to alliance security, then the twin issues of alliance burden-sharing and work-sharing should be addressed. The cost of research and development for space-based systems, the benefits that may be derived from transnational industrial-technological collaboration, and the security problems attending space industrialization will create a series of problems calling for joint action. The development by the Soviet Union of space-based military capabilities would leave the principally civilian space assets of U.S. allies in Western Europe and Japan vulnerable in the absence of an American commitment to their defense. To enter into such a discussion is to extend to space a set of issue areas in alliance relations that have proven often to be interrelated in their earth-bound dimensions. The United States should develop a joint program with its closest allies, especially NATO, for surveillance systems and for the deployment of a manned space station.

Thus space constitutes an important frontier for technologically advanced societies and confronts the United States with important choices in its national security policy in the years ahead. Both for the United States and the Soviet Union, the concept of global strategy is in the process of being broadened to encompass exospheric dimensions. To the present emphasis upon such national security activities as command, control, communications, surveillance, and verification will be added numerous other military and commercial programs and activities. The future holds the prospect that space will be transformed from a simple adjunct to earth-bound endeavors to become an arena of growing importance in its own right and a vast frontier for human activity. If this is the potential or likely course of events, its implications for mankind, and for the terrestrial international system and its constituent elements, may prove to be as profound as the transformations resulting from the age of exploration that produced the Renaissance, the Industrial Revolution, and ultimately the global system of the late twentieth century.

EPILOGUE:
THE HIGH FRONTIER OF STRATEGIC DEFENSE

The proposal for an accelerated program of research for a defense against nuclear missiles contained in President Reagan's speech of 22 March 1983 holds out important opportunities for the United States that would transform nuclear strategy from deterrence of nuclear war based upon the destruction of an adversary to a concept based upon deterrence by the assurance of survival. If neither the United States nor the Soviet Union could threaten credibly to destroy the other, the haunting specter of nuclear annihilation would have been exorcised from the minds of peoples here and elsewhere. To be sure, other forms of warfare would remain, but mankind would be relieved of the possibility that somehow nuclear war, whether by conscious calculation or by accident, would end civilized life.

The idea of a space-based strategic defense represents a compelling alternative to a nuclear environment founded, as it has been since the advent of such weapons, upon dominance of the offense. As long as it was more cost effective to build additional nuclear missiles and warheads to penetrate any strategic defense that an adversary might construct, it was not feasible to expend substantial national resources on defenses against offensive forces. This was the premise upon which the ABM Treaty of 1972 was based. Although the United States was then capable of deploying an imperfect strategic defense, it was reasoned that, by largely forgoing such a system, the Soviet incentive to build larger missiles and greater numbers of more accurate warheads to penetrate the American ABM would be removed.

In retrospect, the fatal flaw in the SALT concept of the 1970s stemmed from the inability of the United States, having been limited drastically by the ABM Treaty of its ability to defend the most accurate portion of the Triad of the U.S. strategic forces, to obtain effective limits on the growth of Soviet offensive forces. In fact, the huge Soviet buildup after 1972—three new generation ICBMs deployed in 10 variants and two new classes of submarines with four types of missiles—gave to the Soviet Union the means, in missile numbers and throwweight, and in warhead numbers and accuracy, to threaten the ICBM and strategic bomber forces of the United States, as well as the command, control, and communications structure of our sea-based force. The expansion of Soviet forces followed a pattern that might have been expected if in fact the United States had deployed a strategic defense with then existing technologies. Opponents of the deployment of ABM could have argued, as surely they would have, that the United States had driven the Soviet Union into an unprecedented strategic force buildup designed to saturate and penetrate the American strategic defense. A decade and more later, in the absence of any such American strategic defense, evidence of the Soviet strategic force buildup that has occurred is abundant. With its predecessors having failed in SALT II to achieve deep cuts in Soviet strategic forces despite the U.S. nondeployment of a strategic defense, the Reagan administration entered the Strategic Arms Reduction Talks with its promised strategic force modernization program as the principal incentive to the Soviet Union to negotiate symmetrical reductions in nuclear arsenals.

In the last decade both the United States and the Soviet Union have made substantial progress in technologies for strategic defense. This includes radars, electronics and micro-miniaturization, interceptor missiles, and nonnuclear means of destroying an incoming missile. There is promise, moreover, that by means of high-energy lasers and particle beam technologies, the offense-dominant environment of the recent past could be transformed so that it would no longer be easier for an opponent to build more missiles to overwhelm a defense than for a defender to construct the means to thwart such an attack. It is presently technologically feasible to deploy a strategic defense to protect, for example, all or a portion of the land-based ballistic missile force of the United States from a nuclear attack that would destroy it. The technologies to which President Reagan referred—space-based lasers and particle beams— could attack a ballistic missile from space just after launch, before it had achieved maximum speed outside the earth's gravitational field, and before its warheads had been released against their intended targets. Although such a system would probably not provide full protection for a city against nuclear attack, it would enhance the certainty that neither side could destroy the nuclear forces of the other side. It would render even more unlikely the prospect that smaller nuclear forces could be used against the states possessing strategic defense. Hence the incentive for nuclear proliferation would be reduced, especially if the United States could extend such a defensive strategic shield to protect allies and friends.

Our arms control policy has failed to place effective constraints on the types and levels of strategic offensive forces. The key to symmetrical reductions in such forces lies in a changed cost/effectiveness ratio between offensive and defensive forces. With the availability of technology for a strategic offense, the United States would find itself in a more advantageous position to negotiate a treaty to reduce Soviet offensive strategic systems which, in any event, would no longer be useful at high levels if they could not overwhelm the strategic defense. We would have established a strategic framework with a clear relationship to arms control. Strategy would provide the basis for technological development, rather than the reverse, as often has been the case, with strategy having been based instead upon available technology. The course which President Reagan has proposed represents a plausible alternative to the idea of a nuclear freeze, which would lock the United States into a position of inferiority in most static measures of nuclear weapons, while doing nothing to enhance nuclear force survivability upon which the deterrence of nuclear war is vitally dependent. Deterrence by means of strategic defense in the high Frontier of Space represents a challenge worthy of American creative energies in strategy, politics, and technology.

Appendixes

Appendix 1

Evolution of the U.S. Military Space Program, 1945–1960: Some Key Events in Study, Planning, and Program Development

BRUNO W. AUGENSTEIN

This appendix will trace the conceptual phase of the military space program, the period in which major studies were undertaken that formed the basis for subsequent developments. Some of these early studies proved remarkably prescient, and a few are still worth reading today; for example, the Rand Feed Back Studies of 1954. Little official or high-level enthusiasm accompanied the early proposals flowing from the studies. In many ways, it was the personal enthusiasm of a few individuals that made the difference.

Naturally, such enthusiasm would probably have been to little avail had not two other major events taken place: the U.S. decision to pursue an aggresive ICBM program, spurred in 1954 by key ICBM development proposals from The Rand Corporation and from SMEC (von Neumann Committee), and the roughly concurrent increased U.S. awareness of the Soviet Union as a major power, whose policies required that the United States develop new means for gathering intelligence. This early period closes with the decision to pursue the WS 117L program, whose main progenitor was the Rand Feed Back study. A number of people associated with the Feed Back study played key roles in WS 117L and later associated developments. The impetus given to satellite work by Rand studies of this era seems mostly forgotten now, but it is doubtful if the programs could have obtained a running start without them. (This chapter does not cover every space issue considered by the United States government, since many early deliberations remain classified.)

The following years, 1956–60, were critically important in the U.S. military space program. Once the decision to undertake the basic WS 117L program had been made, program proposals began to proliferate rapidly. This proliferation was spurred by the Soviet Sputnik launch in October 1957. The U.S. military space program rapidly became very complex. At the same time, there was much "backing and filling" in the military space program. The thorny issues of program allocations to the military departments surfaced into full visibility. Many different organizational approaches to managing the space programs were proposed, within the Air Force, the Joint Chiefs of Staff, the office of the secretary of defense, and at higher levels. The emergence of the Advanced Research Projects Agency (ARPA) as an overall manager of Department of Defense space programs took place. For a short time, while NASA was being established, ARPA managed the entire national space program. Then program management again devolved to the individual services. Within the Air Force much controversy surrounded the issue of proper organization to manage programs. The full scope of the U.S. Air Force ambitions and goals did not prove achievable because of higher-level decisions. Nevertheless, the period essentially decided the basic shape of the programs of subsequent years; for those programs that survived, fundamental policy and developmental decisions were made.

EARLY HISTORY AND ORIGINS: 1945

Early space interests in the post-World War II United States were spurred by a May 1945 report in which Werner von Braun discussed German views on prospects and potentials of satellites. Navy interest in the report was responsible partly for a request in December 1945 to study satellite vehicle potential.

Air Force interest in and awareness of space was formalized in two reports in 1945. In November 1945, the Arnold Report concluded that the design of space ships "is all but practicable today." Later, in a December 1945 report, the Air Force discussed a proposal for "space vehicles, space bases, and persuasive devices... therein."

EARLY STUDIES: 1946–47

In 1946, the Navy proposed combined sponsorship of satellite programs to the Air Force. The Air Force, however, assigned a major satellite study to Project Rand, which was completed in May 1946, as evidence of an independent Air Force program rather than a joint Air Force-Navy program. In July 1946, the Navy assigned contracts to Aerojet, North American Aviation (NAA), and Martin for propulsion and vehicle engineering design work for satellites. These Navy design studies were completed in 1947. In March 1948, the RDB established the "technical feasibility" of earth satellite vehicles, but claimed that no military scientific utility had yet been shown. The RDB proposed that the Navy continue limited development of engines and tanks. In the summer of 1948, however, because of budget problems, the Navy relinquished immediate interest in satellite work. Nevertheless, this early postwar interest in satellites was reflected in December 1948, when the annual report of the secretary of defense noted research on "earth satellite vehicles."

RESULTS OF THE EARLY STUDIES

The accomplishments and prescience of these early satellite studies were in many ways remarkable. The navy work showed emphasis on hydrogen-oxygen propulsion, pressurized structual tanks, and single-stage concepts. Both Martin and NAA developed reasonably detailed design and layout studies for satellite vehicles with substantial payloads (up to 2,000 pounds). In addition, work on nuclear rocket and ramjet propulsion was undertaken.

The Air Force efforts reflect equally serious analysis. The Rand report contained thorough preliminary scientific and engineering analyses of satellite feasibility. Concepts studied included multistage vehicles, meteor problems, reentry considerations, scientific applications, detailed trajectory analyses, and military uses for assisting missile guidance and for reconnaissance, weather surveillance, and communications; the potential impact and significance of the satellite project were also assessed and highlighted.

In February 1947, Rand published a multivolume detailed study amplifying the 1946 work. Accordingly, in September 1947, the U.S. Air Force requested an AMC evaluation of the Rand reports of February 1947. The December 1947 response of AMC verified feasibility, but again had questions of utilization. Doubts were voiced that funding would become available at the appropriate level. AMC suggested establishment of a satellite project to prepare specifications, requirements, and scheduling. The agency noted that guided missile development had priority, but proposed starting on satellite component developments.

FORMULATION OF USAF POLICY AND MORE INTENSIVE STUDIES: 1948–53

General Vandenberg's policy statement (January 1948) was the first clear service statement of space program interest: "USAF . . . has logical responsibility for satellite." The January 1948 policy was put into effect by authorizing Rand to do research and to let subcontracts in the field, even though the military worth of satellites was not yet fully recognized. The Air Force became the sole service authorized to expend funds on satellite vehicle studies.

In November 1950, Rand received support for research to demonstrate the military utility of satellite reconnaissance. Two major Rand reports were issued in April 1951, concerning the utility of a satellite vehicle for reconnaissance and the feasibility of weather reconnaissance from a satellite vehicle. These reports discussed "pioneer reconnaissance," with extensive earth coverage at resolutions (utilizing television) of between 40 and 200 feet, in a 1,000-pound payload and at a vehicle weight of 74,000 pounds. A new U.S. awareness of Soviet military potential—reflected in atomic weapons and related vehicle developments, for example—had posed new requirements for technical intelligence-gathering; the Rand reports were therefore published at an opportune time.

The U.S. Air Force, with RDB approval, authorized Rand to recommend development work in reconnaissance satellite programs—now known as Project Feed Back—in 1951. Air Force reorganization, such as the creation of ARDC, brought more emphasis on research and development aspects of the Air Force mission.

PROJECT FEED BACK ACCOMPLISHMENTS

The USAF-Rand studies of the 1950s—Project Feed Back—produced a series of important results. In November 1951, the Air Force secured AEC cooperation on research into satellite nuclear power sources. In May 1953, the Air Force directed additional feasibility studies on a satellite nuclear power source, and requested the research and development command to begin active direction of the Feed Back program. By September 1953 Rand had recommended "letting a system design contract within one year, and proceeding to a full system development program."

ARDC endorsed that recommendation and developed a unified management scheme. The command established Project 409-40, "Satellite Component Study," and system number WS 117L was assigned.

FROM PROJECT TO SYSTEM: 1954–56

In early 1954, the Rand Corporation and the von Neumann Committee proposed revisions to the ICBM program. These proposals started effort on the large boosters necessary for many versions of militarily useful satellites. The sudden emergence of new evidence on Soviet advances in defense technology demonstrated that new intelligence means were of paramount importance if the accelerating Soviet programs were to be monitored. One result was the initiation of the U-2 program in 1954, which produced an operational system in 1956. At the time, the useful life of the U-2 was judged to be relatively short, because Soviet air defense was considered likely to deny free overflight. Improving the technical intelligence systems was a major goal, and satellites appeared to be a promising means for gaining critical information.

The milestone Rand reports of March 1954 refined the reconnaissance satellite studies. Satellites, the reports concluded, were of vital strategic interest to the United States. Rand suggested a development program lasting seven years at a cost of from $165 million to $330 million. A recommendation that the Air Force continue the program on a full-scale basis was the central point of the Project Feed Back Report.

Project Feed Back was a landmark study that discussed many operational aspects of the program not previously treated, such as development, scheduling, and cost estimates. For these reasons, the Feed Back studies formed a useful preliminary blueprint for the early space program. The studies are still worth reading today for their conceptual and planning foresight.

In May 1954, concurrent with the ICBM decisions, ARDC was directed to study the potential applications of Feed Back, and by March 1955 formal approval had been granted for development of a reconnaissance satellite system. The development charter paralleled Rand's conclusions and called for visual-band reconnaissance, specialized data, and weather data to determine the status of a potential enemy's war-making capability. An operational availability date of 1965 was specified.

By November 1955, Martin and Lockheed were conducting studies aimed at further definition of time and technology requirements for satellite developments under the nickname of "Pied Piper." By early 1956 the program had been transferred from WADC to WDD under General Schriever, and the detailed outlines of the ' project were well established. Finally, on 29 October 1956, Lockheed was awarded the development contract for WS 117L. The military satellite program was now committed to development and testing of actual satellites.

SCIENTIFIC SATELLITE VERSION OF WS 117L

As early as 1954 and 1955, a number of Rand studies had stressed needs for an instrumented test vehicle for space research. In August 1954, Congress approved U.S. participation in the International Geophysical Year (IGY), and launchings of small satellite vehicles were recommended. As a result, in early 1955, the Army and Navy proposed a joint satellite effort, Project Orbiter.

In May 1955, however, National Security Council Directive 5520 stated that no missile intended for military purposes could be used for IGY satellites by the United States. The directive supported President Eisenhower's "peaceful uses of space" concept. Two potential satellites—the Army-Navy Redstone and the Air Force Atlas—conflicted with the directive, so the Navy Viking-based system, Vanguard, had to be chosen.

NSC Directive 5520 notwithstanding, ARDC was requested in August 1955 to establish a scientific satellite program integrated with WS 117L, to satisfy IGY requirements. By January 1956 WDD proposed to orbit a 3,500-pound satellite capable of conducting a number of specific scientific experiments by August 1958, but because the satellite would have used an Atlas C booster, the program was not endorsed. In any event, the Atlas satellite ((Project Score) was finally launched in December 1958, mainly for demonstrative purposes.

OTHER AIR FORCE SPACE-ORIENTED PROJECTS THROUGH 1956

Several Air Force projects had their beginnings in the early period, but either fell by the wayside or were greatly modified as time went on.

Development and flights of the X series of research aircraft, destined to gather valuable "near-space" information, began with the 1944 contract to build the X-1 and led to the X-15.

Boost-glide vehicles were discussed by Rand in 1948. The Air Force finally contracted in 1954 with Bell for further study, and in May 1955 proposed a hypersonic strategic bombardment system. In 1956 the Air Force asked Bell to study bomber systems (Robo) and reconnaissance systems (Brass Bell), and ARDC proposed a research vehicle system called Hywards. In 1957 studies were requested to consolidate these into one system (Dyna-Soar), to lead to global circumnavigation capabilities in three subsequent phases.

Man-in-Space (MIS) proposals were based on early and mid-1950s space biology, balloon, and research craft experience. This background resulted in an ARDC proposal as early as February 1956 for a man-inhabited ICBM capsule. In December 1956 Avco and Martin submitted unsolicited proposals for a Manned Ballistic Rocket Research System, responsive to an Air Force plan approved in May 1956. The Air Force planned to contract for an effort of this sort in April 1957. However, no funds were then available.

None of these projects had any substantial impact on the use of space for military purposes. The projects are indicative, nevertheless, of the great diversity of space plans in the late 1950s. These plans were for the most part aborted or modified by policy decisions, funding constraints, or both.

Even though a military satellite program was underway in 1956, various advanced concepts were still being formulated by early contributors to the space program planning period, such as Rand. At the same time, events soon moved to upset and modify these early plans, and the space program of 1958–60 differed significantly from that undertaken in 1956.

In 1956 Rand and others proposed three projects of potential military significance: the Advanced Reconnaissance System (ARS); the Man-in-Space (MIS) Project; and the Ballistic Systems Research and Supporting System (BALWARDS). The latter, using Atlas, Aerobee, and Sergeant missiles, looked toward landings on the moon and flights in the vicinity of Venus and Mars. Both ARS and MIS were approved as possible projects. The Air Staff also approved BALWARDS. In May 1957 the office of the secretary of the Air Force deleted the interplanetary missions. BALWARDS instead became the near-space project known as the Ballistic Research and Test System (BRATS).

On 4 October 1957, newspapers around the world announced the 184-pound Russian Sputnik. National and international comments on the Soviet victory were not complimentary to the United States. Throughout the American press there was general condemnation of partial measures, hit-or-miss planning, and confused organization. A number of high-ranking U.S. officials attempted to belittle the Russian satellite, but at no level within the Air Force, the Department of Defense, or the administration had there appeared a statement of the ultimate objectives of an American space program.

A committee of distinguished scientists and Air Force officers, headed by Dr. Edward Teller, was formed by the secretary of the Air Force to propose needed actions. The committee's report, completed on 22 October 1957, recommended a unified program, but the result was a divided program that diffused rather than focused any expanded effort.

The first major organizational development came on 7 November 1957, when the president added to the existing organizational structure by appointing Dr. James R. Killian as special assistant for science and technology. On 10 December General Putt announced the establishment of the Directorate of Astronautics, headed by Brigadier General Homer A. Boushey. The Department of Defense, however, reacted adversely to this action. By 13 December General

Putt had canceled his memorandum of 10 December. Although the Air Force remained aware of the need for strong control of space projects, chances for approval for the necessary organization remained poor.

EMERGENCE OF NEW ORGANIZATIONS: 1958

As part of the response to Sputnik, Secretary McElroy established the Advanced Research Projects Agency (ARPA) on 7 February 1958. The new office was headed by Roy W. Johnson and was authorized to direct research and development projects within the Department of Defense. In practice, ARPA reassigned projects to the military departments, other government agencies, or civilian institutions.

On 7 January 1958, the Department of Defense had asked the three services to list their proposed space projects. The Department of Defense wanted this information mainly to assist ARPA in assigning development missions among the Army, Navy, and Air Force. The Air Force interpreted the request quite differently, believing that the Department of Defense might approve a USAF space program. Two weeks later, the Air Force had assembled a program consisting of five major space systems, including Ballistic Test and Related Systems, manned hypersonic research, Dyna-Soar, the WS 117L Satellite System, and a Lunar Base System. These proposals were further divided into twenty-one major projects.

On 2 April, the president asked Congress to approve the establishment of a National Aeronautics and Space Administration (NASA) to conduct all space activities except those primarily associated with military requirements. On 20 July, the president signed the National Aeronautics and Space Act (Public Law 85-568), creating NASA. It had the effect of partitioning the space program into military and civilian segments and was the culmination of an extensive debate within the White House on the relative merits of alternative plans.

On 3 July 1958, the National Security Council (NSC) submitted to the president a policy statement on outer space. The NSC noted that Russian superiority in astronautics would create an imbalance of power in favor of the communist bloc. There were immediate military requirements for weather, communication, and other applications of satellites for additional purposes, such as maintenance and supply depots for outer space vehicles and as reconnaissance stations. The notion of space systems providing support for operational forces received the beginnings of high-level official sanction in this NSC sanction. The president signed this paper on 18 August and by midsummer 1958 the administration had established a space policy that called officially for dual civilian and military space programs. That policy remains in effect today.

THE EMERGING ROLE OF ARPA IN DEFENSE DEPARTMENT SPACE ACTIVITIES

The policies of ARPA became clearer during the spring of 1958. Johnson, with the approval of Secretary McElroy, would organize and operate the agency as a "fourth service" or possibly as a "special task force" within the Department of Defense.

Johnson's authority was further increased when the president determined that ARPA would control civilian as well as military space projects until NASA began functioning. Between 7 February and 1 October 1958, ARPA served as the "national" space agency. Many of the NASA plans depended ultimately on the programs undertaken by ARPA.

In the spring of 1958, Johnson transferred to ARPA several Air Force proposals, including Space Track, a 1.5 million-pound-thrust, single-chamber engine, reactor propulsion, the Advanced Reconnaissance System, and the three-phased satellite for man in space, along with others from the Army and Navy.

By then, ARPA had organized its space projects into four large programs, which were titled Missile Defense against ICBM, Military Reconnaissance Satellites, Developments for Application to Space Technology, and Advanced Research for Scientific Purposes.

On 28 July the president decided to emphasize the civilian space program, giving NASA such nonmilitary projects as lunar probes and scientific satellites initiated by ARPA, along with Project Vanguard. Executive Order No. 10783 began this transfer immediately after the activation of NASA on 1 October. Under this arrangement, NASA assumed responsibility for advanced research for scientific purposes, and for developments for application to space technology. NASA was also assigned projects pertaining to man in space (redesignated Project Mercury), special engines, satellite tracking, communications, meteorology, and navigation.

In September 1958, ARPA had redefined the Advanced Reconnaissance System into separate projects, with new designations. The reconnaissance aspect was renamed Sentry. The vehicle tests, biomedical flights, and recovery experiments were grouped together as Discoverer. The infrared sensing system became Midas. In the last months of 1958, ARPA assigned these three projects to Air Force organizations.

NEW U.S. AIR FORCE AND DEFENSE DEPARTMENT
INTERESTS IN SPACE: 1959–60

In the spring of 1959, significant organizational changes were made in the space program. On 13 April 1959, USAF headquarters gave the Directorate of Advanced Technology authority to coordinate within the Air Staff all USAF space activities, including those conducted for ARPA and NASA.

ARPA recommended in June a Mercury Task Force to assist NASA, and the secretary of defense proposed the reassignment of operating responsibilities for several projects, including Midas and Sentry, the latter soon to be redesignated Samos. Service views were varied. The Army and Navy wanted a Mercury Task Force and a Defense Astronautical Agency to control the space systems. The Air Force objected to both.

TRANSFER OF SPACE ACTIVITES TO THE SERVICES

In September the secretary of defense disapproved the proposed Defense Astronautical Agency and Mercury Task Force. As a substitute he designated Major General Donald N. Yates, USAF, Atlantic Missile Range commander, to direct military support for the project. Secretary McElroy reversed his established policy on ARPA and reassigned the military space program among the three services. Under this arrangement, Midas and Samos went to the Air Force. Transit, a more recently planned navigational project, went to the Navy. A Notus family of four communications satellites went to the Army.

The actual transfer of Samos and Midas occurred in late November 1959. ARPA also relinquished Project Discoverer to the Air Force as a separate action.

As early as 1958 the Air Force chief of staff had commented on the desirability of issuing preliminary long-range concepts for space operations through the medium of an Air Force Objective Series (AFOS) paper. By July 1959, AFBMD had readied a development plan for what it termed the "flag national survival communication satellite," the operational follow-up of the ARPA development program. SAC immediately supported the plan and suggested that the system offered an excellent opportunity to exploit space for peaceful purposes, with industry using the system for commercial interests. The Satellite Communications Act of 1962 and NSC Action Memorandum 338 subsequently specified the interactions between commercial and Defense Department users of satellite communications systems, as earlier envisioned by SAC.

SPACE SYSTEMS FOR DEFENSIVE ROLES

During 1959–60 the Air Force took some tentative steps toward Aerospace Defense Systems, via weapons system development for ballistic missile defense. Deputy Secretary of Defense Gates in effect spurred this action when in October 1959 he indicated that he might soon approve production of Nike Zeus. Air Force studies of ballistic missile defense had investigated three possible modes of destroying ballistic missiles: destruction during the boost (powered) phase; destruction during midcourse flight; and destruction during terminal reentry. The Air Force, with ARPA concurrence, concentrated on what appeared to be a most attractive systems concept—destruction of enemy ballistic missiles in their boost phase. This concept had an ARPA designation of BAMBI (Ballistic Missile Boost Intercept). Convair's SPAD (Space Patrol Active Defense) concept, based on a satellite equipped with infrared sensors, was initially emphasized. The plan was broadened after Ramo-Woolridge submitted a variation of this idea, called the Random Barrage System (RBS). The Air Force hoped to define a system and the component development necessary to start proving the feasibility of the total system concept, with the ultimate objective being to have an operational satellite system available by 1967.

Study of defensive measures against hostile satellites had begun earlier, in 1956, under ARDC sponsorship. In 1958, ARPA had assumed responsibility but retained ARDC as project supervisor. The steadily advancing space technology appeared to some to be a threat in the form of Soviet "bombs in orbit," possible by 1964. A capability to inspect and, if necessary, destroy any hostile satellite therefore seemed desirable or essential in the near future. In August 1959, AFBMD, in cooperation with WADC, submitted a preliminary development plan for such a space defensive system.

Dr. Herbert York approved the start of a program to demonstrate engineering feasibility of a co-orbital satellite system on 16 June 1960. Work on the prototype system was to be restricted to development, but not flight testing, of critical subsystems. Subsequent direction was that all systems emphasis focus on inspection functions, a step related to the president's "Space for Peace" program. Such a plan went to the secretary of defense on 21 July 1960, and gained approval a month later.

THE DYNA-SOAR YEARS

The Air Force and the aircraft industry had long conducted studies on the feasibility of hypersonic (Mach 5 and above) orbital flight with a manned vehicle employing boost-glide principles. These studies had been carried out earlier under such project names as Robo, Brass Bell, Bomi, and Hywards, finally culminating in Project Dyna-Soar (Dynamic Soaring). By the fall of 1958 the Air Force emphasized suborbital performance (for the specific purpose, presumably, of keeping management authority within the Air Force and away from ARPA).

By April 1959, Dr. York (DDR&E) had directed that the primary objective of Dyna-Soar I was to be the exploration of hypersonic flight at velocities up to 22,000 feet per second with a vehicle that was manned, maneuverable, launched by a booster already in production or under development, and capable of controlled landings. Secondary objectives were to be achievement of an orbital capability and provision for installing and testing military subsystems.

By fall 1959 a three-phase development plan called successively for fabrication and testing of a full-size, 5,000-mile-range glider, initially to be airdropped from a B-52 and later ground-launched with a Titan A booster. Later tests were to extend glider tests to global range and orbital velocity, using a larger booster. Finally, advanced systems were to be developed by 1967.

By November 1959 Undersecretary of the Air Force Dr. J. Charyk wanted to be sure that the critical aerodynamic, structural, and materials problems so important to the success of Dyna-Soar had been carefully considered, and allowed only a Phase Alpha to proceed. Phase Alpha results were received from Boeing in late March 1960. On 22 April, Dr. York approved the start of Dyna-Soar development and released the required fiscal Year 1960 funds. The plan was for an unmanned ground launching of a Dyna-Soar test vehicle to occur in late 1963, followed by a manned launching a year later.

QUESTIONS ON SPACE SYSTEMS AND THE 1960 U-2 INCIDENT

The reliability, life, complexity, and priority of several Samos and Midas subsystems were continuously debated. Some Defense Department officials and administration scientific advisors doubted that many of the tests would succeed and envisioned substantial savings by using less sophisticated equipment and subsystems requiring more modest ground facilities. A "fly before you buy" view took hold.

When Gary Powers's U-2 was downed over the Soviet Union on 1 May 1960, the Air Force saw the potential for increased support of the Samos-Midas-Discoverer program, and a plan was developed to exploit early data from Samos flight tests.

During the spring of 1960 and following the downing of the U-2, Congress became intimately involved in Samos-Midas progress, calling for rapid development of both space systems and voting sums far in excess of the administration's requests for Fiscal Year 1961. Even so, uncertainties and indecision on the technical and budgetary aspects of Samos and Midas continued to affect planned operational dates for the two space systems.

The Air Force, in view of its responsibilities for the Samos and Midas programs, called for the Strategic Air Command to operate the Samos system and provide support to Continental Air Defense Command and North American Air Defense Command (NORAD) in the operation of Midas. On 14 March 1960, the secretary of defense forwarded both plans to the Joint Chiefs of Staff and asked for an early reply. The Joint Staff accepted the plans, but argued that NORAD should not exercise operational control of Midas. Army and Navy planners favored a joint organization specifically for military space operations. Processing and dissemination of Samos-derived data by an Air Force command (SAC) were seen by these planners as inconsistent with development of a joint organization. The Air Force planners protested the exclusion of NORAD, arguing that a breach of American-Canadian agreements would result.

At the end of June 1960, after Gates reemphasized use of existing commands for military space operations, it was clear that the issue could be settled only after numerous other Samos and Midas-related problems were resolved. Conflicting decisions and indecision marked the Samos-Midas-Discoverer program during Fiscal Year 1960. Few people were aware of the complex bureaucratic background largely responsible for the piecemeal approach to important programs. Virtually every phase of the projects remained in a constant state of flux. Divergences of view arose continually between civilian and military experts in the technical area, between the secretary of defense and the Air Force in funding, and between the Air Force and other services in the operational areas.

THE STATUS OF SPACE SYSTEMS IN 1960

Much effort had gone into Air Force space programs by 1960, but major changes were soon to occur. The Samos program was radically revised, and the BAMBI and Dyna-Soar programs were canceled. The communications satellite programs were restructured in many ways. Only the Midas program was to carry on as a major national effort.

OVERALL IMPRESSIONS OF THE PERIOD 1945–60

Many of the conceptual applications of satellite vehicles were not only conceived, but also explored in some depth, during 1945–60. The implications of the availability of satellite vehicles—as instruments of national prestige, tools of politics and diplomacy, and means for new capabilities in scientific research—were considered and debated. The technological advances needed to support these visions also developed, although with varying degrees of success.

Following this early period, a significant shift of emphasis occurred, which persists today. Current technology exceeds in nearly all respects the wildest dreams of twenty-five to thirty years ago, but national goals for this technology are no clearer today than in the 1950s. In the near term, technology is capable of supporting missions and operations for which national space policy is unprepared and for which no far-seeing national space plan exists. In short, technological capabilities may not be fully exploited, because no coherent national space program allows rational decisions on whether or how new ventures should be undertaken.

In addition, a significant portion of the nation's ability to respond quickly to emerging needs and developing opportunities has been lost. The pace of development of early space programs seems almost impossible by today's standards. Much of the loss must be attributed to the organizational and management environment within which today's programs operate.

Appendix 2

Evolution of the Soviet Space Program from Sputnik to Salyut and Beyond

MARCIA S. SMITH

The Soviet space program can be divided into the same elements that constitute the U.S. program: manned activities, dedicated military programs, space applications, and space science. Unlike the United States, however, the Soviet Union does not distinguish between military and civil space activities; all launches are conducted by the Strategic Rocket Forces, and the Air Force is responsible for cosmonaut training.

The Soviet Union launches many more satellites per year than the United States, and a large percentage of these have military missions. In 1981, the Soviet Union made 98 successful launches, of which 59 (60 percent) were primarily military. It must be pointed out, however, that Soviet military satellites, particularly those for reconnaissance, have much shorter lifetimes than their U.S. counterparts, thus requiring more frequent replacement, resulting in a high launch rate.

These facts have led to the impression in many circles that the USSR space program is military in character. While the military aspects of its program cannot be denied (nor can those of the U.S. program), the scientific and civil applications components are often overlooked in discussions of the raison d'etre of the USSR space program.

The political nature of the USSR space program is another aspect that should not be underestimated. The achievement of space "firsts" has always been important to the Soviet leaders, even when it is obvious that they are purely for publicity purposes. The Soviet leaders also recognize the value of visible international cooperation in their space activities. While they cooperate with a much smaller number of countries than does the United States, the Soviet leaders advertise these activities. Although many of these countries (such as Mongolia and Vietnam) could have had little to offer in terms of innovative experiments, the public relations advantage is significant. The United States does not seem intent on such visible expressions of cooperation, relying instead on more substantive, but less noticeable, programs, such as utilizing communications and earth resources satellites to assist less developed countries.

The Soviet Union has always had a long-term commitment to its space program (in marked contrast with the United States), and that commitment is important in helping the Soviet leaders achieve the goals they have established: to explore and exploit space to the maximum extent possible for military and scientific applications and for political gain (not necessarily in that order).

This year marks the twenty-fifth anniversary of space flight, a significant event for the Soviet Union, which launched the world's first satellite, Sputnik I, on 4 October 1957. This brief overview of Soviet space activities over the past quarter century necessarily omits a great amount of detail.[1]

SOVIET MANNED ACTIVITES

The Soviet Union launched the first man into space on 12 April 1961. With that historic flight, the Soviet Union began an extensive program of manned activities, which through 1 May 1982, involved 49 flights. The crews have accumulated 51,233 person-hours in space. The Soviet Union has never sent crews to the moon, but instead has concentrated on utilizing near earth space for a variety of scientific, military, and civil applications.

Vostok and Voskhod: 1961–64

The Soviet Union's Vostok and Voskhod programs were essentially similar to the U.S. Mercury and early Gemini flights and were designed to develop experience with a person's reaction to weightlessness and with orbital rendezvous (but not docking). Vostok 1 placed the first man, Gagarin, in space in 1961; Vostok 3 and 4 rendezvoused to within 6.5 kilometers of each other in 1962; Vostok 6 took the first woman, Tereshkova, into space in 1963; Voskhod 1 carried the first three-man crew (1964); and Voskhod 2 featured the first extravehicular activity, by Leonov, in 1965. It should be remembered, however, that many of these "firsts" were designed as just that. The Soviet Union disbanded the small group of women cosmonaut-trainees as soon as the Tereshkova flight was completed, and there are no women in training today. The Voskhod spacecraft was simply a modified Vostok capsule that was forced to contain a three-man crew in very tight accommodations, and its first EVA was only a brief excursion in an extremely bulky spacesuit that did not permit an extended time in the space environment.

In 1961, President Kennedy initiated the Moon Race by establishing a goal of landing Americans on the moon before the end of the decade. From all appearances at the time, the Soviet leaders were intent on getting there first, and the Soyuz program was expected to be the equivalent of the U.S. Apollo project.

The Soyuz Program and the Moon Race

Following the second Voskhod flight in March 1965, the Soviet Union did not launch another manned mission until April 1967. During this time, the United States conducted its Gemini program, which provided extensive experience with rendezvous, docking, and extravehicular activity and extended the duration of flight to 14 days. In January 1967, the U.S. program suffered a tragic setback when the crew of the first Apollo mission was killed in a fire on the launch pad during a prelaunch test. The Soviet leaders, while expressing their condolences, also intimated that the deaths were the result of the Americans placing the desire to be first on the moon above the safety of the astronauts.

On 24 April 1967, the Soviet Union launched Vladimir Komarov in the first flight of its new spacecraft, Soyuz 1. After eighteen orbits, one orbit later than usual, the spacecraft began its reentry cycle, but the parachute lines tangled during descent and the pilot was killed on impact with the earth. The Soviet Union had suffered its own tragedy. Both programs were set back for a year and a half.

When the programs resumed, the United States clearly was ahead in the race to the moon. The first U.S. flight, Apollo 7, was a test of the Apollo command module in earth orbit. The first Soviet flight was a simple rendezvous between the manned Soyuz 3 and the unmanned Soyuz 2. Then, in December 1968, the United States won the moon race by placing three astronauts in lunar orbit with Apollo 8; seven months later, two Americans landed on the surface of the moon with Apollo 11.

The question of why the Soviet Union lost the moon race has been debated for many years. The most frequently cited reason is the fact that it still does not have a launch vehicle with a thrust comparable to that of the U.S. Saturn 5. Rumors have been prevalent since the mid-1960s of several tests of a large vehicle, sometimes designated the "G" vehicle, all of which allegedly exploded on the launch pad. Stories persist to this day that the launch of a large booster is imminent, although this cannot be confirmed from the open literature.

In fact, the Russians (or the Americans) could have reached the moon without a large booster, by using earth-orbital and/or lunar-orbital assembly of the necessary components. The Soviet Union simply may have run out of time, believing up until the last moment that it might reach the moon first. The Soviet leaders have a very conservative philosophy when launching new hardware; they conduct several unmanned tests before committing crews. If the United States had adopted such a policy toward the Saturn 5, it might have decided to launch an unmanned flight to the moon with Saturn 5 rather than sending the Apollo 8 crew on the first lunar-distance flight attempt of that booster. Thus, the Soviet leaders might have thought they had more time to develop their own systems; they have acknowledged that several flights of the Zond series in 1968–70 were unmanned precursors related to a lunar manned program, and in 1981 they acknowledged that Kosmos 434, an unmanned spacecraft launched in 1971, had also tested a lunar cabin. Thus, it seems apparent that they were trying to reach the moon, even after the United States won the race. For whatever reasons, they abandoned that goal (at least temporarily) and turned their attention to earth orbit.

Soyuz 4 and 5, the first Soviet manned flights after Apollo 8, accomplished a rendezvous and docking in earth orbit, and two of the cosmonauts transferred from Soyuz 5 to Soyuz 4 using EVA. The Soviet Union claims this as the first space station, but since there was no direct access between the two ships, that categorization is disputed in the West. Soyuz 6, 7, and 8 (launched after the first U.S. moon landing) accomplished the first group flight, and although the Russians claim that this was their only goal, it has been speculated that Soyuz 7 and 8 were supposed to dock but could not. The Soyuz 6 crew performed the first welding experiment in space. Soyuz 9, in June 1970, was a flight designed to extend the duration of manned spaceflight, and the crew remained in orbit for eighteen days, establishing a new record.

The Space-Station Era

In 1971, the Soviet Union launched the world's first space station, Salyut 1. Since that time, it has launched seven more stations, two of which (Salyut 2 and Kosmos 557) failed in orbit and were never occupied. With each new station, new capabilities have been achieved.

Three of the stations are categorized as military, while four are considered to be primarily civilian in purpose. The most recent, Salyut 7, is probably a civilian station, but such a determination cannot be made until it is occupied. The difference between the two modes of operation is that military space stations use military frequencies for communications, have only military personnel for crews, and are placed in lower orbits to facilitate reconnaissance activities. The civilian stations use civilian frequencies, mixed military/civilian crews, and are placed in higher orbits, which permit both earth resources photography and astronomical observations. A wide range of biological, materials processing, and other experiments are performed as well. Through 1 May 1982, the Soviet Union had sent twenty-eight crews to occupy the space stations, twenty-two of which completed their missions successfully.

1971–75: Salyut 1–4 and Free-Flyers

The Soviet space station program has not been without its difficulties. Salyut 1 was successfully launched in April 1971. A three-man crew was launched to occupy the station shortly thereafter, but although they docked successfully, they could not enter the space station because of a problem with the hatch, and the crew had to return early. The second Salyut 1 crew (Soyuz 11) successfully entered the space station and remained on board for twenty-four days. When the crew returned to earth, however, an improperly closed hatch allowed the cabin atmosphere to vent into space and the crew died of asphyxiation (they had not been required to wear space suits). Since that time, cosmonauts have worn suits during launch and reentry, forcing a return to two-man crews because the Soyuz could not accommodate three men plus the bulky suits and associated systems. Ten years of development were required before a modified version of Soyuz appeared, which could accommodate three-man crews in improved spacesuits.

The Soyuz 11 tragedy was followed by space station failures. Salyut 2, launched in April 1973, suffered a "catastrophic-malfunction" eleven days after launch, and the station broke into pieces. It is thought that this was to have been the first military space station. In May 1973, another space station was launched which failed so early in its flight that it was not given a formal Soyuz designation, but rather was placed under the catch-all Kosmos designation (Kosmos 557). This is thought to have been a civilian space station.

The Soviet Union temporarily returned to free-flying Soyuz spacecraft; Soyuz 12 was a systems test following the Soyuz 11 accident, while Soyuz 13 was an eight-day mission that included astrophysical and other scientific experiments.

The space station program resumed in 1974 with the launch of Salyut 3, the first successful military space station. The Soyuz 14 crew docked with Salyut 3 and spent two weeks on board performing what the Soviet press announced as earth resources photography, but which Western analysts have concluded was for reconnaissance.

Soyuz 14 was a streamlined derivative of Soyuz in that no solar panels were used, meaning that the spacecraft had only about two and a half days worth of power from internal batteries. This was sufficient for ferrying the crew to the space station and home again, but insufficient for them to remain in orbit for longer periods of time if docking could not be achieved. This became an important factor on the next flight, Soyuz 15, which was unable to dock with the space station for unexplained reasons (it has been speculated that they were testing a new automatic docking system that failed); the crew had to return home without docking because they did not have enough power for a second try. Soyuz 16 was a systems test of modifications made to Soyuz for the joint U.S.-USSR Apollo-Soyuz Test Project (see below).

The civilian Salyut 4 space station was launched in 1975 and hosted the Soyuz 17 crew for thirty days, setting a new duration record. The next manned launch to the space station occurred on 5 April 1975, and became known as the "April 5th Anomaly." This is the only known manned flight that had to be aborted before reaching orbit. The third state of the standard A-2 launch vehicle failed, and the crew landed 200 miles north of the Chinese border. The next mission in the series was thereupon designated Soyuz 18, and it docked with the space station for sixty-three days. The mission for the two Salyut 4 crews included astrophysical, atmospheric, biological (including plant growth), and earth resources experiments.

The 1975 Apollo-Soyuz Test Project

Soyuz 19 was the Soviet portion of the joint U.S.-USSR Apollo-Soyuz Test Project (ASTP). Although this mission ostensibly had scientific purposes (for example, several materials processing experiments were flown on the Apollo), it was primarily a show of political cooperation. The three-man Apollo crew and the two-man Soyuz crew shook hands in orbit and visited each other's spacecraft during the flight. It was hoped that this mission would herald a new era in cooperation between the two countries in space activities, and although some programs have benefited from increased data sharing and flight opportunities, the cooling in relations between the two countries over other international matters has been felt in scientific agreements for cooperation as well. In fact, the 1977 agreement between the two countries for continued space cooperation expired in May 1982, and President Reagan has announced that he will not renew the agreement because of Russian involvement in Poland.

1976–77: Salyut 5 and Free-Flyers

Following ASTP, the next Soviet Soyuz flight, Soyuz 20, was an unmanned test of the Soyuz spacecraft. The spacecraft, which carried biological specimens for various experiments, docked with Salyut 4 for ninety days to determine whether the spacecraft could be safely repowered after that length of time, a necessary factor in lengthening the duration of flights.

Salyut 5, a military space station, was launched in June 1976 and hosted two crews (Soyuz 21 and 24) successfully, although a third (Soyuz 23) was unable to dock.

Soyuz 22 was a free-flying spacecraft and carried the first Soviet-implemented experiment of non-Soviet origin on a manned flight. The mission tested an East German multispectral camera for earth resources photography which later flew aboard Salyut 6.

1977–81: Salyut 6 and Soyuz T

On 29 September 1977, the Soviet Union scored an impressive space "first" with the launch of Salyut 6. This is the first space station to have two functioning docking ports, an important advancement in terms of developing permanent earth-orbiting space stations. The second docking port allows resupply of the space station while a crew is on board, and also allows second crews to join the primary crew. Salyut 5 remained in orbit as of 1 May 1982, although no manned crews have docked with the station since Soyuz T-4 returned on 26 May 1981. The unmanned Kosmos 1267 spacecraft (discussed below), has been docked with Salyut 6 since June 1981.

Since 1977, Salyut 5 has hosted sixteen crews (two other crews were unable to dock), all of which have performed a wide variety of experiments in areas such as biology (including plant growth), earth resources photography, materials processing, and astronomy (including the deployment of the first space radio telescope). For the first time since Soyuz 4/5 in 1969, the Soviet Union performed extravehicular activity: in 1977, Grechko (Soyuz 26) performed a one-and-a-half-hour EVA; in 1978, Kovalenok and Ivanchenkov (Soyuz 29) performed a two-hour EVA; and in 1979, Lyakov and Ryumin (Soyuz 32) performed a one-hour-and-20-minute EVA to free the radio telescope they had deployed, but which would not release properly from the space station. (The Soviet Union has developed new EVA suits which are much more flexible than those used in the 1960s.) This gives the Soviet Union a total of approximately 11 hours of EVA experience, compared with over 100 hours of EVA time by U.S. astronauts (not inlcuding EVA on the lunar surface).

Another important development with Salyut 6 was the first refueling of a spaceship in orbit. The Russians use unmanned Progress spacecrafts as cargo ships. In some cases, the Progress ships carry fuel, which is transferred into the fuel tanks of Salyut; in other cases, the Progress ships themselves are used to raise the orbit of the space station. In this manner, Salyut 6's orbit has been raised repeatedly, thus extending its lifetime.

The Soviet Union has more than doubled the duration of spaceflight with Salyut 6 crews. In 1977, they broke the U.S. record of 84 days (on Skylab 4) when the Soyuz 26 crew remained on board Salyut 6 for 96 days. This record was increased to 140 days by the Soyuz 29 crew in 1978, to 175 days with Soyuz 32 in 1979, and to 185 days with Soyuz 36 in 1980. One cosmonaut, Ryumin, was part of the crew that set the 185-day record, and then returned to space six months later for another 175 days in space. Thus, he has spent almost one year in weightlessness. Soviet physicians have reported that although there are measurable changes in the body's systems during extended periods of weightlessness, they have found no factors that would preclude even longer flights.

Nine of the eighteen flights to Salyut 6 have involved international crews. The Soviet Union sponsored the formation of Interkosmos, a formalized structure permitting the participation of Soviet-bloc countries in the Soviet space program. In addition to the Soviet Union, the Interkosmos members are: Bulgaria, Czechoslovakia, Cuba, East Germany, Hungary, Mongolia, Poland, Romania, and Vietnam. One representative from each of these countries has now flown in space (all of these docked with Salyut 6 except the Bulgarian, who was part of the Soyuz 33 crew that had to return early because of an engine malfunction). The Soviet Union also has extensive space cooperation with France and India, and is planning to launch a Frenchman into space in 1982 and an Indian possibly in 1984.

In 1980, the Soviet Union also introduced an improved version of the Soyuz spacecraft, designated Soyuz T. With advanced avionics, a new fuel system, and a return to using solar panels for power, Soyuz T represents a significant advancement in Soviet ferry ships. In 1981, the Soviet Union announced that the Soyuz would be retired from service and Soyuz T would be used exclusively. Four flights of Soyuz T have been made to date: the first was an unmanned test, the second and fourth carried two-man crews to Salyut 6, while the third, in 1981, was the first flight of a three-man Soviet crew since the Soyuz 11 tragedy in 1971.

1982: Salyut 7

The Soviet Union launched a new space station, Salyut 7, on 19 April 1982, the eleventh anniversary of the launch of Salyut 1. As of 1 May 1983 three Soyuz crews and four Progress tankers had been sent to the space station, with the crew of Soyuz T-5 establishing a new 211-day manned flight record. The new station is physically similar to Salyut 6 and will allow the Soviet Union to maintain its manned presence in space.

THE FUTURE: PERMANENT SPACE STATIONS, A SOVIET SHUTTLE, AND BEYOND

The unmanned satellite Kosmos 1267 has received a great deal of attention recently because it is claimed by some Western experts to be an orbiting battlestation. The Soviet Union claims, however, that it is a systems test of the first modular space station and a precursor of future permanent space stations. In either case, it is an important indicator of what the near future may hold for Soviet manned programs. The Russians have also been talking more about their plans for a reusable spacecraft and about manned flights to Mars.

Kosmos 1267 and Permanent Space Stations

The Soviet leaders rarely reveal their plans in advance, but in the case of the desire to establish a permanent earth-orbiting space station, they have let it be known for several years that this is a near-term goal. Salyut 6, with its two docking ports, is a clear step in that direction. In June 1981, the Soviet Union docked the fifteen-ton unmanned satellite Kosmos 1267 with the unoccupied Salyut 6 and announced that this was a test of a modular concept of constructing larger space stations. On several occasions, the Soviet Union has released information about the status of the Kosmos 1267-Salyut 6 combination.

Kosmos 1267 was not a surprise as a modular space station test, but in October 1981 *Aviation Week and Space Technology* announced that it had information showing the spacecraft to be a "battle station" in orbit, armed with clusters of one-meter-long infrared homing interceptors.[2] If true, this would be a surprise. While the Soviets have had an operational antisatellite system for many years, the advent of such a large battle station, based on different technology, together with the political ramifications of a direct connection with a manned system, would be a significant event in escalating space weaponry.

The actual nature of Kosmos 1267 cannot be determined from unclassified reports, so the debate in the West over its purpose has developed into a heated exchange. It is logical for the Soviet leaders to be testing a modular space station system, and it would be uncharacteristic for them to publish reports on the system if it truly were devoted to military purposes. Also, it would not have been politically wise for them to place a weapon in orbit at the same time that they introduced a draft treaty at the United Nations to ban weapons in space. There is no information in the open literature to disprove the *Aviation Week* charge, although the Pentagon has publicly denied having evidence of such a battle station.[3]

Manned Flights to Mars

The Soviet Union has stated that one of the reasons it is interested in extending man's duration in space through missions abroad earth-orbiting space stations is that it plans to send crews to Mars, although it has not specified whether these would be orbital or landing missions. Anatoliy Skripko, the science and technology attaché at the Soviet Embassy in Washington, stated in a speech to the American Astronautical Society on 11 February 1982, that the Soviet Union hopes to accomplish the manned Mars flight in from ten to fifteen years. Since the Soviet leaders have such a conservative approach to their manned space activities, it would not be surprising if they first attempted such flights around or on the moon, although Skripko did not mention such plans.

A Soviet Shuttle?

In that same speech, Skripko acknowledged the development of a Soviet reusable space vehicle. Although he did not provide details of the craft, he stated that more would be heard about it in from two to three years, and it might be "seen" in five years or so. The "Soviet shuttle," which most Western experts do not think will resemble the U.S. shuttle very much at all other than in terms of reusability, has been rumored for years to be on the verge of an actual spaceflight. Skripko's remarks paint a less optimistic picture of the development program; in fact he commented that developing a reusable vehicle is "costly, time consuming, and complicated," something the Americans in the audience already knew. It is expected that, when developed, the Soviet shuttle will be about one-third the size of the U.S. shuttle, and will not have a large cargo bay since the Soviet Union has an ample supply of expendable launch vehicles for placing satellites in orbit.

DEDICATED MILITARY PROGRAMS

Like the United States, the Soviet Union uses space for various military purposes, primarily reconnaissance and communications. There also are satellites called "minor military," which are apparently used for radar calibration, and satellites for geodesy. In addition, the Soviet Union has three special military space programs that do not have U.S. counterparts today: radar ocean surveillance satellites, a fractional orbital bombardment system, and an antisatellite device.

RECONNAISSANCE

Soviet reconnaissance satellites can be divided into the following groups: photographic reconnaissance (of low, medium, or high resolution); electronic intelligence; radar ocean surveillance; and early warning. Reconnaissance missions constitute the greatest number of launches by the Soviet Union, and involved 45 of the 98 successful Soviet launches in 1981. The count of 45 does not include the special class of satellites at 82.3° inclination, which are indistinguishable from the military photorecon flights but are announced by the Russians as earth resources flights. Seven of these satellites were launched in 1981.

The Soviet photorecon satellites are thought to be based on the Vostok and Soyuz manned spacecraft. These satellites remain in orbit for periods of either two weeks (or less if the data is required sooner) or six weeks, and are then recovered with their film packets (the six-week versions have multiple reentry capsules for returning film). An analysis by Nicholas Johnson of Teledyne-Brown Engineering shows that the Soviet Union achieves an ever-increasing number of mission days per year for photorecon satellites by using combinations of shorter and longer duration missions; in 1981, total missions days exceeded those of 1980 by 24 percent.[4]

In 1981, *Aviation Week and Space Technology* reported that the Soviet Union had developed a digital imaging reconnaissance satellite system,[5] but this has not been confirmed by either Soviet or official U.S. sources, and there were no unusual or unexplained Soviet reconnaissance launches in 1981 that might signify such a new program.

As noted in the section on manned space activities, the Soviet Union has launched two space stations (Salyut 3 and 5), which were apparently used for reconnaissance purposes as well.

Electronic Intelligence and Radar Ocean Surveillance

The Soviet Union has a system of electronic intelligence, or ferret, satellites that are launched into 81.2° inclination orbits, with an altitude of approximately 630–90 kilometers. These satellites intercept radio and radar transmission.

A special category of electronic intelligence mission, placed in 65° inclination orbits at an altitude of 425–60 kilometers, is part of the ocean surveillance program and tracks ocean-going vessels by intercepting their radio or radar emissions. Called EORSATs (electronic ocean reconnaissance satellites), they are thought to be powered by conventional solar panels. The Soviet Union also has a system of nuclear-reactor-powered ocean reconnaissance satellites, however, called RORSATs (radar ocean reconnaissance satellites). Although they fly at the same inclination as the EORSATs, they are at a lower altitude (between 250 and 285 kilometers). The satellites are designed so that after the mission is completed, the portion of the spacecraft that contains the nuclear reactor is separated from the rest of the vehicle and maneuvered into a high orbit from which it will not decay until the radioactivity is no longer a hazard. The unexpected reentry of one of these satellites over Canada in January 1978 (Kosmos 954) has prompted a review at the United Nations of what (if any) restrictions should apply to the use of nuclear power sources in outer space. The United States does not use nuclear reactors for powering satellites at the present time, although it does use radio-isotope thermal generators for spacecraft that will remain in space for long periods, and particularly for planetary spacecraft. Although that debate has not been resolved, the Soviet Union resumed its RORSAT flights in 1980. The United States does not have a program equivalent to the RORSAT at the present time.

Early Warning

The Soviet Union has not been as quick as the United States to establish a system of early-warning satellites, and as of the end of 1981, still apparently had not deployed a fully operational system. Those satellites that are thought to have an early-warning function are typically placed in highly elliptical orbits very similar to those of the Molniya communication satellites. It has been speculated that when operational, the satellite system will consist of nine satellites spaced 40° apart.[6]

COMMUNICATIONS, COMMAND, AND CONTROL

The Soviet Union uses several satellite systems for communications, command, and control. The first, for acquiring and storing information for later transmission upon command (called store/dump), is easily recognizable because the satellites are launched eight at a time into roughly circular 1,500-kilometer orbits at 74° inclination. A second series, also at 74° inclination, consists of three satellites in roughly circular 800-kilometer orbits.

The Molniya satellite series is also used for military communications, and Molniya 1 satellites are now thought to be dedicated to military use, with Molniya 3 satellites serving both sectors (the Molniya 2 series has been phased out). Molniya 3 satellites are used for the "hot line" between Washington and Moscow.

Molniya satellites are placed in highly elliptical orbits, with an apogee of approximately 40,000 kilometers that occurs over the northern hemisphere (perigee is approximately 500 kilometers), thus providing perhaps eight hours of coverage to the northern latitudes of the Soviet Union. A constellation of eight Molniya 1 satellites and four Molniya 3 satellites is maintained in orbit to provide full coverage. (The Russians have not yet utilized geostationary orbit for military communications satellites, as the United States has, although they indicated in the late 1970s that they are planning a system designated Gals for some unspecified time in the future.)

SPACE WEAPONS

The Soviet Union has conducted nineteen tests of an antisatellite (ASAT) system since October 1968. With this system, an interceptor satellite is launched to rendezvous with a target satellite already in orbit. The interceptor maneuvers close to the target and explodes, destroying it with shrapnel. The Soviet Union has demonstrated the capability to intercept a target within one orbit, up to an altitude of approximately 2,300 kilometers. The last ASAT test was in March 1981.

In 1977, the U.S. secretary of defense declared the Soviet ASAT system operational, and the United States embarked upon an ASAT development program of its own (the U.S. ASAT device will be launched from F-15 aircraft). At the same time, however, President Carter initiated a series of limitation talks with the Soviet Union on weapons in space. Three sets of meetings were held in 1978 and 1979 without resolution, and the talks have been indefinitely postponed. Part of the trouble was that the Soviet Union claimed that the U.S. Space Shuttle can be used for weapons purposes and therefore should be included in the ban, a contention the United States obviously could not accept.

The Soviet Union also developed a fractional orbital bombardment system (FOBS), which is essentially a very long-range ICBM that could fly a trajectory over the South Pole to the United States, thus avoiding the North American BMEWS radars, which point north. The last FOBS test was made in 1971, and opinion in the West is split as to whether tests were suspended because the system is now considered operational or because the Soviet leaders decided it was unnecessary.

The Soviet Union and the United States are both working on directed energy weapons (lasers and particle beams) for use in space. U.S. Defense Department officials have estimated that the Soviet Union is probably five years ahead of the United States in developing space-based lasers, and since they feel that the United States might be

able to deploy such weapons in approximately ten years, they estimate that the Soviet Union might deploy them in five years or so.

In August 1981, the Soviet Union introduced a draft treaty at the
United Nations calling for a ban on stationing, installing, or deploying weapons in outer space. The Soviet leaders are obviously concerned about the possibility of the United States placing weapons on
board the Space Shuttle, and they included language in the draft
treaty that would ban weapons from "piloted space vessels of multiple
use." The draft treaty has been referred to the U.N. Committee on
Disarmament.

SPACE APPLICATIONS

The use of space for applications purposes—communications,
weather, remote sensing, and navigation—has been an important
part of the Soviet space program from the beginning, although they
have been somewhat slower than the United States in making use of
geostationary orbit for communications and weather, and in using
free-flying satellites for remote sensing.

COMMUNICATIONS

As noted earlier, the Molniya series of highly elliptical satellites is
used for both military and civil purposes. The first Molniya was
launched in 1965, and Molniya satellites were the mainstay of civilian
communications until 1974, when the Soviet Union finally placed its
first satellite into geostationary orbit (a feat the United States accomplished in 1963).

The Soviet Union now uses three series of geostationary satellites
in addition to Molniya: Raduga and Gorizont, voice and television
relay systems that together can reach most of the world, use the same
ground stations as Molniya; Ekran satellites, used for broadcasting
television to the far north and far east (such as Siberia and Mongolia),
use much smaller receivers.

The Soviet Union also has launched satellites for amateur radio
operators, called Radio, which are similar to the U.S.-launched
OSCAR satellites. In 1981, the Soviet Union launched six Radio
satellites at one time, in the same fashion as it launches store/dump
satellites.

The Soviet Union has notified the International Telecom-
munication Union of two additional civil geostationary communication satellite systems that it apparently intends to introduce in the
near future—Volna for mobile communications and Luch for general communications—but no time period was specified.

NAVIGATION

The Soviet navigation satellite system, Tsikada, is thought to be very similar to the U.S. TRANSIT system. The Soviet leaders have said very little about the program, but there is some evidence that there are two different systems, one for the military and one for the civil sector, consisting of a total of ten satellites.

REMOTE SENSING

While the United States began its land remote sensing program in earnest in 1972 with the launch of the first LANDSAT (the fourth LANDSAT was launched during 1982), there is no Soviet equivalent of LANDSAT even today. They do, however, collect remote sensing data from other space systems..

The majority of Soviet earth resources photography has been conducted with the Salyut series of space stations. Salyut 6, which carries the MKF-6 multispectral scanner (it observes in six visible and infrared wavelengths) has been used extensively for this purpose. The resolution of the MKF-6 scanner is reported to be as high as 30 meters (existing LANDSATs have 80-meter resolution, although the next one will have 30-meter resolution).

Recently, the Soviet Union has also begun launching free-flying satellites which it identifies as having an earth resources mission. The satellites and their telemetry are indistinguishable from the two-week version of military reconnaissance satellites, but it is possible that the film that is returned is utilized for nonmilitary purposes.

Data from Meteor weather satellites are used for earth resources purposes, and the Russians have begun flying experimental sensors on the second-generation Meteor satellites (called Meteor 2), suggesting that they recognize the value of such data and will continue such programs in the future. They have also begun launching "Meteor-Priroda satellites into sunsynchronous orbits to collect earth resources data, and they reportedly plan to launch one of these per year. (Priroda, the Russian word for nature, is the name used for the earth resources research center in Moscow.)

A number of satellites identified by the Soviet Union as having "ocean resources" missions have also been flown. They observe the ocean in several wavelengths to study, for example, ocean surface temperatures and ice conditions. In addition to direct observations in visible, infrared, and microwave spectral bands, the satellites may also relay data that is collected by ocean surface buoys. Two such satellites launched in 1981 may be working as a pair. The only U.S.

satellite dedicated to sensing the ocean, SEASAT, failed after only 100 days in orbit because of an electrical short circuit.

WEATHER

The Meteor satellites have been used for gathering weather data for both the military and civil sectors since the early 1960s. The satellites are typically placed in 900-kilometer circular orbits and take readings in the visible and infrared bands. As noted above, some of the data are used for earth resources purposes. The original series of Meteor satellites has apparently been phased out and replaced by Meteor 2 satellites, which are placed in polar orbits.

The Soviet leaders have yet to place a meteorological satellite in geostationary orbit, even though they promised to do so as part of an international weather program in 1979 that involved satellites from the United States, the European Space Agency, and Japan. Why they were unable to keep their part of the agreement has not been revealed, and they still state that they plan to launch such a satellite (called GOMS, for Geostationary Operational Meteorological Satellite), perhaps in 1983.

SPACE SCIENCE

Soviet space science missions can be considered in two groups: earth orbital flights (either on the manned flights or using free-flying spacecraft) and lunar/planetary flights. Although the Soviet Union has not devoted as much attention to earth orbital science as has the United States, such activities seem likely to receive more attention as space station utilization increases. The Soviet Union has accomplished a great deal with its programs to explore the moon and Venus, although it has not been as successful with its Mars flights, and has not attempted missions comparable to U.S. flights to the outer planets. They are planning to send probes to intercept Halley's Comet when it returns to the earth's vicinity in 1985–86.

EARTH ORBITAL MISSIONS

Like those of the United States, the first Soviet satellites were devoted to space science in its broadest terms. After Sputnik, the Kosmos designation for Soviet satellites came into use and was claimed by the Soviet Union to denote satellites being used for scientific purposes. While that might have been true in the very early days of space flight, Kosmos is now used to denote most Soviet satellites, including those whose mission the Soviet Union does not care to reveal; very few Kosmos satellites today are used for science. Instead, free-flying scientific satellites are launched as part of the Interkosmos or Prognoz satellite series.

Twenty-two Interkosmos satellites and nine Prognoz satellites had been launched by 1 May 1982. These satellites are thought to be roughly comparable to U.S. Explorer satellites, which are relatively small and carry a limited number of experiments. The Soviet Union has not launched any free-flying observatories similar to the U.S. High Energy Astronomy Observatories, the Orbiting Solar Observatories, or Orbiting Astronomical Observatories, although some of these types of observations have been made as part of the space station program. Among the areas studied by Soviet scientifc satellites are particles and fields, solar wind, sun/earth interactions, aurora, the ionosphere, atmospheric constituents, and geodesy.

The Salyut space stations, and several manned free-flying Soyuz flights before them, have provided the Soviet Union with extended periods for conducting science in space. The many experiments the Soviet Union has conducted include plant growth (which has not been very successful, because the plants do not produce new seeds in space); astronomical observations in the visible, infrared, ultraviolet, X-ray, and radio wavelengths (including the deployment of the first radio telescope in orbit); materials processing experiments for developing new alloys and making better crystals; a large array of biological tests on cosmonauts to assess the impact of extended exposure to weightlessness; studies of the atmosphere; and laser holography.

LUNAR AND PLANETARY MISSIONS

The Soviet Union has expended considerable resources in its exploration of the moon and Venus and has attempted to explore Mars, although the latter has not been very successful.

The Moon

While the Soviet Union has never landed crews on the moon, it has studied the lunar surface with a variety of unmanned spacecraft, including fly-bys, orbiters, and landers. Twenty-four lunar missions have been accomplished and include an impressive list of "firsts": the first fly-by of the moon, the first photographs of the far side, the first photographs from the surface, the first automated sample return, and the first roving vehicle on the lunar surface.

The latter two categories do not have a U.S. equivalent and

warrant further comment. Three Luna spacecraft (16, 20, and 24) returned small samples of lunar material by remote control. In total, approximately 300 grams of material were brought back. Although this is very small compared to the 380 kilograms returned by the U.S. astronauts, the Russians are proud to point out that they did not have to risk lives to accomplish the task.

Two Lunokhod roving vehicles successfully landed on the moon (Luna 17 and 21) for extended duration studies of the surface. The Lunokhods could move about the surface on treaded wheels, taking photographs and performing chemical analyses of surface samples by remote control. Lunokhod 1 traveled more than 10.5 kilometers on the surface during its almost one year of operation. Although Lunokhod 2 operated for a shorter period of time (three months), it traversed 37 kilometers of the surface.

The last Soviet lunar mission was launched in 1976, and there is no reason to believe the Russians will not resume such missions at some time.

Venus

The Soviet Union sent its first spacecraft to Venus in February 1961. Since that time, thirteen more Venera missions have been launched, achieving the first direct readings of atmospheric constituents, the first hard landing on the planet, the first soft landing, the first surface photographs, and the first soil sample analysis. In short, the Soviet Venera probes have revolutionized scientific understanding of Venus, just as the U.S. Mariner 9 and Viking probes did for Mars.

The most recent Venera flights consist of pairs that soft land and send back geophysical readings and photographs of the surface. Venera 9 and 10 in 1975 transmitted black and white photos and made geophysical readings; Venera 11 and 12 in 1978 were expected to return photographs, but the camera systems failed, so only geophysical data were returned; and Venera 13 and 14, which landed on March 1 and 5, 1982, respectively, sent back the first color pictures and drilled a Venusian rock for chemical analyses. The Venera 13 and 14 pictures show Venus to have an orange sky and brown surface.

Soviet Venus missions are planned far in advance, particularly since they sometimes involve cooperation with other countries (notably France). A French experiment to deploy balloons in the Venusian atmosphere for longer duration readings of atmospheric constituents was planned for the 1984 Venus opportunity, but has been postponed until the next flight because the Russians restructured the flight to include an intercept with Halley's Comet.

Mars

The first acknowledged Soviet mission to Mars was launched in 1962 (it is thought that several failures occurred earlier), but communications with the spacecraft failed. Another Mars mission was not attempted until ten years later, when Mars 2 and 3 were launched. The spacecraft, which carried geophysical equipment only, were combination orbiters and landers. Only the Mars 3 lander reached the surface successfully, and it ceased transmitting pictures twenty seconds after landing. In 1973, Mars 4, 5, 6, and 7 were launched. Mars 4 and 5 were orbiters paired with the Mars 6 and 7 landers. The Mars 4 and 7 spacecraft missed the planet. Mars 5 successfully entered orbit and relayed data from Mars 6 as it descended through the atmosphere, but communications ceased just before it would have reached the surface. No further Mars missions have been attempted.

Halley's Comet Intercept

When it became apparent in 1981 that the United States would not launch a spacecraft to study Halley's Comet, the Russians upgraded their 1984 Venus spacecraft to allow a dual mission in which landers would first be dropped off at Venus and the parent spacecraft would then continue on to study the comet. The spacecraft are expected to carry as many as ten instruments, including three that are primarily French: an infrared spectrometer, a close-up television camera, and a three-channel spectrometer. Other instruments are being provided by the Russians in cooperation with Interkosmos countries, including a mass spectrometer, an ion and solar wind analyzer, a plasma wave analyzer, and a magnetometer. The European Space Agency and Japan are also planning to send spacecraft to Halley's Comet, and an agreement of cooperation has been established among the three groups for exchange of data.

FUTURE EFFORTS

The Soviet Union has a broad program of space activities, covering all aspects of spaceflight. Through 1 May, the number of Soviet launches in 1982 has been about the same as in 1981: 31 were launched in the first four months of 1982, compared with 33 during the same period in 1981. None of these launches was unexpected.

The Russians launched a French "spationaut" to the new Salyut 7 space station in 1982 as part of their highly visible international program of sending non-Soviets into space. Two Frenchmen (prime and backup) were in training for over two years. In the summer of 1981, the Russians had announced that Salyut 6 would not host any more manned crews, and therefore that the French crewman would be sent to the new space station. As the year passed, however, the Russians apparently changed their minds and suggested that Salyut 6 might be reoccupied after all. In the end, though, due in large part to French pressure, the multi-national mission was sent to Salyut 7.

As noted earlier, the Soviet leaders like to publicize their international space activities, and they have begun to express a desire for greater cooperation. This may indicate a new attitude about opening up their program, or may simply reflect the current economic situation where a greater number of partners could reduce the cost of new missions. The Russians have been forthcoming with data from their scientific experiments, particularly in the fields of space biology and planetary exploration; perhaps this will extend to other areas, such as remote sensing, in the future.

It is also possible that the Soviet Union may launch something new in military space systems, although it seems unlikely that it will deploy space-based lasers or particle beam weapons soon. Depending on the global political climate, a new ASAT system based on conventional technology may appear, if it has not done so already in the form of Kosmos 1267.

In short, it appears that in 1982 and beyond, the Soviet Union will continue a broad range of space programs, and its space doctrine—to explore and exploit space for maximum gain in all areas—will remain the same.

NOTES

1. Additional information can be found in two reports prepared by the Congressional Research Service: *Soviet Space Programs, 1971–1975*, published by the Senate Committee on Aeronautical and Space Sciences in 1976; and *Space Activities of the United States, Soviet Union, and Other Launching Countries/Organizations, 1957–1981*, CRS Report 82-45.

2. "Killer Satellites," *Aviation Week and Space Technology*, 26 October 1981, p. 15. See also "Antisatellite Watch," *AWST*, 2 November 1981, p. 15; and "Cosmos Threat," *AWST*, 30 November 1981, p. 17.

3. "Pentagon Says It Has No Evidence of Soviet Space Battle Stations," *Defense Daily*, 28 October 1981, p. 279.

4. Nicholas Johnson, *The Soviet Year in Space: 1981* (Costa Mesa, Calif.: Teledyne Brown Engineering, 1982).

5. "Killer Satellites," p. 15.

6. Johnson, *The Soviet Year in Space*.

Appendix 3

Soviet Draft Treaty on Weapons in Outer Space
Excerpts from 1972 Anti-Ballistic Missile Treaty

UNITED NATIONS GENERAL ASSEMBLY   11 August 1981

Thirty-sixth session

REQUEST FOR THE INCLUSION OF A SUPPLEMENTARY
ITEM IN THE AGENDA OF THE THIRTY-SIXTH SESSION

CONCLUSION OF A TREATY ON THE PROHIBITION OF THE
STATIONING OF WEAPONS OF ANY KIND IN OUTER SPACE

Letter dated 10 August 1981 from the Minister for Foreign
Affairs of the Union of Soviet Socialist Republics
addressed to the Secretary-General

The Soviet Union requests the inclusion in the agenda of the
thirty-sixth session of the General Assembly of an item entitled
"Conclusion of a treaty on the prohibition of the stationing of weapons of any kind in outer space."

In 1982, mankind will observe the twenty-fifth anniversary of the
beginning of the conquest of space, which is one of the greatest
achievements of science and technology in the twentieth century.
The use of outer space is already producing considerable benefit to
mankind today in such areas as communications, study of the earth's
natural resources, meteorology, navigation, and many other areas. It
may be said that people are beginning to make space "habitable."

At the very beginning of the space age, as early as 1958, the
Soviet Union made a proposal in the United Nations envisaging the
banning of the use of cosmic space for military purposes. Over all the
years which followed, it invariably stated and continues to state that

space should be a sphere of exclusively peaceful co-operation. And it is gratifying to note that much has been done in this regard.

1963 saw the conclusion of the international Treaty banning nuclear weapon tests in the atmosphere, in outer space and under water. The 1967 Treaty on Principles Governing the Activities of States in the Exploration and Use of Outer Space, including the Moon and Other Celestial Bodies, provides for the use of the moon and other celestial bodies exclusively for peaceful purposes and also specifies that no objects carrying nuclear weapons or any other kinds of weapons of mass destruction should be placed in orbit around the earth or stationed in outer space in any other manner. The 1979 Agreement Governing the Activities of States on the Moon and Other Celestial Bodies develops and spells out the obligations of States to ensure the exclusively peaceful use of the moon and other celestial bodies within the solar system.

However, none of these international instruments precludes the possibility of the stationing in outer space of those kinds of weapons which are not covered by the definition of weapons of mass destruction. Consequently, the danger of the militarization of outer space still exists and has recently been increasing.

The Soviet Union considers that this is inadmissible. It believes that outer space should always remain unsullied and free from any weapons and should not become a new arena for the arms race or a source of strained relations between States. In the opinion of the Soviet Union, the attainment of these goals would be promoted by the conclusion of an international treaty on the prohibition of the stationing of weapons of any kind in outer space.

The draft treaty on this subject proposed by us is enclosed with this letter.

I should be grateful if you would consider this letter as an explanatory memorandum in accordance with the rules of procedure of the General Assembly, and circulate it and the draft treaty as official documents of the General Assembly.

(Signed) A. GROMYKO
Minister for Foreign Affairs of the USSR

Draft treaty on the prohibition of the stationing of weapons
of any kind in outer space

The States Parties to this treaty,

Motivated by the goals of strengthening peace and international security,

Proceeding on the basis of their obligations under the Charter of the United Nations to refrain from the threat or use of force in any manner inconsistent with the Purposes of the United Nations,

Endeavouring not to allow outer space to become an arena for the arms race and a source of strained relations between States,

Have agreed on the following:

ARTICLE I

1. States Parties undertake not to place in orbit around the earth objects carrying weapons of any kind, install such weapons on celestial bodies, or station such weapons in outer space in any other manner, including reusable manned space vehicles of an existing type or of other types which States Parties may develop in the future.

2. Each State Party to this treaty undertakes not to assist, encourage or induce any State, group of States or international organization to carry out activities contrary to the provisions of paragraph 1 of this article.

ARTICLE 2

States Parties shall use space objects in strict accordance with international law, including the Charter of the United Nations, in the interest of maintaining international peace and security and promoting international co-operation and mutual understanding.

ARTICLE 3

Each State Party undertakes not to destroy, damage, disturb the normal functioning or change the flight trajectory of space objects of other States Parties, if such objects were placed in orbit in strict accordance with article 1, paragraph 1, of this treaty.

ARTICLE 4

1. In order to ensure compliance with the provisions of this treaty, each State Party shall use the national technical monitoring facilities available to it, in a manner consistent with generally recognized principles of international law.

2. Each State Party undertakes not to place obstacles in the way of the national technical monitoring facilities of other States Parties performing their functions in accordance with paragraph 1 of this article.

3. In order to promote the implementation of the purposes and provisions of this treaty, the States Parties shall, when necessary, consult each other, make inquiries and provide information in connexion with such inquiries.

ARTICLE 5

1. Any State Party to this treaty may propose amendments to this treaty. The text of each proposed amendment shall be submitted to the depositary, who shall immediately transmit it to all States Parties.

2. The amendment shall enter into force for each State Party to this treaty accepting the amendment when the instruments of acceptance of the amendment by the majority of States Parties have been deposited with the depositary. Thereafter, for each remaining State Party, the amendment shall enter into force on the date when that Party deposits its instrument of acceptance.

ARTICLE 6

This treaty shall be of unlimited duration.

ARTICLE 7

Each State Party shall in exercising its national sovereignty have the right to withdraw from this treaty if it decides that extraordinary events related to the subject-matter of this treaty have jeopardized its supreme interests. It shall notify the Secretary-General of the United Nations of the decision adopted six months before withdrawing from the treaty. Such notice shall include a statement of the extraordinary events which the notifying State Party considers to have jeopardized its supreme interests.

ARTICLE 8

1. This treaty shall be open for signature by all States at United Nations Headquarters in New York. Any State which does not sign this treaty before its entry into force in accordance with paragraph 3 of this article may accede to it at any time.

2. This treaty shall be subject to ratification by signatory States. Instruments of ratification and instruments of accession shall be deposited with the Secretary-General of the United Nations.

3. This treaty shall enter into force between the States which have deposited instruments of ratification upon the deposit with the Secretary-General of the United Nations of the fifth instrument of ratification.

4. For States whose instruments of ratification or accession are deposited subsequent to the entry into force of this treaty, it shall enter into force on the date of the deposit of their instruments of ratification or accession.

5. The Secretary-General of the United Nations shall promptly inform all signatory and acceding States of the date of each signature, the date of deposit of each instrument of ratification and accession, the date of entry into force of this treaty and other notices.

ARTICLE 9

This treaty, of which the Arabic, Chinese, English, French, Russian and Spanish texts are equally authentic, shall be deposited with the Secretary-General of the United Nations, who shall transmit duly certified copies thereof to the Governments of the signatory and acceding States.

Excerpt from the 1972 Anti-Ballistic Missile Treaty

Article XII

1. For the purpose of providing assurance of compliance with the provisions of this Treaty, each Party shall use national technical means of verification at its disposal in a manner consistent with generally recognized principles of international law.

2. Each Party undertakes not to interfere with the national technical means of verification of the other Party operating in accordance with paragraph 1 of this Article.

3. Each Party undertakes not to use deliberate concealment measures which impede verification by national technical means of compliance with the provisions of this Treaty. This obligation shall not require changes in current construction, assembly, conversion, or overhaul practices.

Article XIII

1. To promote the objectives and implementation of the provisions of this Treaty, the Parties shall establish promptly a Standing Consultative Commission, within the framework of which they will:

(a) consider questions concerning compliance with the obligations assumed and related situations which may be considered ambiguous;

(b) provide on a voluntary basis such information as either Party considers necessary to assure confidence in compliance with the obligations assumed;

(c) consider questions involving unintended interference with national technical means of verification;

(d) consider possible changes in the strategic situation which have a bearing on the provisions of this Treaty;

(e) agree upon procedures and dates for destruction or dismantling of ABM systems or their components in cases provided for by the provisions of this Treaty;

(f) consider, as appropriate, possible proposals for further increasing the viability of this Treaty, including proposals for amendments in accordance with the provisions of this Treaty;

(g) consider, as appropriate, proposals for further measures aimed at limiting strategic arms.

2. The Parties through consultation shall establish, and may amend as appropriate, Regulations for the Standing Consultative Commission governing procedures, composition and other relevant matters.

Index

Abrahamson, James A., 107
Advanced materials technology, 161
Advanced Reconnaissance System, 277
AEG Telefunken, 178
Aerobee, 277
Aerojet, 272
Aerospace Corp., 158
Aerospatiale, 181, 185
Afghanistan, 237
Africa, 180, 235
Agreement Governing the Activities of States on the Moon and other Celestial Bodies, 214
Agreement on the Rescue of Astronauts, the Return of Astronauts, and the Return of Objects Launched into Outer Space, 214
Airborne Warning and Control System (AWACS), 100
Airpower, 28, 62, 96, 99, 100, 111, 258. *See also* U.S. aircraft; USSR aircraft
Allen, Lew, Jr., 72
AMC, 273
American Astronautical Society, 294
American Telephone and Telegraph (AT&T), 186, 187, 196, 199, 200; TELSTAR, 196
Antarctica, 235
Antisatellite weapons, 12, 41, 42, 70, 71, 73, 80, 81, 85, 87, 97, 104, 110–112, 122, 123, 135, 216, 237–239, 264, 297; homing, 133; potential for arms control

constraints of, 21, 22, 70, 87, 97, 104, 121, 122, 123, 132, 134, 135, 218, 237, 297; Soviet, 12, 55, 70–73, 82, 104, 108, 121–123, 132, 133, 143, 219, 234, 257, 258, 293, 294, 297, 304
Antisubmarine warfare (ASW), 99, 129; P3C Orion aircraft, 129
Antitank missile (TOW), 68
Arianespace, 179, 185–187
Arizona, 127
Arms control, 11, 12, 17, 18, 20–22, 24–26, 27, 29, 59, 60, 62–64, 69, 87, 93, 97, 106, 108, 110, 112, 119, 121, 131, 136, 137, 148, 213, 218, 221–242, 259, 262, 263
Assured destruction strategy, 132
Asteroids, 39, 40, 42, 44
Atlantic Alliance, 123
Atlantic Ocean, 126, 194, 199
Atmospheric dispersion, 32
Augenstein, Bruno, 261
Austria, 177, 215
Aviation Week and Space Technology, 124, 128, 293–295
Avco, 276

Ballistic missiles, 19, 26, 62, 72, 73, 75, 76, 78, 92, 93, 95, 96, 128, 132, 180, 213, 258, 267
—defense (BMD), 23–25, 41, 42, 59–64, 68, 69, 76, 110, 112, 119, 122, 123, 131, 132, 259, 264, 266, 280
    antiballistic missile (ABM), 25, 41, 42, 51, 60, 61, 64, 80,